HISTORY OF THE UNITED STATES OF AMERICA

History of the United States of America

N. JAYAPALAN

ATLANTIC
PUBLISHERS & DISTRIBUTORS (P) LTD

ATLANTIC
PUBLISHERS & DISTRIBUTORS (P) LTD

7/22, Ansari Road, Darya Ganj, New Delhi
Tel.: +91-11-4077 5252, 2327 3880
E-mail: orders@atlanticbooks.com
Web: www.atlanticbooks.com

Reprint 2025, 2023, 2022, 2018, 2016

Published by Atlantic Publishers & Distributors (P) Ltd.

Printed & bound in India by Atlantic Print Services

Preface

Eversince my student days I have been attracted by the developments in the United States of America. While specialising in History it was my good luck that I had to offer 'History of the United States of America' and the 'History of Europe' for my postgraduate course. Hence, I have always cherished the hope of writing a book presenting their glorious struggle against England and the various phases of their History to the students in an objective manner.

Before writing this book I took up a thorough study of the subject presented by various distinguished writers, oriental and occidental. My teaching experience at the college level classes added another dimension to my study which helped me to present this book to the earnest readers.

In this book I have given the historical events in the chronological order in a simple manner so that the students can easily follow the events pertaining to the United States of America.

In this book I have drawn the sources from the brilliant works of reputed writers. I very sincerely acknowledge their authority and express my gratitude to all their publishers.

I am thankful to M/s Atlantic Publishers and Distributors, New Delhi for readily agreeing to publish this book and bringing it out expeditiously and efficiently.

I shall be grateful to the readers of this book for their valuable suggestions, if any, for the improvement of the book.

N. JAYAPALAN

Contents

PART II

PART I

1

Colonisation

The exploration and discovery of America was the biological result of a series of happenings which began centuries before. Such occurrences can be enumerated as follows:

(1) The lure of the orient has made Europeans to face East for a longer period than they have faced West. Oriental wares, spices and fine fabrics had compelled them to explore a new sea route which ultimately brought them to America.

(2) The crusades had their impact upon seafarers and adventurers through its mythical tales of the Levant and Eastern Asia which encouraged people in the geographical explorations.

(3) The growth of geographical knowledge gave a fillip to geographers. The Franciscan missionaries who in their proselytisation activities had visited and resorted on countries like Persia, India, China and Japan. Merchants like Polo brothers and Marcopolo who visited China in the 13th century, stirred the imagination of the Europeans about the fabulous wealth of the East and revived the East-West trade.

(4) The expanding European business activities made credit and 'Investment Capital' easier which in turn enabled overseas ventures to be undertaken.

(5) One among the reasons of exploration was the religious motive. The crusaders were in search for great treasures to finance new crusades. Another religious reason was the necessity of protestants to escape from the turmoil and turbulence of religious feuds made them to migrate to America.

(6) The rise of the nation states was also another significant factor for the flourishing international trade which made the exploration feasible.

(7) Above all, the renaissance which dawned in the 15th Century, shot hopeful rays of light through the middle ages. Better maps, Mariners' Compass and Printing presses had created a healthy spirit of optimism, self-reliance and venturesomeness.

All these factors had ultimately heralded the "Age of Explorations".

Establishment of Commercial Empires

Portuguese Path-Finders. Portugal was the first European country to search for the Far East under the able guidance of Prince Henry, the Navigator, who founded a School of Navigation. Thus, resulted in reaching the western shores of India by Vasco da Gama in 1498. Pedro Cabral discovered Brazil in 1500.

Spanish Attempts of Exploration

Christopher Columbus, an Italian Seaman and geographer secured adequate outfitting and finance from the Spanish King and Queen, Ferdinana and Isabella. Columbus was a man of vision, energy and resourcefulness. He tried to find out route to East Asia by sailing westward on the basis of his conviction of the globular shape of the world. Megallen sailed westward in 1519 and reached the eastern coast of Brazil. In his four voyages Columbus discovered Bahama islands in October 12, 1492 and later on Haitis, Trinidad and the coast of Honduras. Thus, Columbus stumbled upon a New World, the parts of the America.

But even prior to Columbus many explorers had discovered America and the claim of Norseman of Scandinavia only is corroborated by evidence. It is true that about the year 1000 A.D. Norseman discovered Iceland, Greenland and North America where there was abundance of the wild grapes which they named Vinland. Later on, they were abandoned.

Thus, the New land discovered by Columbus was called as New world until it was named America in honour of America Vespucci, an Italian mariner who after three voyages to the New world had given a sensational account of the land.

Spanish Conquistadores

Later on, Spaniards explored still more lands and founded colonies in the American continent. The City of Santo Domingo was founded by Bartholomeo Columbus, brother of Columbus in 1509. Puerto Rico, Jamaica and Cuba were also colonised in 1513. Balboa discovered Pacific Ocean by crossing the foaming waves of Panama Isthmus. Spaniards were more successful in the establishment of colonies in South American continent than in the North. Mexico and Peru were also explored and colonised by Spaniards in 1518 by Cortez and 1535 by Pizarro respectively. Spaniards were also concerned with spreading their culture and religion in such colonised countries. Missionaries started the conversion work on indigenous people and educated through their schools.

The Founding of New France

By the time Spain had conquered Mexico, France had become a powerful force in European politics which started challenging Spain and Portugal in their colonial activities of fishermen on the New Foundland banks of fur traders. Their attempts of settlement in Brazil and Florida ended in tragic failure due to the rivalry of Portuguese. But they had good fortunes in Canada. Samuel-de-Champlain, a hardy and vigorous man explored St. Lawrence Basin and founded the City of Quebec in 1608. He may be suitably awarded the tittle of "The Father of Canada". Fur trade had become the economic backbone of New France. French expansion towards West was swift and they reached almost the rocky mountains before the British had founded half of the "old thirteen" colonies of North America. In 1682, La Salle explored the river Illinois and named the Valley Louisiana in honour of King of France.

Dutch Commercial Empire

The Dutch Netherlands after their secession from Spain, in 1581, had become a keen competitor for Spain and Portugues maritime commerce. The New Netherland Company and the West India Company had established settlements in Guiana, West Indies, and Valley of Hudson River. Ultimately the Dutch settlers settled in Manhattan island (now New York)

Swedes in America

Sweden's merchants established a trading post on the Delaware river in 1638 but since it was not well supported. It was conquered by the Dutch in 1655.

Early English Explorations

The English were the latest to enter into this scramble for colonies in America. England was affected by the internal rifts of political and religious ideologies and its long drawn war with Spain distracted the nation from dreams of Imperial grandeur. But slowly the ideas of economic self sufficiency, relief of over population became the strongest motives and they turned England into a capitalist and trading state. The anti-Spanish exploits of Sir John Hawkins, Sir Francis Drake's accounts of his world round voyages, Sir Humphrey Gilbert's attempt to colonise New foundland and Sir Walter Raleigh's mission of planting a colony in North Carolino encouraged the Englishmen to launch still more strong colonising activities.

But the defeat of Spanish Armada (invincible) had marked the beginning of the rise of British Navy to the first rank on the Seven Seas.

It was a red letter event in England History for it dampened the fighting spirit of Spain and the triumph of England ensured the naval dominance making her Mistress of the seas.

VIRGINIA — The English Beach Head or the Child of Tobacco

The initial failures of the English explorations had made them to learn a lesson that only a concerted effort could yield success in colonisation. Hence, a number of adventurous traders founded companies and obtained charters from the Emperor. One among them was Virginia company which was granted charter in 1606 by King James I. The first settlement was at Jamestown, 50 miles inside the James river in 1607, but it was unsuitable for habitation. The colonisers had to face encumbrances like diseases, contaminated water, uncongenial climate conditions which resulted in high mortality rate. John Smith saved the colony from ruin. John Rolfe showed the possibilities of profit from raising tobacco. It was in Virginia that twenty Negro labourers were first introduced from the Dutch and the institution of slavery was introduced.

The most valuable gift of Virginia company to this country was the introduction of House of Burgesses, a representative assembly of the colonies of James Town in 1619. It was the first such body in America which was capable of becoming an organ of free and representative self-Government. So the displeased Emperor revoked the charter in 1624 and Virginia hence forth was brought directly under the crown as a Royal Colony.

NEW ENGLAND COLONIES

(a) *Plymouth :* The next successful settlement was that of the venerated "pilgrim fathers" in 1620 at Plymouth, Even the Plymouth Company was chartered in 1606 and it was sold to pilgrims in 1620. The pilgrims were dissatisfied Protestants against that of the Church of England. They first migrated to Holland and then proceeded to America in "May Flowership" and landed at Plymouth. Before disembarking, the pilgrim fathers drew up and signed the seven line "May Flower Compact". In 1691, this colony was joined with Massachusetts Bay colony.

(b) *Massachusetts :* A neighbouring settlement Massachusetts Bay was chartered in 1929. It was a religious refuge for puritans during the civil war period in England. Unhappy about the "Romish" tendencies in the English Church, the stock-holders of Massachusetts Bay Company agreed in Cambridge agreement to migrate to America. Twenty thousand Puritans had migrated to this colony within next twelve years. It remained a self-governing unit, with Boston as its capital. It was also called as "Bible Commonwealth". The success of this colony was all due to the services of conscientious and prudent English Squire John Winthrop.

(c) *Connecticut* : Puritans still sought to plant new settlements on rivers or harbours. One dissident group from Massachusetts migrated to Connecticut valley under the leadership of Thomas Hookes in 1635. They were followed by a group of London Puritans who came to New Haven via Boston. The founders of Connecticut drafted a series of statutes together called the Fundamental orders of Connecticut by which they established a representative Government. In 1662, Connecticut obtained a Royal Charter from King Charles II, which served as a "State Constitution".

(d) *Rhode Island* : This was formed by dissenters and exiles of Massachusetts. Roger Williams, a young clergy with radical ideas defended native Indian claims to the soil and separation of Church from State. He was banished from Massachusetts. He founded the City of Providence with the aid of Indians. He built the first Baptist Church and declared freedom of religion. The colony of Rhode island was formed by the Union of four towns — Providence, Portsmouth, New Port and Warwick. The colony secured charters from England in 1644 and 1663. The Second Charter explicitly guaranteed liberty of conscience, a freedom legally unknown in England.

PROPRIETORY COLONIES

All those colonies that were mentioned earlier were corporate for they were founded on the basis of charters granted to joint stock. Companies. There were other colonies whose charters were issued to individuals with the authority of acting as constitutional monarchs on those lands. Such of them are as follows:

Maryland

This was the first proprietary colony. George Calvert, the first Lord Baltimore, a Catholic peer was granted Maryland in 1632. He planned to establish a Catholic haven for they suffered discriminations and persecutions from the hands of Anglicans in England. The colony was named after the queen Henrieta Maria by the King Charles I. Since George Calvert died soon, it was renewed in favour of his son Cecilius Calvert, the Second Lord Baltimore. The first settlement was made in 1634. The government of Maryland was based on feudal principle. The representative assembly imitated the English Parliament. Maryland was the second plantation colony and tabacco growing became profitable. An Act of Toleration was enacted in 1649 which provided religious freedom to all including the Protestants.

New Hampshire and Maine

Two adventurous proprietors of England obtained joint patent from the Council of New England to promote settlements. They were Sir Ferdinand George and Captain Mason. The territory that was allotted to George was Maine and Mason was Hampshire. The settlers of these colonies were non-Puritans and hence Puritan dominated Massachusetts had annexed it in 1643. The case was referred to the court in England and independence of these colonies were confirmed in 1677. Hampshire was made a royal colony in 1679. Maine was united with Massachusetts in 1691 through a Royal Charter but it was separated in 1820 and became independent.

New Jersey

James, the Duke of York gave a sub-grant, that part of his proprietorship between the Hudson and Delaware rivers to Lord John Berkeley and Sir George Carterat who in turn sold to an ever increasing number of other proprietors. Ultimately the colony called New Jersey came to be owned by twenty-four proprietors. The quaker proprietors established legislatures in their areas. A conflict ensued between New York and New Jersey on the matters of collection of quit-rent and business affairs. Incessant frictions forced the proprietors to surrender the whole of New Jersey to the Royal Government in 1702.

North and South Carolina

With the restoration and installation of Charles II on the English throne in 1660, the English National policy favoured southern expansion to compete with Spain and the Carolinas were the result. Charles II wanted to reward all those who assisted him in his restoration and hence conferred on Anthony Ashley Cooper and eight others the proprietary rights over the Carolinas. This territory lay South of Virginia and North of Spanish region of "Florida". It was named Carolina after the Latin "Carolinas" meaning Charles. The first permanent settlement near present Charleston was made in 1670. These settlements were separated by vast tract of uninhabitated land and for the purpose of administrative convenience, they were divided into North and South Carolinas. The settlers in South Carolina were highly dissatisfied with the administration of the proprietors who were engaged in personal gains. Hence, there were frequent friction between them which forced the proprietors to sell the colony to the King and made it a Royal Colony in 1719. The North Carolina followed suit in 1792.

Pennsylvania

This colony was founded by William Penn, a quaker. James II granted this great province in 1681 as a payment of debt owed to his father. Since the quakers were persecuted in England they founded their own colony. The territory was named Pennsylvania by the King himself. This province was the most fertile of all and possessed rich minerals. The capital city Philadelphia meaning brotherly love was founded by Penn. This colony attracted many Germans of the Lutheran faith, Scotch proselyterians and Irishmen. It remained the largest American City till independence and surpassed all other cities in population.

LATER COLONIES

New York

It was initially established by the Dutch West India Company in 1624 on the course of the river Hudson. Since it was an area rich in furs, it attracted thousands of colonisers. They founded the City of Amsterdam on the Manhattan Island and the whole colony was named New Netherland. It became an eyesore to the English because it was like a separating wedge between English colonies north and South of it and it was captured by an English fleet in 1664. King Charles II granted this colony to his brother James, the Duke of York and thereafter it was renamed New York.

Delaware

Another Dutch Colony seized by the English was Delaware and Duke of York had sold it to William Penn in 1682 who had attached it with Pennsylvania. Since people became uproarious about economic and political control, Delaware was granted a representative assembly in 1703 and became a separate colony.

Georgia

The last of the mainland colonies was Georgia. It was founded by a philanthropic Board of "Trustees of Georgia" headed by James Edward Oglenthorpe in 1732. It was named after George II. It was valued by the English Crown chiefly as a buffer which would serve to protect Carolinas from Spaniards of Florida and Frenchmen of Louisiana. It was a charity colony for the imprisoned English doctors. It was also a haven for the persecuted Protestants of European countries. This colony grew slowly due to many prohibitory orders. Finally, in 1752, this was made a Royal Colony.

2

British-French Wars in America

The British Imperial Policy

Great Britain had adhered to the same mercantilist policy in the American Colonies too. The mercantilist policy stipulated that the colonies should be kept in subordination and be subservient to the mother country as a source of revenue and necessary raw materials. The available raw materials were to be shipped to England, and the English manufactured goods were to be purchased in return. This made the British empire as far as possible, a self-sufficient economic unit independent of her foreign rivals. This policy was enforced by means of the Acts of Trade and Navigation.

Navigation Codes

The Acts of Navigation consisted of three clauses. The colonies must have all their trading activities only in British ships; they must have purchases mostly from the mother country and must do most of their selling to the mother country. In addition to these laws, the Parliament of Great Britain legislated a Staple Act in 1663 according to which the colonies could not buy goods directly from any European country except through England. These laws were incessantly violated by the New England and Bostan Merchants. Hence, the British Government had taken severe steps to check the illegal trade of the colonists.

The colonial industry was cursed by the Woollen Act of 1692 which was repeatedly imposed in 1732 and 1750. Of all these, the most unpalatable act was the Molasses Act of 1773, according to which a duty of six pence a gallon was placed on molasses imported from the French West Indies. This was designed to stop the trade between the Colonies and the French and the Spanish West Indies. Thus, Great Britain had established well its imperialism in America.

French 'Empire' in America : 'New France'

France entered in the scramble for America only at a later period. They established settlements on the banks of the river Lawrence and in the regions like Florida and South Carolina. Even though they all had soon disappeared, their attempts had borne fruit in the form of a new country called Canada. One of the explorers of France namely Samuel de Champlain had followed, up the St. Lawrence river and founded the City of Quebec in 1608. It was the first French settlement in North America and this earned for him the title of the "father of Canada" in later days. The French explorers were highly ambitious in finding out regions as fertile as the Spanish Colonies and also regions abounding in mineral wealth. They extended their sway by their missionaries, soldiers and fur trappers to the interior regions. Fur trade became the economic backbone of Canada which was also called as 'New France'. The French westward expansion was fast enough. Even before Britain could found half of her thirteen colonies, the French "Woods runners" had reached the Rocky Mountains. They wanted to put restraints upon the British encroachments in the Ohio river valley. In 1682, Robert de La Salle sailed down the Mississipi river and claimed the entire valley for France. This Mississipi Valley was named as Louisiana with New Orieans as Capital. The French authorities had established a city 'New Orieans' in 1718 and thereby curtailed the intrusions of Spain. Not having been contented with this, the French explorers tried to explore fields new in the North America. They found out regions extending from Texas in the South to Arkansas, Missouri and Manitopa in Canada. They had also explored the Rocky mountain ranges in 1743. This French empire consisted of a series of trading posts, mission-stations and forts with very few French settlers. Even in 1760 French Canada had no more than 50,000 whitemen. They were more friendly with the Indians and even married their women. The Frenchmen had limited their authority and influence only in Canada even though they found out vast regions through their explorers.

CAUSES OF ANGLO-FRENCH WAR

(1) There was a long standing commercial and colonial rivalry between Great Britain and France for both of them were imperialistic. They wanted to satiate their land hunger through occupying more and more territories.

(2) The French forts along the river Mississippi were considered to be stumbling blocks in their way of westward expansion by the English.

(3) The Englishmen were not ready to tolerate the flourishing and lucrative fur trade and fisheries of the French people in the North Atlantic Regions.

(4) The English people wanted to wipe out the Red Indians from the continent. On the contrary to their plan of extermination of Indian tribes, the Frenchmen had befriended them and even had marital relationship with them. Besides, they armed and supported the Indian tribes. This irritated and infuriated the English.

(5) The Anglo-French Rivalry prevailed every where in the world for a very long time, The New world was not an exception to this rivalry. As it was expressed that whenever France had a cold the whole Europe sneezed, whenever there was a confrontation between Britain and France in any part of the world, it had its reflection in the New world also. There were four rounds such war fought in American theatre, which lasted from 1689 to 1763.

King William's War 1689-97

The first of such wars which broke out during the last quarter of the 17th Century was 'War of the League of Augsburg' in Europe. It was called as King William's War in America. Of course, there were frequent clashes between the English and the French in the border lands between New England and New France. But the first actual war was King William's War which was fought in between 1689-97. During the war Frontenac, the Governor of New France raided New Hampshire, Maine, Massachusetts and New York in the frontiers of New England. The English too tried and failed to conqure Quebec and Montreal. The war was ended by the treaty of Ryswick in 1697 and the conquered territories were restored in the Colonies.

Queen Anne's War 1701-13

Soon Britain and France entered into another confrontation known as war of Spanish succession in 1701. As usual this war had spread to America also where it was called as Queen Anne's war, The French and the Indian tribes attacked the English Colonies in the north and the Spaniards of Florida raided Carolina in support of the French. The English colonial troops succeeded in taking and destroying a few French and Spanish towns. The war brought to an end by the Treaty of Utrecht in 1713. Britain gained Hudson Bay territory, Acadia and New foundland. This gave Britain a foothold in Canada. She also acquired the right to engage in trade with the Spanish American Colonies.

King George's War 1744-48

During the next two or three decades, France and Spain tried to expel Britain from America. The French pushed down its course to the gulf of

Mexico near which they built the city of New Orleans. They developed the Colony of Louislana and began building a chain of ports to connect their areas from the north to the south and incidentally prevent English Colonies from expanding beyond the Appalachians. The English Colonists were aware of the growing French menace and during the Austrian War of Succession (1740-48) captured Louisburg in the Cape Breten Island and wanted to take Quebec. The war came to an end with the Treaty of Aix-la Chapelle in 1748. All the conquered territories were restored. Louisburg was returned to France in exchange for Madras. The treaty brought no real peace in America. The Virginians twice tried to capture the French fort of Duquesne under George Washington in 1754 and under General Braddock in 1755.

Seven Years War in America (1756-1763)

The first three Anglo-French Wars had their origin in Europe and spread subsequently to America. But the fourth war started in America and it engulfed the whole world into it for a period of seven years. Since the countries belonging to the seven seas participated in it, it can be also called as seven seas war. The attack of George Washington on the French fort Duquesne in 1754 was a spark which developed into a dreadful fire within two years and had made the French imperialism to vanish in America.

In the initial stages of the war, the English people had met only failures. The British Government despatched a force of 1,200 Europeans under General Braddock to capture Duquesne. But Braddock was defeated and killed. Under the circumstances, William Pitt the Elder assumed office as British Prime Minister in 1757. Now the tide of fortune turned in favour of Britishers. British troops became victorious. They captured Louisburg in 1758, Quebec in 1759 and Montreal in 1760 under the generalship of Wolfe. The war still continued and ultimately France and Spain were completely wiped out from North America.

The Treaty of Paris

The war ended with the Treaty of Paris in 1763 and it marked a turning point in the history of the colonies. It also marked the high-water mark of English colonial power in the 18th century. The French surrendered Canada and the Western Country as far as the Mississipi Valley to Britain. Spain ceded Florida to Britain and received Louisiana from France in compensation. Thus, with the expulsion of France, North America was divided between Great Britain and Spain, the Mississippi river being the boundary line.

Causes for the Victory of Great Britain

(1) The Englishmen in the New England were 100,000 in 1688 who outnumbered the French in Canada numbering about 12,000 only.

(2) The territories occupied by the English were compact though small in size. But the French had possessed areas vast and extensive in size which were also in scattered condition.

(3) Moreover, the Englishmen enjoyed superior naval-strength and dominated in trade and finance. The Frenchmen were inferior in all these aspects to English people.

(4) Of course, France enjoyed two advantages namely centralized political control and the presence of a strong army in the strategic forts. But soon they were neutralised.

As a result of the number of advantages enjoyed by the Britishers, they were able to conquer Frenchmen and expel them from North America.

Results of the Triumph of Great Britain

(1) The most significant result was that it freed the colonies from French fear and made them less dependent upon Britain for military protection. The war necessitated the colonies to come closer and organise things in common for the colonies.

(2) The colonial militia raised during the Anglo-French wars in support of the Great Britain had enabled the colonists to gain self-confidence which later on encouraged them to declare independence.

(3) The ultimate victory of Great Britain in the wars had doubled her territories in North America, which had considerably increased her responsibilities too.

3

American War of Independence

The American War of Independence was an epoch-making factor not only in the annals of America but also in the history of the whole world. The tyrannical practices of colonising and inhabiting many tracts of lands had been in vogue from the times immemorial, but America was the first country to launch a war of independence against oppression, enslavement and exploitation. This movement opened a new era of liberalism, revolution and independence in the dictionary of nationalist movement.

The causes for the American war of Independence were deeply embedded in the life of colonists. The idea of revolt was surging in the minds of the people, for the mother country had became a great hindrance rather than that of help for the development of colonies. The day of American independence was precipitated by the passage of laws of British Parliament to establish a strong imperial organisation in the colonies.

CAUSES OF THE REVOLUTION

1. **Spirit of Liberty of Americans.** The settlers in America had developed a kind of self-reliant attitude for there was enormous growth of their economy, agriculture and trade. This resulted in the emergence of a spirit of liberty for, most part of the settlers were dissenters and radicals expelled from Britain. The divergence of these people from England had enabled them to develop new ways of life. A sense of national awareness was unfolded by Americans. The self-reliance, self-government and a fairly religious freedom had developed a spirit of liberty among the Americans which ultimately was accomplished by an unavoidable conflict with Britain. The vigorous southern planters wanted to escape from the burden of debt to British merchants. The energetic northern traders felt that their developing trade was being crushed by

the imposition of British trade regulations. Moreover, the urban mechanics and some farmers were clamouring for more political and economic freedom. The whole episode of American Revolution was the work of such minority people who were bestowed with superior ability, courage, liberality and dynamic enthusiasm.

2. **Mistress Attitude of the Britishers.** Simultaneously Great Britain too had been developing an exactly opposite attitude against Americans. Their conviction was that the colonies existed primarily for the benefit of the Mother Country and must, therefore, be kept in subordination. Hence, many colonies like Virginia, Plymouth, New York etc. were brought under royal control. Governors and military Commanders of all these colonies were appointed by the British Government. The imperial control was increased and hence frictions between Governors and Assemblies had became frequent. The conflict was between the imperialism of Britain and Colonial autonomy of Americans.

3. **Act of Mercantilism and Navigation.** The basic philosophy under which the English settlement were ultimately exploited was Mercantilism. This meant roughly that the colonies existed for the benefit of the Mother Country, they should add to its wealth, prosperity, and self sufficiency. This policy led to the passage of a number of Navigational Acts.

   Navigation Act of 1651 insisted that all goods entering England must be carried in ships owned and manned by British citizens.

   In 1660, Enumerated Commodities Act provided a long list of commodities like sugar, tobacco etc., prohibiting their export to other countries. The same list was expanded in the year 1706 and 1722.

   Subsequently, the Staple Act of 1663, The Duty Act of 1673, the Enforcement Act of 1696 and the Molasses Act restricted the colonial trade to the benefit of Britain and to the detriment of Americans. So, the American merchants and manufacturers were annoyed, irritated, infuriated and denounced these Acts as an infringement of their rights obtained under Royal Charters.

4. **Freedom from the Gallic Peril.** The defeat of France in the French and Indian Wars had eliminated its menace in northern and western America. Along with it, the need for the military reliance of Americans over their Mother Country too had vanished. After the seven years war the relations between England and the colonies completely changed. The colonies had acquired valuable military training and expanded their militia during these wars.

They had also developed inter-colonial co-operation in facing common problems. Thus, colonies slowly strengthened their positions and gradually tried to sever their connection with the Mother Country.

5. **Proclamation Act of 1763.** After the war with France, the natives of Virginia poured across the Appalachian ranges into the Ohio Valley. The native Indian tribals under the leadership of Partiac fought back the whites which caused the enormous loss of men and money. In order to avoid further clashes with tribals and to preserve the already existing trade centres on the coastal region, the British Government issued a Proclamation prohibiting any settlement beyond the Appalachian ranges. Besides, the British Government decided to maintain an army of 10,000 troops in North America, in order to guard against possible Indian raids and French attempts at reconquest. Since they had to be posted for the defence of the colonies, they were required to pay part of the cost. George Grenville, a brother-in-law of Pitt, the Elder, became Prime Minister and he set himself in raising fresh resources by strictly enforcing the custom duties and preventing smuggling.

6. **The Grenville Measures.**
   (a) *Sugar Act,* 1764 : Smuggling of Molasses from French and West Indies was carried on at a large scale, transgressing the Molasses Act of 1733. Grenville wanted to make this Molasses trade a source of revenue by reducing the duty of six pence per gallon to 3 pence. He passed the Sugar Act in 1764 to this effect and collection of the duty was made strict. Besides, new taxes on wines, silk, indigo and other luxury items were imposed.

   (b) *The Currency Act,* 1764 : It prohibited the Colonial Assemblies from the issue of any more paper currency. By this Act the colonial debtors were prevented from setting their debts in depreciated currency.

   (c) *The Stamp Act,* 1765 : Sugar Act was followed by the Stamp Act in 1765 which declared that Stamp Duties were to be paid on Newspapers and legal and commercial documents. This tax was calculated to yield a revenue of 100,000 pounds for meeting one third of the cost of the army stationed in America. This was considered to be the first direct tax levied by the British Government.

   (d) *Storm of Protests of the Colonies* : Lawyers, Ministers, Legislators and Editors expressed their resentment over this Act. Considering it as violation of their fundamental and natural rights. Massachusetts led the other colonies in organising their protest against this Act. Virginia exhibited its vigorous opposition through its resolution called "Virginia Resolves". These acts raised a storm of indignation of the Americans against the British Government. "Sugar Act made the people to think and Stamp Act to talk". They could not tolerate the tyranny of taxation without representation.

(e) *Stamp Act Congress* : In response to the call given by Massachusetts to formulate protest against the Stamp duty, nine states assembled in New York in 1765. The first meeting to take concerted action in the history of U.S.A. published a "Declaration of Rights and Grievances" which challenged the right of British Parliament to tax Americans.

(f) *Stamp Act Agitation* : A revolutionary organisation called "Sons of Liberty" was founded. Its exponents like Sam Adams of Boston, Charles Thomson of Philadelphia had caused a lot of havoc and made life miserable for the British agents appointed to sell the stamps. Riotous popular demonstrations became rampant. The most effective weapon used against the Stamp Act was a general agreement to stop importing British goods.

(g) *Quartering Act* 1765 : This Act enforced the colonists to provide lodging and supplies for British troops whenever they were stationed for a time in their towns.

(h) *Repeal of Stamp Act* : British merchants suffered heavy losses and urged the Government to give way. Sympathisers like Pitt, Burke and Fox too opposed the right of British Parliament to tax the colonies. Practically the Stamp Act was not implemented and it became defunct, for transactions were carried on without stamps. Hence, Marquis of Rockingham, the successor of Grenville repealed the Stamp Act in March 1766, lowered the molasses duty to one penny and passed a "Declaratory Act" which affirmed the principle of Parliamentary supremacy over the colonies.

TOWNSHEND DUTIES

Rockingham was succeeded by the Earl of Chatham. Charles Townshend was his Chancellor of Exchequer. Since Parliament reduced the taxes in England, Townshend had to turn to colonies in order to make up the deficit and passed the Duty Act in 1767 which imposed import levies on glass, lead, paints, tea and paper. Townshend also suspended the

New York Assembly since it transgressed the Laws of Quartering Act of 1765 by refusing to provide supplies for the troops stationed in the colony.

Opposition Against Townshend's Policies

(a) *Non-Importation* : John Dickinson, a Pennsylvanian Lawyer wrote a series of "Letters from a farmer" which questioned the right of British Parliament to tax the colonies, condemned the Townshend Acts and suspension of New York Assembly. Agreements were signed to refrain from importing British goods in August 1768 by merchants. Merchants engaged in illegal trade were protected from customs officials by the 'Sons of Liberty'.

(b) *Boston Massacre* : Two regiments of British troops were stationed in Boston to prevent smuggling. The 'Sons of Liberty' aroused popular hostility to the presence of these troops. On March 5, 1770, a ding dong battle was fought in which soldiers opened fire upon the crowd which provoked the altercation by throwing snowballs. This resulted in the so-called Boston Massacre of five Bostanians.

7. **Lord North and Conciliation.** Lord North, King George's favourite became the Prime Minister in January 1770. He promised to heal the breach that had been developing between the colonies and the Mother Country. He persuaded the Parliament to repeal all Townshend duties except a small tax on tea in order to assert the principles of parliamentary authority. Peace prevailed in the period between 1770 and 1773 due to the conciliatory policy of Lord North. His conciliatory attitude strengthened the conservatives in the American colonies, who wished to avoid trouble. But the radicals who disputed North prepared to meet any future infringement of their political and economic rights. In 1772 Sam Adams and his associates set up throughout Massachussetts a net work of 'Committees of Correspondence' composed of men who would carry an agitation and organise resistance.

8. **The Final Crisis.** (a) *The Tea Act of 1773* : None of the frictions excited many people until the British Government under Lord North committed the most crucial mistake of passing Tea Act of 1773. It was a clever scheme to dispose of the East India Company's surplus tea by means of bypassing the American wholesalers. What made the scheme unacceptable to the Americans was that the East India Company was given a virtual monopoly of the colonial tea market.

(b) *Boston Tea Party :* The result was that many of the merchants again joined forces with the 'Sons of Liberty'. The Tea Act was opposed everywhere. When the first shipments of tea arrived in the autumn the ships were compelled to sail back. But in Boston Hutchinson the Governor of Massachussetts, was determined of unloading the ships, for the consignees were his own sons and a nephew. Hence, a group of 'Sons of Liberty' disguised as Indians, boarded the ships and threw the tea worth of 15,000 Pounds in the harbour. This Boston Tea party precipitated the crisis.

9. **The Intolerable Acts.** The Bostonians were promptly punished by the passage of the 'Intolerable Acts' which closed the Boston Port until compensation should be made royalised the Government of Massachussetts re-enacted the Quartering Act and provided for the trial of accused royal officers outside the colony.

Quebec Acts

Parliament also passed the Quebec Act which extended the boundaries of the Quebec to include all the areas West of the Alleghenies and North of the Ohio river. It also permitted collection of tithes by the Roman Catholic clergy. This act was passed in accordance with the wishes of the French Canadian population. Thus, the Quebec Act seemed to the Americans to be quite as intolerable as the coercive Acts.

First Continental Congress

These coercive Acts made it obvious that Americans were not entitled to any legal right. Nearly all the colonies expressed solidarity with Massachussetts. The Virginia House of Burgesses passed a resolution calling for the First Continental Congress to meet in Philadelphia. Fifty six delegates representing all colonies except Georgia assembled on 5th September 1774. Eventhough there were three factions radicals, moderates and conservatives, they unanimously adopted "The Declaration of Rights and Grievances" and petitioned King George for a redressal of political and economic grievances. They appealed to the French Canadian to join them and once more adopted an economic boycott of Britain.

A "Continental Association was formed to watch the effective adherence of the boycott. The people of Massachussetts were busy gathering arms and ammunitions and were training themselves as "minutemen" ready to fight at a minute's notice. In the Second Continental Congress at Philadelphia it was resolved to adopt the New England Militia as nucleus of a continental army. One of the most fortunate decisions of the Congress was its choice of George Washington as its Commander-in-Chief of its forces.

Developing desire for Political Separation

The colonists were licensed by the policy of the British Government in hiring foreign mercenaries to fight Englishmen in America. Before, General Washington took the command of the army the colonials were pushed off Bunker Hill near Boston at a terrible cost to the British, who evacuated Boston nine months later. During the seize of Boston, Americans began to conclude that independence from Britain offered the only safety for their liberty. Press and pulpit along with Thomas Paine's argument in his pamphlet, "Common Sense" expressed this common sentiment.

THE DECLARATION OF INDEPENDENCE

The Irrevocable Step

During the Spring of 1776, several colonial legislatures instructed their delegates in the continental congress to work and vote for Independence.

Richard Henry Lee of Virginia moved a motion for Declaration of Independence. One of the strongest arguments for such a step was that it would make it easier for the Americans to secure help from France. The Congress responded by naming a committee headed by Thomas Jefferson to draft a Declaration of Independence. The Declaration, largely the work of Jefferson, was accepted by the Congress on July 2nd and was formally signed by most of the delegates on July, 4th 1776.

The Declaration was designed to strengthen the radical cause in America and to win foreign support for the American rebellion.

It was also a Revolution

The American War of Independence barely lasted only eight years and in a broad sense the American revolution was not the same thing as the American war of Independence. But the American revolution commenced even when the first Permanent English Settlers set foot on the new continent and the revolution lasted over a century and a half. Insurrection of deeds always followed such revolutionary ideas. The revolutionary ferment was burning in the minds of the people in America even before their bullets began to fly. America was a revolutionary force from the day of its discovery.

This revolutionary spirit was the natural result from the dissenters, radicals and descendants of discontented people who migrated from Britain. They emigrated with a view to enjoy large share in Government, richer portion of properties and an opportunity to worship God in their own way. American continent gratified all their expectations. After crossing three thousand miles of ocean, the settlers were relatively free and enjoyed independence. The deep and dense fertile forests had changed the patterns of living and consequently habits of thought. When the Americans attained maturity they set up their own parliaments and adopted the parliamentary methods of Britain.

It was not a revolution in the sense of a radical or total change. It was not a sudden and violent overturning of the political and social frame work as occurred in France and Russia later on. Significant changes were ushered in but they were not breath-taking. What happened was accelerated evolution rather than outright revolution.

Results of the War

The American War of Independence had accomplished a number of things which are placed in the first order. It was the war which liberated a colonial country and elevated to the level of a democracy in which emerged a written Constitution, with federal features for the first time in the annals of the history of the world. The Constitution of U.S.A. came to include the Bill of Rights, seeking to protect the rights and liberties of the citizens.

All the thirteen colonies which were functioning as separate entities were now brought under a single national Government. This helped the development of the National Culture of America.

The effect of the American revolution was almost immediate over France. It had indirectly hastened the French Revolution. The examples of American Diplomats like Adams and Franklin were followed by the French Philosophers and the heroic qualities of Washington was greatly practised by the French leaders. In short, the example of America was very valuable for the leaders of French Revolution.

The tyrannical despotism of George III was brought to an and. The ministry under Lord North fell down and was replaced by responsible ministry. The bitter experiences of Britain in America forced Britain to give up the policy of exploitation. To compensate the loss of America, Britain began to focus its concentration on India. The Victory of Americans inspired and encouraged the Latin American countries, too, to fight for freedom.

Ultimately the Declaration of Independence promulgated during the war became the clarion call for the Human rights and liberties of people all over the world.

4

Federation

Purposes of the Federal Constitution

The convention of Philadelphia had its first session of meeting in May 25, 1787. It was attended by 55 delegates from twelve out of Thirteen States (except Rhode Island) with a view to examine amendments to the Articles of confederation. The delegates were men of practical experience in the management of business who were much concerned with drafting a concrete and workable plan of action. George Washington was elected Presiding Officer of the convention and Madison with immense knowledge of theory and practice of Governments was a very active and useful member.

The constitutional committee examined various plans proposed by the delegates.

Virginia Plan

This was proposed by Edmund Randolph of Virginia and prepared by James Madison, Virginia plan suggested a bicameral legislature. Lower House was to be directly elected by the people and representation was in proportion to population. It offered an indirect election to the upper house. The theory of separation of powers was advocated. After a fortnight discussion, it was abandoned.

New Jersey Plan

This was proposed by William Patterson of New Jersey. This plan insisted on the proportional representation for both houses of legislature. It retained confederation and power of taxation was to be conferred to the Congress whose laws should be treated as supreme.

After examining these two plans, the convention resolved to draft a new Constitution on the basis of Virginia plan. The Framers of the Federal Constitution were faced with many controversial issues. Let us consider them elaborately.

1. **Controversy over the Nature of Government.** In the first place, they wanted to create a central government strong enough to maintain order, pay its debts, promote economic development and protect American interests abroad. Hamilton wanted a Central Government with extensive powers and subordination of state to the centre. The small states considered that their freedom would be jeopurdised. They wanted confederation type of weak National Government whose Congress could be entitled with the power to tax and regulate commerce. Under these conditions of extreme contradictory ideals, a federal system in which sovereignty would be divided between the nation and states became essential and acceptable to both.
2. **Question of the Rule of Majority.** The second purpose of this convention was to impose certain limitations on the rule of majority based on democracy. Many delegates explained their distrust of democracy and their main aim was to protect the rights of individuals and of minorities. Madison declared that one of their aims should be "to protect the minority of the opulent against the majority". Madison argued that society always became divided into different economic faction groups like rich and poor etc. Under such circumstances, a good Constitution should prevent any one of these groups from acquiring exclusive control of the Government and exploiting the others. In order to prevent such mutual oppression, a balance in property and numbers should be arrived at and a federal form of Government would provide for such a balance of interests.
3. **Issue of Separation of Powers.** There was consensus among the delegates of the convention regarding the frame work of the Constitution. They had a firm faith on the division of the Government into legislative, executive and judiciary branches, each one independent of the other. Eventhough the greatest exponent of this theory of separation of power was the French scholar Montesquieu, Americans had already been accustomed to the practice of this theory.
4. **Rift over Representation.** The most crucial problem confronting the convention was the question of representation of the states in the Congress. Should it be based wholly upon population as was desired by the large states or should states have equal powers as the small states instead. Small states were afraid of discrimination by the large states. Hence, they threatened to secede from the confederation if large states' demands were conceded. The small

states insisted on the equality of representation to give equal opportunity in the administration of the whole territory.

5. **Row over Slavery.** The question of slavery also became one of the points of confrontation. The southern states were much dependent upon the slaves for their plantation. They demanded that slaves should also be included as part of their population, on the basis of which representation of their states should be determined. The northern states were not ready to accept this demand.
6. **Disputes between the States of North and South.** The Northern States were interested in the protection of American shipping. But the Agricultural South disliked anything that might interfere with the export of its products to Europe. They thought that the regulation of Navigational laws would adversely affect their agriculture.

Necessity of a Compromise

Under these circumstances, where controversies were rife, a compromise had become the most crucial need of the hour. Angry debates heightened by a stiffing heat wave, led to the deadlock. The danger seemed that the convention — would break up in complete failure. Even skeptical old Benjami Franklin proposed that the daily sessions be opened with prayer by a local clergyman.

Hammering out a Bundle of Compromises

After bitter and prolonged debates the "Great compromise" of the convention was hammered out and agreed upon. The compromise provided in the plan was suggested by Connecticut. It consisted of twenty three fundamental resolutions. A committee of five members was formed which drafted the Constitution. The convention debated the draft Constitution and enunciated the provisions. After receiving it on September 20, 1787, the provisions, the Congress resolved to submit the draft constitution for the ratification to the legislatures of the States.

Features of Compromises

(1) At first the setting up of a strong or weak central government was decided. It was resolved to have neither too powerful nor too weak a central government. This delicate problem was solved by establishing a federal system of government in which sovereignty would be divided between the Nation and the States. It was an unique achievement.

(2) On the question of limiting the rule of majority a balance of interests was achieved more easily in the federal form of

Government. The majority rule was limited by giving direct representation to wealth by laying down high property qualification for election to the Senate. The House of Representatives would have popular representation while the Senate would be more independent of popular pressure. Its members would be chosen by the States Legislatures.

(3) On the controversy of representation in the Congress the compromise sponsored by Connecticut was accepted by both large and small states. It was agreed that the legislature should have two houses. The Houses of Representatives should be constituted of members represented on the basis of population. In the case of Senate (the Upper House) each state should be equally represented. In fact this compromise was regarded as more of a victory for the small states.

(4) Regarding the slave population, it was agreed that a slave might count as three fifths of a man for the purpose of determining the number of congressmen. Hence, it came to be called as 'three fifths compromise'.

(5) As regards the question of the clash of interests between the states of North and South, a compromise was arrived at. It was agreed to empower Federal Government to make Navigation Laws for the benefit of the North in protecting its shipping. In order to conciliate the South, export taxes were prohibited and the importation of slaves in the country was permitted for twenty more years till 1808 A.D.

(6) Another vital compromise that was effected was on the method of electing the President. It was agreed to elect the President indirectly by the Electoral College, rather than by direct means.

Ratification

The convention finished its work on September 17th. The constitutional document was signed only by thirty delegates. Hence, it was decided that ratification should be made by conventions especially elected in the several states. The convention also decided that the constitution should go into effect when ratified by nine states. In the process of actual ratification, Massachusetts insisted on the incorporation of Bill of Rights which constituted the first eight amendments.

5

George Washington

George Washington, the Commander-in-Chief of the American colonial forces, was the unanimous choice of the electoral college for the presidency. Washington's presidency was inaugurated in New York on 30 April 1789. In his inaugural address he declared that "the preservation of the sacred fire of liberty and the destiny of republican model of government are justly considered, perhaps as deeply, as finally staked on the experiment entrusted to the hands of American people".

His Early Career

He was born in February 22, 1732 at Bridges Greek, Virginia. Washington lived for most part of his life in Mount Vernon. He served in the French and Indian War in the rank of a colonel. When he became a member of the Virginia House of Burgesses, he married Martha Dandridge in 1759. He was a delegate to first and second Continental Congress and was chosen to command the Continental Army in June 1775. Though at the initial stages he suffered some defeats, later he won marvellous victories at Trenton and Princeton. York town victory had crowned him with the greatest credit.

Creation of Governmental Machinery

Washington's foremost duty was the creation of Governmental machinery as practically there was no machinery of National Government. Three important departments were created by the Congress. Thomas Jefferson took charge of Secretary of State to handle foreign affairs. Alexander Hamilton assumed the office of Secretary of Treasury and Henry Knox occupied the post of Secretary of War. Besides, Edmund Randolph was appointed Attorney-General. They constituted the first cabinet of America. Cabinet was expanded to offer efficient administration. The first significant service that the Congress rendered was the amendment of the Constitution which incorporated ten important measures in the year

1791. They were called as Bill of Rights which guaranteed fundamental rights like freedom of speech, etc.

The establishment of Judicial System was the next important task of the Congress. According to Judiciary Act of the Congress, 1789 thirteen district courts at the rate of one for a State was established. There were three circuit courts above them and a Supreme Court at the apex of Judicial System. John Jay was the first Chief Justice of the Supreme Court.

Domestic Policies

The main task confronting the new government was to work out a programme for dealing with financial and economic problems. This was the responsibility of Alexander Hamilton. Washington generally approved all his recommendations and he quickly became a dominating figure in the administration. Hamilton financial programme consisted of five essential features. They were : (1) Providing the Revenue; (2) Protective Tariffs; (3) Funding the National Debt; (4) Assuming the State Debts and (5) Establishment of a National Bank.

Providing the Revenue

The foremost duty of Hamilton was to provide finance for the administration. The confederation had handed over only a depleted treasury and Hamilton had to replenish it through the principle of economy. An excise tax on Liquor erupted whisky insurrection in 1794 which was at once suppressed to demonstrate the power of the Federal Government.

Handling the National Debt

Hamilton proposed that the United States "fund" its national debt, which had been incurred during the Revolution and the confederation period. He provided for the payment of all federal obligations, those held by foreigners as well as by citizens of the United States at full face value. Even though there was opposition, this measure was adopted by the Congress.

Payment of State Debts

Hamilton asked that the Federal Government assume the debts of the states, on the ground that they were incurred in a common defence in the Revolutionary war. Opposing Congressmen who blocked this proposal were persuaded to vote, through the acceptance of Hamilton's friends to vote for the National Capital on the Potomac.

National Bank and the Currency

In order to establish a sound currency, Hamilton suggested, and Congress after a long and sometimes bitter debate passed a bill for the chartering of a Bank of the United States modelled on the Bank of

England, with 10,000,000 dollars capital stock — one fifth subscribed by the Government and the remainder by the public in 1791. It was to be the fiscal agent of the Nation. The controversy over this bill centered on the interpretation of the Constitution. Jefferson an advocate of states' rights applied a "Strict Construction" with his argument that incorporation of a National Bank was not a power delegated to the Congress in the Constitution. Hamilton an ardent nationalist, countered with a 'loose construction' of interpretation in his assertion that the legislation was necessary and "implied" with constitutional powers of the Congress. President Washington signed the Bill.

The Bank was authorised to issue notes backed partly by gold and silver but chiefly by Government lands. By the Mint Act of 1792 a mint was established and the present decimal system of currency was enacted.

Protective Tariff

Hamilton's Report on Manufacturers strongly urged to adoption of a protective tariff to aid American industries and to stimulate new industries which might develop under favourable conditions.

Development of Political Parties

As Hamilton scored success after success in all his proposals, an opposition began to take form. Soon, a split developed and the two party system of politics came into existence. The first two parties were the Federalists and Democratic Republicans. The Republicans enrolled in their ranks, the defenders of States' rights, city workers and farmers. The Federalists drew support from financiers, importers, wholesalers, ship owners and those who appreciated the value of a strong central government and the rights of property. The Republicans showed more trust in the good sense of the average man, the Federalists thought of Democracy as mob rule. Hamilton and John Adams were the leaders of Federalists while the Republicans were led by Jefferson and Madison. Very soon, a heated press war broke out, full of vituperation and invective. The outbreak, full of vituperation and invective. The outbreak of French Revolution sharpened the differences between parties. Republicans admired it while Federalists detested it.

But George Washington who always held himself aloof from party bickerings, generally favoured Hamilton and disliked the animosities of the press.

Foreign Policies

The diplomatic difficulties of the American Republic were greatly aggravated of world-wide revolution. Lukewarm Federalist's approval of the early revolution, turned almost overnight, to heated opposition.

The sober-minded Jeffersonian Republicans regretted the blood shed during the Jacobin's reign of terror. But even then they justified it saying that a few thousand aristocratic heads were a cheap price to pay for human freedom.

1. **Washington's Neutrality Policy.** When the war between France and England broke out, it gave both problems and ample opportunities for the growing American diplomacy. Since the France-American Alliance of 1778 was still on the books, France expected United States to defend its West Indies from the attacks of British fleets. Jeffersonian Republicans favoured honouring the alliance. The Federalist Hamilton argued that it was a treaty with a French King and since monarchy had been abolished it was no longer binding them. But President Washington, was not swayed by the clamour of the crowd. He displayed an invaluable realism and coolness of judgement. Washington issued a proclamation of Neutrality in April 22, 1793. He declared that America was neutral to both the warring Nations — France and Britain. He also sternly warned American citizens to be impartial towards both armed camps. It was America's first formal declaration of aloofness from old world quarrels. Thus, Washington resisted both Federalist pressure for involvement on the side of Britain and Republican pressure for aid to France. Washington's neutrality proclamation clearly illustrates the truism that self-interest is the basic cement of all alliances.
2. **Genet's Mission.** The Girondin rulers of France sent their first diplomatic representative namely Edmond Charles Genet with a hope to obtain sympathy and economic assistance. Genet landed at Charleston and was greeted by the enthusiastic Jeffersonian Republicans. Ignoring the proclamation of Neutrality, he used American Ports as bases for French privateers, enlisted American citizens for an invasion of the Spanish colonies and meddled with American internal politics. When Genet was reminded of the Neutrality proclamation by Washington he criticised him as "a week old man under the British influence". As he began to directly appeal to the people, Washington demanded his recall into France. Fearful of being guillotined, by the Jacobins, Genet remained in America as a private citizen marrying the daughter of Governor Clinton.
3. **America's Relations with France After Jay's Treaty.** A threat to American neutrality came from the British navy which made a blockade of France and French Colonies. Britain began to seize the American ships carrying French goods, impressed men of

bonafide American birth, occupied a number of places South of Great lakes and aided Indian tribes against Americans. To settle all these issues Washington despatched Chief Justice John Jay who signed a treaty with Britain in November, 1794 known as Jay's Treaty. This treaty naturally made France enraged over America for accepting the British blockade. Accusing that the United States was violating its own Neutrality Act by befriending Britain, the Directory ordered the French Navy to capture ships trading with Britain. Even the French privateers had seized more than three hundred merchant ships.

John Adams Peace Manoeuvres

By this time John Adams had become the President of United States. He wanted to follow the same policy of peace of Washington and wanted to make the relations with France more cordial. He sent the Federalist Charles Pickney to Paris his ambassador. Adding insult to injury, the Paris regime haughtily refused to receive American envoy and even threatened him with arrest.

Embroilments with Britain

Another threat to American neutrality came from the British Navy which imposed a blockade of France and its colonies including West Indies. The British began to seize American ships carrying goods that belonged to French citizens of bringing to French ports, articles declared to be contraband, despite American protests. Even more flagrant violating of neutral rights was the practice of impressment. Britain regarded that any one with British birth was a British subject. British naval officers in need of men began to stop American ships, search them for British subjects, and in a number of instances, they proceeded to impress men of bonafide American birth.

In addition to blockade, and impressment Britain also occupied a number of places South of Great Lakes. She also rendered military assistance to Indian tribes who had defeated Arthur St. Clair with the aid of British weapons.

The two countries were drifting towards a collision. However, Washington by his cool sense of Judgement decided to draw a treaty with Britain. He despatched Chief Justice John Jay who signed a treaty with Britain in November, 1794 known as Jay's treaty.

This Jay's treaty was a diplomatic defeat for the United States. By this treaty, Jay accepted the British blockade and gave Britain several trading advantages in America. But he made no mention of the compensation to be paid by Britain for the loss caused by her to America. When the terms of the treaty were made public there was a howl of protests and Jay's effigy was burnt.

However, it assured temporary peace and established friendship between Britain and United States.

Treaty with Spain

The diplomatic failure in London was made up by a success at Madrid. In 1795, Spain became an ally of France and visualising a war with England resolved to establish friendly relations with the United States. Washington taking stock of the situation sent Thomas Pickney to Madrid to negotiate a treaty. This treaty of San Lorenzo (Pickney Treaty) provided for the unlimited use of the Mississippi and it also granted the right to deposit duty free goods at New Orleans for export. Spain accepted 31st parallel as the boundary line between Georgia and Florida. The treaty recognised Mississippi as the southern boundary of the United States.

Washington's Retirement

Worn out by the duties of the office of president, Washington insisted on retiring at the end of his second term in 1797. Eventhough he was urged by his friends to stand for the third term, he declined. His farewell address exhorted people to "observe good faith and justice towards all Nations". He passed away peacefully in December 1799.

6

Thomas Jefferson (1801-09)

In the election of 1800, Thomas Jefferson and his running mate Aaron Burr had shared equally the electoral college votes. The deadlock was to be broken by the House of Representatives. With the intervention of Hamilton whose supporters cast blank ballots, it was possible for Jefferson to be elected as President. The new President was a philosopher, a neutralist and a scientific agriculturist. He was not only a shrewd politician but also a dreamer. Though a slave owner, he believed in the principles of liberty and equality. He believed that men were naturally good, but they were corrupted by bad institutions. He stood for state's rights, low tariff and agricultural economy. He was preferably a thinker than a man of action. He declared that best government was that which governed least.

Internal Affairs

Jefferson's first term was a prosperous one. As the Republicans had won control of the Congress, it was possible for the administration to introduce and implement a number of changes.

(1) The administration allowed the Alien and Sedition Acts, the reactionary laws of the Federalists to expire in due course.

(2) The whisky excise implemented by Hamilton was now abolished.

(3) Gallotin, Secretary of the Treasury, took number of economic measures such as economy in government expenditure and rapid payment of the debt.

(4) As Jefferson considered the Federalist bureaucracy as a stumbling-block for his intended reforms, he removed some officials to make room for republicans. This middle of the road plan had drastic effects in the history of U.S.A. It led to floor crossing in the national life.

The Judiciary

There was bitter conflict between the executive and the judiciary organs of the Government. As most of the judges were Federalists and showed partisanship in enforcing the laws, the Republicans regarded their conduct as an abuse of judicial power. The views of Chief Justice Marshall in the case of Marbury *vs.* Madison in 1803, further alarmed them. Marbury was one of "midnight appointments" to the bench. As his commission was withheld by Madison, the Secretary of State he appealed to the court for a writ of Mandamus. Chief Justice Marshall held that the Court had no constitutional authority to issue writs of Mandamus and thereby avoided a direct conflict with the administration. He had also asserted that the Supreme Court had the right to review and invalidate acts of Congress.

Finally, the Republicans decided to remove the judges by the method of impeachment. In 1804, a district judge was impeached on the grounds of insanity. But they failed to impeach Justice Chase of the Supreme Court. Jefferson also failed to replace the existing judges since most of them lived a longer life. A few Republican judges too were influenced by Marshall. But the judges were forced to be more impartial in their views. For a few more decades the judiciary was in the hands of the Federalists.

The Louisiana Purchase

Jefferson achieved considerable success in diplomacy. Louisiana, a large territory extending from Mississipi to the Rockies had been Spanish since 1762. By a secret treaty of San Ildefonso of 1800, Spain had handed it over to France. The Spanish officials still in its occupation of Louisiana withdrew from American citizens the "right of deposit" at New Orieans in 1802. As Napoleon was planning new conquests in the New world it would block the American expansion in the west. The U.S.A. may also be drawn in the European conflicts. So Jefferson sent his Ambassador James Manroe to Paris with instructions to buy New Orleans from France. By the time Manroe reached Paris, Napoleon had already decided to sell Louisiana. The attack of Napoleon on the black Republic of San Domingo had failed. The European war was about to be resumed. France could not defend Louisiana against the British. If France sold Louisiana to U.S.A., then it would make way for U.S.A. in 1803. The purchase of Louisiana was regarded as a spectacular achievement in the history of U.S.A.

Foreign Affairs

During the second term of Jefferson, American foreign policy was mostly influenced by the Napoleonic wars. He vainly tried to safeguard American rights against the warring powers of Europe. After conquering most of the European continent, Napoleon had turned to subdue Great Britain. Against the Berlin and Milan decrees of Napoleon, Britain passed the orders in Council of 1807. Britain also impressed deserters found on American ships. The British ship Leopard attached Chesapeake, an American ship and forcibly took off three Americans. The Chesapeake affair forced President Jefferson to take some precautionary measures. Believing that American trade was essential to Britain, Congress passed the Embargo Act in 1807. As American trade was not essential to Britain, this Act brought only ruin to American economy. It resulted in commercial stagnation and steep fall in the prices of all commodities. As it was very difficult in enforcing the Act, the Congress repealed it in 1809.

Being a dreamer, he often preserved a compromise formula rather than a direct action. By purchasing Louisiana, he achieved the greatest gain for U.S.A. when he became President, the rich were terrified of many revolutionary changes, but he made only a few positive innovations. His presidency ended unhappily because of European conflict. He may be remembered as it was found in his epitaph: "Here was buried Thomas Jefferson, Author of the Declaration of Independence, of the Statute of Virginia for religious freedom and Father of the University of Virginia". Jefferson owes a special place in history of U.S.A.

7

Hamilton and Jefferson

The study of the policies of Alexander Hamilton and Thomas Jefferson will offer a picture of diametrically opposite characters. Alexander Hamilton was a staunch supporter of traders and other wealthy sections of the society. Aristocratic in his personal tastes and political ideas, he distrusted the common people. He was of the view that the rich deserved their riches and the poor their poverty and that only the rich had intelligence and statesmanship. Whereas, Jefferson believed that all men were created equal and possess certain inalienable rights like life, liberty and pursuit of happiness.

Alexander Hamilton

He was the Secretary of the Treasury in the new government under George Washington. He was born in 1757 in Nevis of West Indies to a Scotish father and Huguenot mother. He had his law course in King's College, New York. Completing his education he served as Private Secretary and aide-de-camp of Washington. He married Elizabeth, the daughter of Philip Schuyler, a land lord and became a lawyer in New York City.

His Philosophy

He had a strong conviction that law, order and good government and individual liberties could be preserved only through the rule of an aristocracy and despised democratic as idealists as docrinarire and impractical. Hence, he wanted to establish an alliance between the Federal Government and the wealthy class. He was a man of great personal charm and his financial integrity was remarkable.

Financial Policies of Hamilton

Hamilton was entrusted with the responsibility of chalking out a programme in dealing with financial and economic problems.

Hamilton's financial programme was embodied in a series of reports submitted to Congress. It consisted of five important features. They were: (1) Providing the revenue; (2) Policy of protective tariffs; (3) Funding the National debt; (4) Assuming of state debt of Federal government and (5) Establishment of Central Bank and issue of a National Currency.

1. **Raising the Revenue.** The confederation had bequeathed only a depleted treasury And it was the first task of Hamilton to replenish it through the principle of economy. The National debts were paid off and thus reduced the recurring amount of interest. An excise tax on liquors was imposed which brought about a revolution called whisky insurrection in 1794. The farmers of Carolina, Virgina and Pennsylvania convened a convention and resolved to launch an insurrection. This was quickly suppressed and obedience was exacted from the people.
2. **Tariff Policy.** Hamilton adopted protective tariff to safeguard the existing industries and to encourage new one. He ordered for protective duties on manufactures. Raw materials were exempted from custom duties. He depended much on manufacture for enhancing the National Income as opposed to the Jeffersonian ideal of agriculture. Later on Hamilton's policies were very much hailed by manufacturers.
3. **Funding the National Debt.** The most important aspect of Hamilton's financial programme was the funding of National debt. In his report on public credit he recommended that the debts inherited from the confederation totalling about 50,000,000 dollars should be paid at its face value even if it drained the already depleted treasury. For such a policy would strengthen the Federal Government by winning the support of all public creditors, while at the same time it would provide the moneyed classes with capital for new business. The main objection to this policy was that much of the public debt was now held by a relatively small number of speculators who had bought them at heavy discounts. Hamilton was of the view that money accumulated in the hands of small class of speculators would be redeployed for investment purposes. Hence, the Congress voted by a substantial majority to fund the debts of the confederation.
4. **Payment of State Debts.** Hamilton also recommended that the Federal Government should also assume the debts of the States which amounted to 20,000,000 dollars. These debts had been incurred by the State during the war of Independence. Congress passed a Bill by which payment of the State Debts was assumed.

Besides, the states who had not paid war debts were asked to contribute towards the construction of the New Capital in the newly formed district of Columbia.

5. **National Bank and Issue of Currency.** Another important measure was the creation of a Bank of the United States in the British model. It was to assist the Government by holding its funds and when necessary by making loans. It was chartered for twenty years. It was empowered to issue notes, receive deposits and open branches to promote economic expansion out of the total capital 10,000,000 Dollars-one fifth was to be contributed by the Government and the balance by private investors.

Controversy over the Constitutional Provision

This Bank policy of Hamilton was opposed tooth and nail by Jeffersonians. Jefferson felt that the Bank would give excessive power over the national economy and small group of investors would make large profits out of it. He opposed on the ground that the chartering of it was not explicitly authorised by the Constitution. Jefferson based his views on the "Strict Construction" of the words of the Constitution. Hamilton retarded it by developing a theory of "Implied powers" according to which it was to be assumed that a vast body of powers had to be assumed that a vast body of powers had to be implied by general clauses and one of these authorised Congress to "make all laws which shall be necessary and proper" for carrying out other powers granted. Washington supported Hamilton and in 1791, the bank was established by Congress. In 1792, Congress passed the Mint Act which authorised the bank to issue currency. A mint was established at Philaadelphia to mint gold and silver coins.

Finally, Hamilton established Sinking Fund, which would gradually be accumulated by Government in order to provide for paying off the principal of the National Debt.

Growth of Political Parties

The divergent ideals and economic interests among the people, divided them into two opposing groups. Hamilton's financial programme served as a catalyst. Its supporters called themselves federalists, while their opponents assumed the name of Republicans. Hamilton's policies benefited only the rich, the merchants and financiers and particularly it was more advantageous to North than to the agricultural South. Hamilton believed the Government to be governed by an elite group composed of "the wise, the rich and well born", had framed every measure for the benefit of the rich men and hence was opposed to Agriculture and Democracy.

His policies were severely criticised and opposed by Jefferson and Madison. Madison was formerly one of the spokesmen of Federalists also turned against Hamilton in 1790. He believed in a balance between opposing interests of the different classes — Madison was joined by Jefferson and Aaron Burr, a young lawyer of New York. The purpose of Republicanism was to maintain the ideals of American revolution, popular Government, the right of man and protection for the interests of the masses. Jefferson believed that Hamilton's "Implied powers" would undermine the authority for popular liberty and hence he preached "strict construction" by which the Federal authority must be limited as per the words of the constitution. The key word of Jefferson was liberty where as Hamilton insisted on Discipline. Washington though sympathetic of the Federalists and supported Hamilton, he never allowed himself to be controlled by either party.

Thomas Jefferson

Jefferson was the President to be inaugurated from the new National Capital. Born in 1743, in Marticello of a Virginian agrarian family had his education in William and Mary and soon came to be a versatile genius. He owes his special place in the history of U.S.A., primarily to the fact that he could express his ideas more pointedly and unforgetfully than any other statesman except Lincoln. His eloquence is testified in his draft of the Declaration of Independence. After serving as Governor of Virginia and Minister of U.S. to France, he assumed the office of Secretary in the New Government. Finally, he preferred to resign since he was consistently outvoted at cabinet meetings.

Philosophy of Jefferson

He was a staunch follower of National Philosophy. Throughout his long career, he asserted that men were endowed with rights and the primary purpose of the Government was to protect these rights. He was animated by the optimum of the enlightenment. He insisted that men were naturally good and inclined to follow the guidance of reason. He believed that men might be corrupted by bad institutions.

Faith in Rural Democracy

He realised that agriculture was the only way of life that can promote moral and political virtues. He accused the cities that made men corrupt.

Laissez Faire Policy

He sincerely believed that the best government was that which governed least. That is why he wanted the Federal Government to perform minimum functions. But he was more effective as a thinker than as a man of action and, therefore, his policies as president turned out to be milder than his statements had led people to expect. Eventhough, he called the election of 1800, equivalent of a revolution, he had not followed any revolutionary policy in administration. He contented himself with reversing some of the Federalist policies and introduce few innovations. With regard to external relations he promised a policy of peace, commerce and honest friendship with all nations, entangling alliances with none. To sum up, his principles were embodied in limited government economy and harmoney.

Simplicity and Economy

Jefferson had firm faith in simplicity of administration and economy of expenditure. He stopped the expansion of navy and reduced the size of the army to effect economy. He insisted that funds should be allocated for specific purposes rather than lump sum grants sanctioned to various departments.

Hatred of Slavery

His faith in the quality of men made him consider slavery as an evil institution which must be gradually abolished. His democratic attitude is evident from his views on slavery.

Independence of Judiciary

Jefferson never tried to meddle with the judiciary rather he wanted it to be impartial. The judiciary was completely manned by Federalists who enforced the Sedition Act rigorously. Besides, Chief Justice Marshall made a forceful assertion of the right of the Supreme Court to invalidate the acts of Congress in the case of Marbury *vs.* Madison in 1803. All these activities of the judiciary alarmed the Republicans.

The Republicans decided to impeach such judges. In 1804, an insane judge was successfully impeached and the proceedings against Justice Chase of the Supreme Court failed for want of evidence of his recrimination of the Republicans. Hence, Jefferson got a bill passed by which Additional District Courts and Circuit Courts of Appeal were created. Jefferson appointed judges of his own party to these courts. The ultimate result of all these proceedings was that judges, henceforth, were more careful to show a proper impartiality and to refrain from direct participation in the political conflicts.

8

James Madison's Presidency — the War of 1812

James Madison was the President of America for two terms from 1807 to 1817. He was serving as a secretary of Foreign affairs in the Ministry of Jefferson. He had sound knowledge and experience in the international relations and his chief efforts were to restore good and cordial relations with Great Britain and other countries. The early history of the 19th century was dominated by the Napoleonic wars which made America to follow an aggressive policy and as a result of this policy adopted by the various countries, America was forced to enter in the war of 1812 with England. There were many causes for the outbreak of this war between U.S.A. and Great Britain.

Causes of the War

1. **Decrees of Napoleon.** Napoleon who was desirous of conquering the entire Europe. He wanted to establish his authority over Great Britain after the battle of Trafalgar. So Napoleon issued Decrees from Berlin in 1806 and Milan in 1807, whereby he forbaded the English or neutral vessels to enter any harbour controlled by France or her allies and these decrees checked the progress of trade of the neutral countries like America.
2. **Blockade of Great Britain.** Great Britain issued orders in council to retaliate the decrees of Napoleon. Accordingly no neutral ship was permitted to have a trade with France and her allies. When the American cargoes shipped through the blockades, they were confiscated by the British Navy.
3. **Affect The American Trade.** Due to introduction of the decrees of Napoleon and orders in council of Great Britain, more than 200 American ships which were carrying commodities in the sea waters of France and Great Britain were seized by both

countries and this greatly affected the American trade, self-respect and honour. Consequently United States condemned that the blockade was illegal and protested against the capture of the American ships which strained the cordial relation of America and Great Britain.

4. **Impressment of American Seamen by the British.** The British Seamen deserted their navy and joined in the service of American navy. The Seamen joined in the USA navy were forced by Britain to come back to UK which was an insult to USA. It was further aggravated that Chesapeake, an American warship was attacked by the British ship Leopard and four members of the American crews were impressed into the British navy. So the prestige and honour of America was greatly hurt and the relation of USA and UK was much strained.

5. **Diplomacy of Jefferson.** The Jay Treaty between USA and UK was about to expire. Jefferson, the President of USA wanted to revise this treaty in such a way that the practice of impressing American sailers should be abandoned and illegal capture of American vessels should be stopped. But the effort of the President was not fruitful and the British Secretary for Foreign Affairs was obstinate and did not permit renewal of the treaty. This diplomatic failure further estranged America's relation with England.

6. **Non-Importation Act.** Jefferson decided that the commerce of USA was much important to England and if USA restricted her trade with England, she would come to terms with USA. So he passed the Non-Importation Act by which he denied permission to British manufactured goods to the American ports.

7. **The Incident of Chesapeake (June 1807).** Chesapeake, an American frigate sailed in Mediterranean ocean under the command of Captain Barron. This frigate Leopard demanded the release of the deserters. Since Chesapeake was a warship and outside the purview of inspection by another warship, it did not allow the UK ship for search of deserters. On this refusal, the British ship opened fire and enfound one deserter and carried him along with three seamen who were the American citizens. After this incident, USA adopted stern action of imposing economic sanction against Britain.

8. **Embargo Act of 1807.** America passed Embargo Act by which she stopped the import of British manufactured goods in to America and forbaded the American vessels sailing to foreign ports. America thought that by introducing this act, she could punish

both France and Britain for their activities and the outcome of this act was not fruitful. So the American exports fell and the commerce suffered a great set back. Finally, the Embargo Act was repealed by Non-Intercourse Act which forbaded the commerce only with France and England.

9. **Demand of War Hawks.** War hawks were the persons who were interested in expansion of trade with the west and advocated the conquest of Canada. A few war hawks like Henry Clay and John C. Calhoun demanded for war with England for her illegal capture of American vessels and the glory and prestige of America should be maintained. They requested the President of America to declare war with Britain.

10. **Indians War With America.** By the treaty of Greenville of 1795, the Indians were given lands in the west but the white had been continuously encroaching upon this territory. The Indians were supported by the British who wished them to remain in their place itself. The Indians formed a confederation of fighting men to arrest the march of white people in their dwelling place which infuriated the American because they discovered that the Indians had British guns and ammunition. So WarHawks who were against the stiff attitude of the British forced the President of America to declare war with Britain. But he wanted to settle down the outstanding disputes amicably. When the President found that the British statesmen were stubborn and unmindful of their behaviours, the President of America had to declare war on Britain.

11. **War.** When the British minister in Washington informed that Britain cannot repeal the orders in council, James Madison was compelled to ask the Congress to declare war on Britain and the war was declared on June 16, 1812 between England and America.

Course of War

(1) When war declared in 1812, USA was not prepared to put up a stiff resistance with Britain. The army was not sufficiently well equipped and trained to meet out any outside dangers. The navy consisted of only twelve vessels out of which only three were the large frigates. Whereas the British Navy had 830 vessels in good condition. So America made up her mind to increase the number of soldiers and navy frigates with-in a short time.

(2) At the time of war, America lacked financial sources. So they borrowed a huge sum from other countries and increased her revenue so as to meet the cost of the war preparation against Britain.

(3) The plan of campaign of the United States consisted of three pronged attack — an expedition against Montreal; an attack on the Canadian Centre across the Niagra river and an invasion of Canada.

(4) Hull led an expedition with 2000 men against Canada from Detroit. But he came to know that the Indians were marching towards the city of Detroit and the supply of provision and means of communication to this city was cut off. So Hull did not like to fight with the Indians and on August 16, 1812 he surrendered.

(5) After the expedition of Hull, Von Reusslaer undertook another expedition against the British. The British were pressed hard and General Brock was killed in the process of driving back the US forces. This expedition was not successful to the USA because the British forces received reinforcements and the supplies of the American forces were cut off.

(6) The third expedition undertaken by Dearborn against British did not like to proceed beyond Lake Champlain due to the fear of the British troops and hence he returned to Plattsburg. Thus, all the three expeditions against British were not favourable to USA and she lost the city of Detroit and Michigan territory. So the people of America became angry and wanted to get back their lost places.

(7) In 1813 Captain Oliver Perry defeated the British Squadron on Lake Erie. Another American Commander Harrison recaptured Detroit, drove away the British and defeated them again at battle of Thames where the Indian leader Tecumseh was also killed. This proved to be a graveyard for the Indians. At the end of 1813 neither side had made any real advance.

(8) In the summer of 1814, the Americans attacked Canada and succeeded in defeating the British. In the month of August the British seized Washington the capital of USA and took up the control of the capital after a feeble resistance by America. The President and members of his cabinet took their heals from the capital. The white house and other public buildings were destroyed by the British. When America was defeated in one place, she gained success in Orleans under the leadership of Andrew Jackson.

Battles in the Sea

Though there were many defeats in land, America was able to get a number of victories at the sea because of experienced seamen and excellent fighters. In August 1812, Captain Porter Captured British ship Alert and little later, Captain Isaac Hull captured British frigate.

Commodore Perry, one of the important captains made a victory over the British and controlled the lake Erie which paved the way to advance American forces to Canada. During the year 1813-14, the British blockaded the American ships to carry goods in the sea water controlled by Britain which affected the commerce of America. The British proceeded to Baltimore to capture Fort McHenry and captured it. Finally, there was a fierce naval battle between the two countries for the possession of New Orleans in which the British ran away to their ships which greatly enhanced the glory and prestige of America. Andrew Jackson who took part in this war earned the title of 'Hero of New Orleans' and before the commencement of the battle of New Orleans a peace treaty had already been signed at Ghent in Belgium.

Negotiations for the Treaty

In the absence of clear victory to both countries, the negotiation was dragged on and neither side wanted to review the fighting to bring to an end. The political atmosphere in Europe had changed after the Congress of Vienna and Napoleon who was exiled, came back to France and started his aggression. These factors made European countries to realise the gravity of the situation and so British changed her stiff attitude towards America and the treaty of Ghent was concluded between America and UK.

Provisions of the Treaty of Ghent (December 24, 1814)

(1) Restoration of the territorial *status quo* was accepted by both countries.
(2) The demand of the territorial concession and creation of separate Indian States were not accepted in this treaty.
(3) No country should interfere into the internal affairs of another country.
(4) Boundary disputes between USA and Canada were to be settled by joint commission.
(5) No mention was made about the impressment, neutral blockade and other maritime differences.

Results of the War of 1812

(1) Britain lost her supremacy and monopoly over the sea which encouraged America to become equal naval power with England.
(2) There was a great loss of men and money in the war. The American currency was debased and devalued. As the economy of USA was broken, she wanted to improve the financial conditions. So she adopted the policy of isolation for the next hundred years and during this period improvement took place in all fields.

(3) As America was developing in all fields, and the European powers began to realise that America was an emerging state and she deserved due respect.
(4) The blockade policies adopted by France and Britain encouraged the growth of modern industries in USA particularly the textile industries.
(5) It resulted in peace settlement of the problems of the two countries.
(6) The support given to the Indians by the British was withdrawn.
(7) The war instigated the people of South America for their freedom struggle.
(8) The war made the people of America to realise the value of unity and integrity and they began to fight against the common enemy. A sense of patriotism developed among the Americans and they worked for the progress of the nation from dawn to dusk.
(9) Great Britain retained its power to govern and control Canada.

Way did the War of 1812 Consider as the War of Second Revolution

(1) The war of American Independence was the first Revolution for attaining political freedom and dignity whereas the war of 1812 gave economic freedom. In this war the policy of blockade adopted by great Britain made Americans to have concentration in the industrial progress of the nation. Thus, Americans awoke from their sleep and made the country towards the path of Industrial Revolution.
(2) The American War of Independence was started for political, legal an territorial rights of the people where the war of 1812 took place not for the rights but for the territorial expansion of America.
(3) The prevention of the American industrial and commercial development to far the outbreak of the second revolution.
(4) The British helped the Indians living in America in all possible ways and this assistance was considered as an Anti-American Act. So the Indians took up arms supplied by British in both wars against Americans.
(5) In both the wars the confronting countries had won victories and sufferings also. Both the wars were indecisive and inconclusive. When the people became tired of the war, they ended the wars too.
(6) After the first Revolution of American War of Independence, she followed the policy of non-interference in the internal policy of the foreign countries and the policy of isolation from the rest of the world was adopted after the war of 1812.

(7) In both the wars, Americans fought against British for the welfare of the people.

(8) The policy of isolation adopted by America after the two wars made the people to realise the spirit of nationalism, patriotism and dignity of labour.

(9) In both occasions, America had an idea of establishing her authority over Canada but her dream was not fulfilled. Hence, the war of 1812, to some extent, may be regarded as a Second Revolution.

9

James Monroe's Administration

James Monroe was elected President of America in 1816 after James Madison. He occupied a significant place in the history of USA. Before he was elected as the President of America, he served as an ambassador to France and Britain. He was the ablest Foreign Secretary during the period of Madison. For the first time in the history of USA the spirit of party rivalry seemed dead due to the extinction of the Federalist party and so his period of administration has been described as "Era of good feelings".

1. **Rush-Bagot Agreement for Peace.** The chief moto of James Monroe was to restore peace in America for which he wanted to settle down all the disputes unsolved by the Treaty of Ghent with Britain. A smooth and cordial relation was maintained with Britain and in return, Britain was also willing to extend her friendship. The help given to the Indians by the British against America was stopped. As the climate of friendship was favourable to both countries, the American Ambassador Rush and the British Minister Bagot signed an agreement in 1817 which came to be known as Rush-Bagot Agreement. It paved the way for peaceful settlement of all the disputes between the two countries.
   (a) Both countries decided not to ply their ship on the Great Lakes.
   (b) A commission was constituted to draw the boundary line between USA and Canada and it was fixed 49th parallel. The territory of Oregon could be settled by both American and British people and later on it was partitioned in 1846. Thus, the settlement of the outstanding disputes between the two countries gave a sense of peace and relief to both countries.
2. **Purchase of Florida.** Florida, a Spanish colony gave asylum to the runaway slaves and white desperadoes of Plantation. It was served as a base to harass the people of the border areas. Further,

Creek and Saminole Indians raided the American settlers. As the menace and atrocities of these Indians were intolerable, Andrew Jackson led an expedition against these people, drove them and took possession of the two Spanish posts. He captured two traders one a Spanish national and the other an English who were inciting the Indians and they were executed. This incident aroused a sense of horror and excitement in both countries and it was decided to settle off this problem through diplomacy Spain which was extending her helping hand to the Indians of Florida could find that her condition was very weak and she offered to handover Florida to USA. So in 1819 Quincy Adams and the Spanish Minister Louis de Oris signed the Florida Treaty. According to this treaty Spain abandoned her control over Florida and sold to USA for 5 million dollars. The amount had to be paid to the Americans in Florida who had claims against Spain. In return for this, the United States relinquished her claims on Texas.

3. **Declaration of Non Colonization.** Russia which was seeking colonies for her industrial products had established her control in Alaska and she would like to extend her interest in Oregon territory. So in 1821, the Czar of Russia published an ukase which claimed a large part of the western, coast as part of Alaska. Knowing the intention of Russia, America decided to tighten her control on the entire American Hemisphere from the clutches of the colonial empires. So America declared her policy by which the countries of the American Hemisphere should be closed to other European countries for colonization.

4. **The Missouri Compromise.** During Monroe's administration, the controversial dispute of slavery flared up once again between North and south which aggravated the political condition of America. At this time five more new American States of Louisiana, Mississippi, Alabama, Indiana and Illinois were admitted in the Union of American States and by adding these states, there were eleven free states and eleven slave states in the Union. The northern free states had more representation in the House of Representative but the representation of North and South States was equal in the Senate. In 1819, Missouri applied for admission as a slave state. If Missouri was to be admitted as a slave state, the representation of the slave state would be more in the Senate. So Missouri was asked to abolish slavery gradually and would become a free state and only on this condition she could be permitted to join in the Union of American States. So Missouri felt that her economic and political freedom should be shattered if she would become a free state in the course of time

which resulted in a heated discussion among the states about the question of admitting Missouri either as a Free State or a slave state. The dispute was solved temporarily when Maine applied for admission as a free state. Missouri was admitted as a slave state and Maine detached from Massachusetts, was admitted as a free state. This formula came to be known as the Missouri Compromise of 1820. When the problem was yet to be solved Jefferson declared that "this momentous question, like a fire ball in the night, awakened and filled me with terror". John Quincy Adams commented that "the present question is a mere preamble — a title page to a great tragic volume".

5. **The Monroe Doctrine.** In the beginning of the 19th century, Napoleon, the war monger of France wanted to bring the entire European countries under his rule for which he was on and off waging wars and when Europe was under turmoil, the South American countries decided to fight against the colonial powers and started their war of independence. In 1822, the five American States namely Argentina, Chile. Colombia, Mexico and Peru had become independent and they were soon recognised by USA and the independence of the American States was welcomed by both Britain and USA, because they wanted to root out the influence of Spanish colonial system so they could promote their trade and commerce.

After the fall of Napoleon, Europe was dominated by the Holy Alliance comprising Austria and Russia and the Alliance authorised France to suppress the riots in Spain. France which was regaining her strength and vigour made up her mind to send her army to South America to re-establish colonial rule, which was a threat to the security of the American colonies. So USA and Britain proposed to put up a joint fight against the aggressive tendencies of France in South America. Adams preferred to act alone and the famous Monroe Doctrine came into existence. This doctrine formed a part of the President's message to Congress on 2nd December 1823. It declared that American States should be for Americans just as the European Countries for Europeans. The intervention of the European Countries in the internal affairs of the American States could be considered as an act of aggression and USA could not tolerate the colonisation of the South American States by the European Countries. The Monroe Doctrine was to be considered as part and parcel of the American foreign policy towards Caribbean countries. It implied the supremacy of USA over the whole American Continent. By following this policy USA often intervened in the affairs of South American countries to make them to be its sphere of influence.

10

Monroe Doctrine

1. **Emergence of the Monroe Doctrine.** When Monroe was the President of America, the European Countries desired to extend their sphere of influence in the South American states. There was a keen competition among the countries to establish their colonial rule so that the colonies could be used for their market. This commercial tendencies of the European Countries were strongly objected by USA and stated clearly that the American states should be closed to further colonization by European powers. When the danger and security of the South American Countries were felt, USA decided to protect the democracy and independence of the colonies by extending all possible assistances. Then the new policy which proclaimed that "America was to be for the Americans alone" became to be known as Monroe Doctritine. Whenever time and tide favoured it the succeeding presidents simply implemented this doctrine in Caribbean region. Many causes were responsible for the declaration of Monroe Doctrine in 1823. It is only to be regarded as part of American foreign policy in Caribbean region. It may also be regarded as a combination of the Doctrine of Non-Colonization and the policy of isolation.
2. **Political Condition in Latin America.** After the fall of Napoleon of France, the Spanish Colonies in Latin America rose up from their bondage and started their rebellion against the aggressive aggressor *i.e.* Spain who could not crush the rebellion. The freedom fighters like Simon Boliver of Venezuela and San Martin of Argentina countinued the struggle and helped to liberate a number of colonies which resulted Argentina, Chile, Colombia, Peru, Mexico and Brazil proclaiming their independence. Spain appealed to the Holy Alliance to get back their lost colonies. To avert Republican Revolution in Europe these powers were ready to

assist Spain. So there was a real danger of European intervention in South America.

3. **Interest of UK and USA in Latin American Countries.** Both UK and USA had their interest for their own welfare. America extended her maximum support to the South American Republic and vehemently objected the European interventions. The expulsion of European imperialism would give safety and security to the American Hemisphere. The elimination of Spanish influence would serve as a market for the American goods in South America and the declaration of independence for the South America would enhance the prestige and power, America. Further, the American Countries could introduce and improve their developmental activities on their own accord without outside interference. Great Britain had too deep interest in Latin America. The distinction of Spanish influence would help Britain to expand her trade in Latin America. It was also possible for her to check the influence of USA in this region. So both countries had intense interest in establishing their sphere of influence and further they wanted to check Russia which claimed ownership on many Latin American Countries.
4. **Confrontation with Russia.** In 1821, the Czar of Russia issued an order warning all foreign vessels not to come within 100 miles of any port of the Pacific Coast of America and she claimed over a large territory of Latin American Countries. Therefore, Secretary of Sate Adams announced that United States would not admit the right of the Russia to any territorial establishment in North America and would act on the principle that "the American continents are no longer subjects for any European colonial establishments".
5. **Efforts of Spain to Recolonise the Latin America.** After the Napoleonic war the Hapsburg dynasty was put back on the throne of Spain and Austria and the political condition in Europe was also changed. The Holy Alliance was formed in 1816 by the Czar of Russia by which the countries Russia, Austria, Russia and France took a pledge that they would rule the people in accordance with the christian principles and further these countries extended support to Spain to recolonise her lost Latin American Countries. It created a wild protest from USA because she recognised the freedom and independence of these countries. Great Britain who had trade interest in these countries decided to help all the countries to fight against the move the European Countries.

Consequently Great Britain approached America to make a joint declaration of policy and check the move of reactionary European powers.

6. **Drafting the Monroe Doctrine.** George Canning, the British Foreign Secretary proposed to Richard Rush, the American Ambassador that both countries should protest the intervention of the reactionary European powers in Latin American countries. But America did not accept the proposal of the U.K. Monroe, the American President had consultation with Adams and other important cabinet members and finally had arrived at a conclusion to make a declaration himself and not in collaboration with England. This declaration was called "Monroe Doctrine" and the message of this declaration was sent to Congress on 2nd December 1823.
7. **Provisions of the Monroe Doctrine.** The main principles of the Monroe Doctrine are given here :
   (1) The American continents were not to be considered as subjects for future colonization by any European powers.
   (2) The political system of Europe was entirely different from the political system of USA and any attempt of the European Countries to introduce their system to any portion of the American hemisphere would be dangerous to peace and security of USA.
   (3) The interference of the European countries into the internal affairs of the liberated Latin American Countries would be considered as an unfriendly attitude and potential danger to safety of USA.
   (4) The American Continents are no longer subjects for any European Colonial establishments. Just as the Europe was for Europeans, so America was to be for the Americans.
   (5) The United States would not interfere with existing colonies or dependencies of any European power.
   (6) America would not involve into the internal affairs of the European Countries and she would not join in the wars of the European powers. The Monroe Doctrine was nothing but the establishment of American supremacy over her hemisphere.
8. **Application of this Doctrine.** The application of this Doctrine was not effective because America was not bold enough to implement it and further the declaration of this doctrine was not actively considered by other European powers. In fact no country took it seriously and challenged it during the 19th century. Great Britain was more powerful than USA and in case of rivalry

between the two countries, the victory always favoured Britain. The liberated Latin Countries liked to have diplomatic relations only with UK. They thought that their security and independence could be restored only with the help of Great Britain rather than America. Hence, the declaration of this doctrine and the expansion of American influence over the Latin American Countries were treated as a potential threat to the existence of their independence. Consequently there was no cordial relations between the two parts of the American Continent for a long time. When Britain captured Falkland islands, Honduras and Nicaragua against the principles of USA, USA could not check the aggressive policy of the UK because of its military weakness. Actually, it was considered by the American as an expression of opinion by President Monroe.

9. **Implementation of this Doctrine by President Polk.** When the application of this doctrine was practically absent, President Polk gave life to it in 1845. Britain and France had shown special interest in Texas and the expansion of British influence in other Latin American Countries was going on increasing gradually which alarmed and awoke the American people who made up their mind to arrest the influence of Britain. Polk, the President of America was an expansionist who wanted to introduce the Monroe Doctrine in letter and spirit. He had stated that Monroe Doctrine had become a permanent feature of American policy and had warned the European diplomatic interference of other nations with American affairs.

10. **The Dispute of Venezuela.** There was aboundary dispute between Venezuela and British Guiana in 1895. As Venezuela was the American Country, the President of America, Cleveland had to involve in this dispute. So he wanted to apply the doctrine of Monroe. The President of America stated that the dispute should be solved through the arbitration but Britain refused to concede the demand of USA. Consequently the President declared that USA was practically sovereign on American continent and the British refusal to arbitration would invite the USA to resort to force. The war was about to start. But it did not take place as UK was involved in a dispute in Africa and UK accepted to settle the broader problems by means of arbitration by an International Board. From the beginning of the 20th Century Britain expressed its acceptance of the Monroe Doctrine and the American predominance in the Caribbean region.

11. **Application of this Doctrine in the 20th Century.** In December 1904 President Roosevelt extended this principle by issuing the corollary to the Monroe Doctrine. He asserted the right of the United States to intervence in the domestic affairs of the Latin American Countries. In 1917 President Wilson also invoked the Principle to keep America out of the European wars and politics. In 1941 USA stopped her policy of isolation and entered in the second world war not as an aggressor but the protector of her interest.

When Kennedy was the President of USA, Castro, the Cuban dictator had developed a cordial relation with Russia. It was a threat to the American Continent and further USSR established her missile bases in this island. The President of America warned USSR to dismantle the missile bases failing which there would be another global war over the Cuban crisis. Khruschev, the Russian Premier, yielded to the demand, demolished the bases and averted the war between the two super powers.

12. **Results of the Doctrine.**

(1) As a result of the Monroe Doctrine, the political system of the American hemisphere was essentially Republicanism and it strengthened the forces of Democracy.

(2) As this doctrine prohibited the involvement of USA in the power politics of the European countries, America was able to exploit her natural resources for her industrial progress which resulted that she became one of the biggest powers in the world.

(3) As America was cut off her relations with outside world, she was able to have concentration on economic and political developments. When European countries were preoccupied with internal changes and conflicts America primarily occupied in the nation's developments and expansion. By the turn of the century, economically America became a stronger country.

11

Chief Justice John Marshall

As per the provision of the Judiciary Act of 1789, a Supreme Court with six members was set up. In the early period of its existence, its function was not definite and it could not play a vital role. It was not sure whether it could invalid any law passed by the Congress because the Supreme Court did not represent members from the House of Congress. Consequently, in 1798, when the Alien and Sedition Act was passed by the Federal Government, the Supreme Court remained passive. John Jay, the Chief Justice of Supreme Court was succeeded by John Marshall in 1801. The Supreme Court under Chief Justice Marshall played a vital role and attained the heights of reputation unknown earlier. The decisions of the Supreme Court had much influence on American development and rights of the property of the people.

Justice Marshall and his Methods

(1) He was very careful and cautious in his rulings. He gave his judgements which would not be changed by constitutional amendment.

(2) Marshall tried to strengthen the national Government by keeping all the Governments within their constitutional limits.

(3) He enforced that the Supreme Court was the highest court and all the Federal Courts and State Courts must be the subordinate courts.

(4) He stated that the judges could invalid the unconstitutional statutes.

(5) He argued that the decisions of the inferior Courts could be modified or changed by the Supreme Court which had the power of final verdict.

The Policies of Justice Marshall

He had followed many principle in giving the verdict. His chief policies were :

(1) Supreme Court as the sole Arbitrator.
(2) A strong Central Government.
(3) Protection for the private property.
(4) Protection for the business establishments.
(5) Limited powers to State Governments.

1. **Supreme Court as the Sole Arbitrator.** The Supreme Court established its authority of supreme arbitrator in all disputes regarding the functioning of the American Constitutional system.
   (a) In the case of Marbury *vs.* Madison in 1803 the Supreme Court clearly stated that the Congress had no power to define the powers and priviledges of the court.
   (b) Similarly in the case of Fletcher *vs.* Peck (1810), the court declared the act of Georgia as unconstitutional on the ground that it conflicted with the rights of the individuals.
   (c) In the Martin *vs.* Hunter case, the supreme Court confirmed its right to review the decisions of the State Court when constitutional issues were involved.
2. **A Strong Central Government.** In another case of McCulloch *vs.* Maryland in 1819, he defended the sovereign powers of the federal government and thereby restricted the activities of the State Government to impose heavy taxes, on the banks. John Marshall gave a colour to the 'implied powers' theory of the constitution and declared that the government of the union was created by the people and not by the states and so the states had no power to hinder the Federal government in the exercise of its constitutional powers. Hence, he concluded that Maryland had no right to hinder the bank by taxation.
3. **Protection for the Private Property.** Justice Marshall was the protector of the private property and his verdicts were against the principles of nationalisation. Any law hostile to the right of the private property was declared as invalid and unconstitutional.
   (a) In the Dartmouth College, he gave constitutional protection to the private institutions. It was a College run by the private individual. New Hamphire State wanted to bring out a change in the charter of the College and thereby transformed it into a state institution. When the case was referred to the verdict of the Supreme Court, it held the view that the charter of the college was a contract and, therefore, could not be changed by the State of New Hamphire against the will of the college.
   (b) In the case of Fletcher *vs.* Peck in 1810, he regarded the sanctity of contracts as a kind of religious dogma.

(c) The Government of Georgia sold lands at the cheapest price in 1795. Many members of the legislator bought the land and earned huge profit. In the next election, new legislature came in and declared the acts of former legislature as invalid. When the case brought before the Court, Justice Marshall had declared that the sale was legally a contract and so the sale could not be invalidated.

4. Limited Powers to State Government.

(a) In the case of Gibbon *vs.* Ogden (1824), the Supreme Court declared its verdict that the State Government had no power to interfere with interstate commerce. The power of controlling interstate commerce and foreign trade were vested only with the Federal Government.

(b) Further, Marshall stated that the grant of monopoly given by the New York State to a steam boat company for interstate water ways was illegal and the Federal Government had the absolute power over this subject.

Case of Indians

The Indian tribes suffered a lot during the Presidency of Jackson. The territory of Cherokee Indians of Georgia had been guaranteed to them by a treaty with Federal government. When gold was found in it, Georgia wanted to grab their land. When the matter was appealed to Supreme Court, John Marshall declared that Georgia had no right to interfere with the Indian territory. On hearing this decision, Jackson said that John Marshall alone should enforce his own decision. No wonder that the Indians interests were deeply buried within a short span of time.

The verdicts of Marshall were significant and popular and these verdicts nade the Federal Government to be strong and powerful. Justice Marshall was interested to protect the Constitution from the arbitrary acts of the majority. He protected the private property and Private commercial establishments. On the other hand, his verdict of giving constitutional protection even to the corruption filled contracts was not conductive and ruinous to the interests of the nation. It was bitterly criticised by the critics. John Taylor said "Marshall's doctrine becomes the protector of political frauds; it compels a nation to be an accomplice in its own ruins; it takes from it the right of self-preservation". So it was stated that the Supreme Court was protecting the privileges of the vested interest. Though there were many criticisms against the verdicts of the Supreme Court, the role of the court was highly praised and it transformed the Constitution from the abstract ideas to the living reality which was very helpful for the progress of the nation.

12

John Quincy Adams (1825-29)

John Quincy Adams was born on 11th July, 1767. He was an expert in all fields. He studied in the Haward University and became a barrister. He had a rich experience as a barrister. He knew French and Dutch languages. As he had adequate knowledge in the international relations, he was sent as an ambassador to Russia in 1809. He was much interested in the revolutionary concepts. He worked for the advancement of America. America must come out from the conservative ideas and lead the other nations in the American hemisphere were his progressive principles. He was selected as a minister of state in the ministry of James Monroe.

Election of 1824

Election for the President of America was held in 1824 in which four candidates entered the field. John Quincy Adams of Massachusetts, Andrew Jackson of Tennessee, Henry Clay of Kentucky and William Crafford of Georgia were the candidates in the election. Though Andrew Jackson had secured more votes than the other candidates he was not elected as the President of America because no candidate had secured absolute majority votes in the election. So the Congress of America had to decide it and finally Adams was declared elected as President of America which led to formation of two rival groups in the Republican party. The group headed by Adams and Clay came to be known as the National Republicans and other group headed by Jackson came to be known as the Democratic Republicans. The important achievements of Adams were the internal improvements, tariff of abomination, settlement of Red Indian Problems and construction of Erie canal.

Internal Improvements

President Adams wanted to tone up the economic condition of America by boasting trade and commerce. He requested the American Congress to pass on laws for the welfare of the nation so that he could take steps effectively to fulfil his ambitions. He encouraged the scientific exploration and increased the means of transport by constructing roads, canals and railway lines. He wanted to set up a national university and observatory. He promoted science, art, literature and agriculture. In general there was development in all fields. Though he took steps for the improvement of the nation, it was not welcomed by the Congressmen because they were only interested in the next election rather than the internal improvements.

The Tariff of Abomination

Adams wanted to protect the American producers by imposing taxes on imported goods and so a new tariff bill was enacted in the house of Congress in 1824 with the aim of introducing improvements in the country. But woolen traders and sheep raisers were not satisfied about the bill and they declared that fresh protection should be extended to them. As a result of their compulsion, the bill was revised and introduced in 1827 which provided for increase in import tax and protected home commodities. Though this bill extended more protection, it was not passed in the Senate which was again redrafted in a manner so as to satisfy the producers of the raw materials.

(a) There was wild protect to this bill from the southern provinces. The South Carolina termed the tariff as unconstitutional and unjust and resolutions to this effect were also passed by some other states like Georgia, Mississippi and Virginia. The Jacksonians, the opponent of Adams, had succeeded in discrediting Adams which resulted in his defeat at the next Presidential election.

(b) Tariff was levied on Woollen, Cotton, Sugarcane, Salt and Coffee in 1819-20 which affected the manufacturers of Southern States. So this tariff was objected by the people of southern states and the bill of this tariff was defeated by the Senate.

Settlement of Red Indian Problems

Indians were living in Georgia. As their problems were mounting a compromise was effected between Georgia and Federal Government in 1802 which provided the western part of Georgia for the accommodation to the Indians who were asked to live in the allotted places. In 1821, the Federal Government entered a treaty with Indian chief with a view to secure their removal from the territory but soon after the chief was murdered and the process stopped till another treaty was concluded in 1826. As the process of settlement of Indians was stopped, the Governor of Georgia wanted to get back the allotted area and ordered for the survey of the land. But the President of America requested the Governor to be calm and wait in this matter. The Governor threatened to use force on the plea that Georgia was a sovereign state within her own territorial limits and could,do anything. Meanwhile the Indians of Georgia declared themselves independent. This incident led to complication between the State of Georgia and Federal Government which could not be solved during the administration of Adams.

Construction of the Erie Canal

The construction of Erie Canal was one of the important achievements during the administration of Adams. The construction of this canal was started in New York in the year 1817 with the advice of Gleanton. The length of this Canal was 363 miles and it served as a bridge between eastern and western states. As it was a big scheme, it involved huge expenditure. So the people began to critise the utility of this canal. But the expectations of the people were in smoke and it was highly useful for the trade and commerce. It was stated that goods could be carried through this canal to other parts of the nation with limited money and time and New York City emerged as a flourishing and prosperous city later on.

Panama Congress

Adams wanted to protect the weak nations in American hemisphere. At that time the Americans lived in Spain convened a meeting at Panama and requested Spain to give freedom to the colonies of Spain in American Continent. Adams who was anxious to protect all the American Nations, wanted to send delegates to this Congress but his decision was turned down in the American Congress. Although permission to attend the Panama Congress was not accorded, Adams sent his delegates by using his arbitrary powers. The outcome of the Congress was not fruitful to fullfil his ambitions.

Foreign Policy

Adams had been known for his diplomatic potentialities but he could not succeed in achieving the expected goals. He could not solve the outstanding disputes with Great Britain. His efforts to take part in the Panama Congress was not welcomed in the House of Congress.

The Administration

John Quincy Adams was on the whole a failure both in the domestic and foreign spheres because his staunch enemies Jacksonians tried to discredit and overthrow him. Jackson and Calboun blocked his steps in the congress and hampered the smooth sailing of the administration. The atmosphere in the cabinet was also tense that led to the weakening of the hands of the President, who despite his capabilities failed to achieve anything. So the administration of Adams was called as an Era of Hard Feedlings.

13

Andrew Jackson (1829-37)

Andrew Jackson was born in South Carolina in 1767. His father died before his birth. So he run away from his house at the age of fourteen and served in the local militia. He was imprisoned in the revolution by the British and after his release, he worked as an assistant to a saddle maker. During this period, he continued his study and became a barrister. He was appointed as a Public Prosecutor in the district court of Nashville at the age of twenty one. He was a member of the State constitutional convention in 1796. Later on he entered into politics and he was elected a member of the House of Representatives from Tennessee in the same year. He joined in the militia and served successfully and hence he was promoted to the rank of Major General in the U.S. army. He took part in the war against British at New Orieans. Then he was appointed as Military governor of Florida in 1821 but resigned. In 1823 he was elected to the Senate but resigned from there also in 1825. He contested in the Presidential election of 1824 and secured more votes but the Congress due to the intrigues of Adams and Clay, decided the election against him. Then he became the President of America in 1829. He was the first President who came from the poor family and the previous Presidents belonged to aristocratic family.

Jobs for the Commoners

As Jackson hailed from common family, he strongly opposed the policy of giving important posts to the privileged class. He believed in the theory of equality and all the posts should be given to all sections of the society irrespective of their status. So he removed ten per cent of the privileged class from their jobs and those posts were filled up by the Commoners belonging to the Republican party. Thus, Jackson unconsciously gave rise to the system of spoils based on the principle "to the victor belong spoils" The system introduced by Andrew Jackson was being followed by the subsequent Presidents which resulted that thousands of people joined with the President in the next election campaigns with a view of getting jobs. This practice led to inefficient administration and was ultimately replaced by the system of civil service recruitment.

His Policy Towards the Bank of United States

The Bank of United States was guided and controlled by the moneyed aristocracy. Jackson was against the function of this bank which failed to protect the interests of the commoners. In 1831 when the pro-capitalist congress passed the bill extending the life of the Bank of United States by another ten rears, Jackson vetoed the bill on the plea that this bank was advancing loans only to the privileged people who were enjoying all the benefits at the cost of the people. He alleged that "the Bank enabled the rich and powerful to bend the acts of Government to their selfish purposes and the humble members of the society — the farmers, mechanics and labourers, who have neither time nor the means of securing like favours to themselves, have a right to complain of injustice of their Government". He strongly stated that Banks should help to the poor and downtrodden people so as to enable them to come up in their life. As he supported the common people, he was able to get elected in the second time and he stated that his victory was in favour of closing the second National Bank. In pursuance of his policy, he withdrew the Government deposits from the bank and subsequently the Bank was closed. Thus, the privileges enjoyed by the aristocratic were stopped once for all and all the citizens of America were equally treated.

Emergence of Party Politics

Jackson ended the non partisan politics and realised the importance of a national political machinery which could influence the policies of the Government. The political party should represent the will of the people and serve for the progress of the nation. Commenting on this policy of Jackson, Prof. Graebner had said "In overthrowing the nonpartisan tradition so dear to Monroe and Adams, the Jacksonians had employed new techniques of campaigning whereby politicians might bid successfully for popular support. In short Jacksonians in guiding and sustaining the political revolution of the 1820 had given the American people a political vehicle for making their democracy effective".

Decentralization of Powers

He was in favour of giving more powers to the State Government. The previous Presidents had stood for strong central Government whereas Jackson deviated this policy and pleaded for the rights of the common man and the rights of the states. He wanted to introduce many internal improvements in the states. These things had been executed through the states. The Federal Government rendered necessary assistants to the state governments to meet out the financial expenditure of the internal improvements.

Suppression of the Secessionists in South Carolines

There was a threat of existence of the union during his administration. In 1828 the Tariff Law was passed which helped the wool manufacturers and sheep raisers. This law was highly objected by the South Carolina on the plea that it did not give any concession to the cotton growers. Jackson tried to pacify them by amending the bill in order to meet some of the demands of the South Carolina. But the amendment was not accepted by it and passed the Nullification Ordinance in 1832. By passing the Nullification Ordinance, she refused the collection of duties within the state with effect from 1833. The actions of South Carolina were disliked by Andrew Jackson and he made up his mind to collect the taxes by force for which he made the Congress to pass Force bill in January 1833. So Jackson decided to use force for the collection of taxes in South Carolina and at the same time he made negotiation to meet out the objection of the Southerners and passed a Compromise bill. Thus, he tactfully tackled the secessionists tendencies and preserved the Union.

Jackson and Congress

The relation between Congress and Jackson was not cordial. He wanted to be an independent administrator and not under the control of the Congress which consisted the members of the privileged classes. However, Jackson a commoner, could not maintain cordial relation with Congress mainly composed of representatives of the privileged classes. As the relation with the Congress was not good, he used Veto powers many times and he was the first President to make use of the "Poket Veto". The use of Veto was criticised in the Congress but Jackson justified the use of Veto to protect the Constitution and fullfil his obligations to the people.

Jackson and his Cabinet

When Jackson was elected as President, he formed the cabinet which contained mostly his friends and unwise statesmen. He deliberately excluded the talented and privileged people. The practice of consultation with the cabinet was not adopted by him and he treated all the members of his cabinet as Departmental Heads. Thus, he started the practice of consulting only with friends and so his cabinet came to be known as the 'Kitchen Cabinet'.

Differences in the Cabinet and Breakup

Jackson had included many supporters of Calhoun in his cabinet and a rift was soon developed between the followers of Calhoun and Jackson. The rift was further widened when Mr. Eaton's wife was boycotted by the Washington Society and there was a rumour that the supporters of Jackson formed a plot to topple the cabinet of President Jackson. There was a final break between the two groups. The rift had its influence in the cabinet and resulted in the break up of the cabinet. Thus, Jackson dissolved the cabinet and subsequently organised a new cabinet containing new members who would support the President and maintain cordial relation.

The Spoils System

In the beginning of Jackson administration, he boldly attacked the system of partisan appointment to offices. He stated that ability and honesty should be considered for the appointment and later on he abolished the practice of keeping one man in the particular office for life. He preferred a system of rotation and the post was to be rotated amongst different incumbents. When he became the President, he found out many incompetent and old employees and he wanted to get rid of them because he wanted to give jobs to his friends who had worked for him during the election. Thus, out of 10,000 Federal Officials who were custom collectors, post masters, clerks and holding other offices, Jackson removed 1000 and replaced them with his friends. The policy of appointment was based on the principle 'to the victors belong the spoil.' The policy was being followed by the subsequent Presidents which resulted thousands of people joined in the election campaign with the view of getting jobs. This, practice soon came to be discredited and was ultimately replaced by the system of civil service recruitment in 1881.

Jackson's Policy Towards Indians

The policy towards Indian was harsh and stiff. During his administration, he concluded ninety four treaties with Indians by which he recognised the Indians as the citizen of America. Further, they were asked to settle down in the allotted places. He paid compensation to the Indians for the lands surrendered by them The tradition and customs of the tribes or Indians were also preserved. In certain eases, he resorted to force, if the Indians offered resistance to accept the principles of Jackson. He forced the Indians to migrate to the Trans-Mississippi valley and ultimately the menace of Indians was rooted out.

Jackson's Internal Improvements

He carried out many internal improvements and made a special reference to this effect in his first message to the congress. He diverted the surplus Federal funds to the states for executing the works of internal improvements. Many roads, canals and bridges were constructed. A bill was moved in the Congress which provided for the purchase of assets of some Twinpike Companies which was constructing roads connecting Cumber-land in Ohio with Florence. However, Jackson vetoed this bill on the ground that the road passed entirely through one state and Federal money cannot be spent for that purpose. It led to controversy in the cabinet and ultimately with the help of Henry Clay he put an end to it. Later on Jackson sanctioned many measures which were not exclusively Federal in character. The total amount sanctioned by him for the internal improvement came to about $ 10.5, millions.

Loco-Focoism

The supporters of Jacksonian in the North East came to be known as "Loco-Focos". A meeting was being arranged in New York by the Radicals, but it was disturbed by the conservative by putting off the lights. However, the meeting was conducted by Jacksonians by striking safety matches. Hence, these radicals came to be known as Loco-Focos and they fought for elimination of monopoly and banking corporation which supported only the capitalist.

Objectives of Jackson

The chief objectives of Jackson were as follows :

(1) The Government must be for the welfare of the planter, the farmer, the mechanic and the labourer and not for privileged class.

(2) The Commoners should be defended against the industrialist and aristocratic people who possessed ample powers in their hands.

(3) A union of labourer and agricultural people is inevitable to meet out the challenges of the rich and upper class people.

(4) The Government shall strictly follow *laissez faire* policy and shall protect the small property owners.

(5) Special privileges granted to the banks and big business corporations should be withdrawn.

(6) The government lands must be sanctioned to the commoners on easy terms.

(7) The Constitution and National integrity should be preserved at all cost.

(8) The common people should come up in all walks of life.

He got support from the democratic and debtor farmers of the west, from the southern planters for his support of slavery, from the middle class and working class people in Northeast and also from small businessmen. The humanitarian measures of abolishing imprisonment for debt, the growth of public school system, the extension of democracy to the common people and other social welfare measures made him popular and true representative of the plain people and democracy.

Foreign Policy of Jackson

As he was fully occupied in the internal problems and administration, his foreign policy was not significant. He followed a fresh approach in the foreign policy. A policy of conciliation was adopted by him. He made negotiation with Britain and succeeded in reopening the British Colonial ports to U.S. Trade and Commerce and maintained a cordial relation with UK, though there were many misunderstanding and irritation with British. In 1831 he concluded a treaty with France by which the two countries agreed to pay compensation for the spoliation committed against each other's subjects. As the French delayed in paying the amount, the relation with her strained for sometime. Ultimately the issue was settled through British mediation in 1836.

By going through the achievements of Jackson, one can come to the conclusion that he was undoubtedly a famous President in USA. He performed yeomen service for the welfare of the plain people. He suppressed the influence of the privileged class and big industrialist. He undertook many internal improvements. He was the liberator of poor and downtrodden people from the bondage of slavery.

14

Westward Movement

Before the war of American Independence, the American settlements existed only between Atlantic Coast and the Appalachian ranges and in between the Appalachian and Pacific, Coast the Indian were living. This area was thinly populated and most of the area was not used by the people. As a vast stretch of land was available, people began to settle in this area and this process was known as the Westward Movement. In 1803, America purchased the territory on the West of Mississippi upto the Rockey Mountains known as Lousiana. Further, France and England made their encroachments in the Western direction which was a threat to USA. So USA decided to annex the unused western lands. America acquired Florida and Texas. The acquisition of the territories by United States upto 1829 formed the first phase of expansion and is popularly known as early westward movement.

Beginning of the Settlers

There were three stages in the development of Westward movement :

(1) The hunters and Roman traders entered the dense forest in the western direction of America and established their settlements. They constructed roads and made cordial relation with the Indians who were already living there.

(2) Those who were badly in need of pastures for grazing their cattles and the persons engaged in mine works were the next settlers. These persons were followed by Squatters who held no legal titles to the lands. They removed the thick forest and started cultivating the forest.

(3) The agriculturist who learnt the fertility of the soil started to migrate to this place. They began to plough the lands, build churches, schools and houses and start business establishments and institutions and in the course of time, their settlements emerged as a state and joined with the Federal State.

Settlement in the Appalachian Region

In 1769 some families of Scotch-Irish origin established their settlement in the Watanga river In 1775, the North Carolina judge, Mr. Henderson, who was anxious to form a colony, inaugurated a colony which he named Transylvania. Then roads were opened which encouraged the people to rush to the area for living. When Henderson appealed to the Virginian Government for recognisation, the Government refused the same. So he gave up that area and moved to the Central Tennessee. He bought lands and planted another colony. Then Kobertson, another important man established a colony near Nashville. Thus, three separate colonids were planted in the Kentucky and Tennessee regions. Many improvements were executed in these colonies. As a result of more facilities, fertility of the soil and economic prosperity of the place, there was a flood of people who crossed the mountain and settled in the Kentucky Tennessee area. The number of settlers rose upto 3 lakhs in 1800. The newly started colony attained its recognition from the Federal Government. Kentucky became as state in 1792, and North Carolina in 1796 with John Servier and Andrew Jackson as Governors of the states respectively.

The North West Ohio

The next state was in the North West direction. Settlements started in this region of Ohio, Indiana and Illinois states. Ohio company purchased lands from the confederation and sent a group of settlers from New England to settle there. But the settlement was blocked by Indians. As they were defeated by general Wayne in the battle of Fallentimbers in 1794 they surrendered their lands to the white settlers by signing the treaty of Greenville in 1795. The defeat of Indians resulted in a mass movement into Ohio. After the treaty of Greenville most of the tribes surrendered and more people migrated to this region and Ohio became a state in 1803.

Indiana and Illinois

The next states to be admitted to the Union were Indiana and Illinois. The territory of Indiana was in the west of Ohio. The movement into the territory had started when the governor of Indiana had got the land law of 1800 passed by the Congress. The resistance of Indiana was Shattered in the war of 1812 and the people of the east moved further to the west. As the flood of people was rushing to Indiana for settlement, the area soon got conjected and it attained the nature of state. So Indiana was admitted to the union in 1816 as a free state. After establishing their settlements in Indiana the people started their movement further towards the west and planted a new colony called Illinois. Illinois too had become organized into a territory with sufficient population and their own government. She too was admitted to the Union as a free state in 1818.

Michingan, Iowa, Wisconsin and Minnesota

The Erie Canal was constructed in the year 1825 which accelerated the tempo of settlement further to the west. The defeat of the Indians in the Black Hawk war of 1832 opened vast areas of territory for new settlements. Agriculturist, fur traders and mine workers moved to the west and thus the new settlements Michingan, Iowa, Wisconsin and Minnesota came into existence and these states were annexed with the Union Government. The immigrants included nationals from Germany and other European Countries.

Settlements in the South West

The area along the Gulf of Mexico attracted the settlers and the first settlement took place in 1798 in Mississippi territory. The white people could not be settled there because of the menace of the Indians. Five powerful Indian tribes—the Cherokees, Creeks, Chickasaws, Choctaws and Seminoles-held this area under their jurisdiction, but their control was broken after the war of 1812 and in the subsequent years all the other tribes were also subdued and they all entered into treaties.

Thus, the white settlers made their way into the Gulf territory in large numbers. Then President Monroe announced his policy towards the Indians in 1825 by which the Indians were asked to settle down beyond the Missouri and in the next twenty five years all the Indians shifted their settlement to the west. When the Indians were compelled to give up their places, they resorted to war but their rising was completely destroyed by the union. By 1842 the last rising of Indians was crushed and this completed the process of evacuating the territory of Indians. Thus, a boundary line was drawn across the country from Minnesota down to Texas and the Indians were given the territory west of this region on the condition that it would not be further encroached by whites.

Settlement in the Gulf Territory-Louisiana

Louisiana was a vast tract of rich and fertile land and President Monroe wanted to purchase it from Spain. The land was transferred to America by Spain in 1800 as a result of secret treaty of San Ildefonso and after the acquisition of this land, the westward movement gained momentum and Louisiana was admitted to the union in 1820.

Alabama (1819) and Mississippi

The territory of Alabama and Mississippi was claimed by Georgia as it was within the boundary of Georgia. It was also claimed by United States. The legislature of Georgia granted this land to four companies for $ 500,000 and later on this grant was nullified and the companies questioned the nullification of Georgia's legislature. A case was referred with Supreme Court which decided that the contract with the company was the original grant and it could not be changed. So Georgia entered a pact with the United States in 1812 by which United States purchased the land for $ 1,250,000 and the Indians settled here were removed. Then this region was converted into states of Alabama and Mississippi and admitted with the Union Government as a slave states because the number of white settlers were small as compared to the slave population which gave rise to bitter controversy.

Arkansas, the adjacent state of Louisiana was admitted with United States in 1836.

New Orleans became the member of the Union on acquiring the full statehood status in 1817.

Admission of Maine and Missouri

The next stage was the question of admission to the slave states. In the beginning only free states were admitted and later on the slave states were also admitted. When Missouri applied for admission with the Union government, there was a furor in the Congress about the question of admission to the slave states. So a new State was created out of Massachusetts and was admitted to the Union along with Missouri as per the terms of the Clay's compromise formula. Missouri was admitted as a slave state and Maine was admitted as a free state with the Union Government.

Effects of the Westward Movement

1. **Evolution of Democratic Principles.** The Democracy came into existence after the westward movement. Equality was maintained between the immigrants of various provinces. There was no hierarchy in the society and all were equal. The people who were depressed and neglected had gone to other settlements where they enjoyed absolute freedom and right. The Union Government insisted that slavery should not be practised and all the decisions of the colonies had to be taken by all the inhabitants of the concerned colony. Thus, the evolution of democratic principles came into existence.
2. **Natural Integration.** The westward movement provided natural unity and integration of America. The independent colonies and colonies under the control of foreign countries were brought into integration with union Government which developed a sense of patriotism and nationalism. The people forgot their regional, linguistic, and parochial interest and promoted their unity and

cooperation. Their previous state and regional loyalties were broken and national unity was established. The continuous mobile of the people did not permit the feeling of separation to grow. Most of the people thought that a strong central government must be necessary to protect their interest. Thus, national unity and creation of a strong central government were the important effects of the westward movement.

3. **Growth of New Culture.** The significance of the westward movement would be seen in the evolution of American civilization and the resolution of its culture. According to Prof. Parkes the most significant feature of the westward movement was that "the pioneers took with them the essential institutions of civilization". After establishing their settlernents in colonies, they practised their customs and civilization. They set up their law courts, schools, churches, printing presses and so on and thus a new civilization came into existence in America.
4. **Internal Improvements.** The new colonies required lot of improvements and consequently improved means of transport and "communication, construction of canals, hospitals and schools, etc. came into existence. The Cumberland road and many other projects were undertaken. In 1790 Lancaster-Turnpikes Road was built in Pennsylavania. The fund was sanctioned by American Congress to meet out the expenditure of these projects.
5. **Growth of Population.** As the colonies were offered many facilities and improvements, there was a flood of people rushed to those places from Europe and eastern regions. The population had gone upto 12 million from 3 million and the number of states was increased from 13 to 24. Since the land was cheap and fertile, it attracted most of the settlers.
6. **The Other Effects.** (1) It promoted fraternity among the frontiersmen and it prevented the exploitation of the proletarians. (2) The native inhabitants lost their own territory, culture and civilization and finally allowed to live in reserves and deserts. (3) The expansion of the frontiers led to the wars with Britain and Mexico. (4) The westward movement cropped up the thorny question of slavery and consequently civil war started between north and south America. (5) As the newly acquired territories had rich in natural resources, it helped for the prosperity of America. (6) Finally, the western territory gave birth to the imperialistic ideals in later days. The ever moving frontier had influenced, changed and shaped the Americanism in the history of USA

15

Mexican War of 1846

During the administration of President Polk the relation between America and Mexico had strained. He adopted the policy of expansion and prevented the interference of European Countries in the American affairs which led to the war of Mexican in 1846. The causes for the war are given below :

1. **The Claim of Mexico.** The Spanish were the pioneers in exploring South America and settled there. So they held control over many colonies. Their rights over New Mexico, Texas, California, part of Kansas and Wyoming were recognised by the Adams-Onis Treaty. In the course of time, Mexico fought with the Spain and achieved its independence. After its independence the control of the other southern provinces was passed into Mexico which could not effectively execute its control. So Texas separated from the control of Mexico and declared independence and she was immediately recognised by the United States. The recognition by America to Texas sown the seeds for a war with Mexico.
2. **Annexation of Texas.** In 1836, the Americans in Texas proclaimed its independence and appointed Sams Houston as Commander of the army to face the Mexican forces. There was a fierce battle between America and Mexico in which the President of Mexico was arrested and later on released when he accented the independent there was a danger of attack from Mexico. So, when Polk was President of America, a resolution was introduced in American Congress for the annexation of Texas and finally Texas was annexed with the Union. The annexation arose a boundary dispute which led to the outbreak of a war in 1846.
3. **Border Disputes.** After annexation of Texas, Polk, the President of America decided to fix up the boundary line between Mexico and Texas. Lot of differences existed between the two on this point. The Texans claimed Rio Grande as the southern boundary while

the Mexicans claimed that Nuces to be the natural boundary. Polk refused to give any consideration to the claims of the Mexican Government which led to the war of Mexico.

4. **Non-Payment of Debts to America.** Another important cause for the war with Mexico was the non payment of American debts. In 1839 there was revolution in Mexico in which many Americans lost their lives for which Mexico had agreed to pay a compensation $ 20,00,000 to America. Mexico which was against America, refused to pay the debt later on. However, during the administration of President Andrew Jackson, when Mexico was threatened by warships, she accepted to pay it and paid only three instalments. The non-payment of further instalments to America by Mexico to compensate the losses incurred by the Americans resulted in war with Mexico in 1846.
5. **Desire to Annex California.** Polk adopted a stiff attitude towards Mexico. America wanted to secure California where gold was found in plenty and Polk thought that Mexico would sell California to Britain. His assessment was wrong and if he followed a right path, he could have got California. In this connection, he should have adopted an attitude of appeasement. So the tactless handling of the issue by President Polk led to the war with Mexico.
6. **Mission of John Slidell.** President Polk sent a mission under John Slidell to Mexico for the purchase of California and settle the boundary dispute with Mexico. When the talk was in progress, a revolution broke out and as a result the President of Mexico was overthrown and General Paredes came to power. When revolution was started, the hope of getting California could not be achieved through negotiation.

War Declaration

When the mission of Slidell failed to attain its goal, Polk declared that the territory lying between Nueces and Rio Grande belonged to America and Mexico should surrender the lands to USA

At this time some incidents took place on the border and war became imminent. President Polk despatched forces under General Zachary Taylor to occupy the disputed area and the same was conquered along with Point Isabel on the northern side of the river. In the fierce battle sixteen Americans were killed and forty people were imprisoned by the Mexican. Polk who was informed about the loss of American soldiers and imprisonment of American people by Taylor, sent a special message to the Congress on 12, May, 1846. He said, "Mexico has crossed boundary of the United States; has invaded our territory and shed American blood upon American soils and war exists, not-withstanding all our efforts to avoid it, by acts of Mexico itself". On seeing the report of the President Polk, the American Congress made a Declaration of War with Mexico without inquiring the fact and it sanctioned money and 50,000 soldiers and thus war was started between America and Mexico in the year 1846.

The Main Incidents of the War

The Mexican army was bigger than America. But at the same time, they lacked sufficient military training, food and weapons and they were reluctant to fight with American soldiers who were well equipped and trained. Thus, in the war the Americans emerged victorious on all the fronts. The course of the war could be studied under two heads.

1. **Annexation of California.** Polk who had an ambition of captuing California, sent Colonel Kearny to capture the same. He first captured New Mexico and from there he proceeded to California. He was joined by Fremont and Sloat at Los Angels. When the attack was going on, the Americans living in Mexico were instigated to raise the banner of revolt against the Mexican Government. In July 1846, the people of Sacramento Valley declared independence and planted their own flag in their place. The revolt could not be suppressed by General De Castro of Mexico. Mexicans took their heals from California. Fremont was proclaimed the military Governor of the province. Thus, the entire region from the West of Texas to the Pacific Ocean was brought under the control of America.

The Siege of Mexico Province

After capturing California, USA attacked Mexico in all directions. Taylor launched attack from Texas, Scott through the Gulf of Mexico and Doniphan and Wool attacked from the north. The army of Taylor fought against the enemy army at Palo Allo and then at Resaca de la Palma and in these fierce battles, the Taylor's army was victorious and he took the possession of the Matamoros. After three months, Taylor again proceeded to Monterry in 1846 and made an armistice with Mexico. The armistice created suspicion to Polk who refused to approve it. Consequently Polk sent an army consisting of 10,000 troops under Scott to attack Mexico and on knowing the matter, the Mexican General Santa Anna requested Taylor to surrender or face humiliation. The request was not considered by Taylor who accepted the challenge of the Mexican force and fought with them. Finally, Santa Anna was defeated and the Americans gained control over the North eastern parts of Mexico.

Doniphan who advanced to Mexico from northern side reached the province of Chipuahera and defeated the Mexicans at El Brazito. Then the City of Mexico was captured by General Scott. He put up a fierce fight to the Mexicans who finally surrendered on March 27, 1847. Scott again advanced to Puchla in August 1847 and made further advance and reached within the five miles of Mexico. Ultimately Scott reached on Mexico and defeated Santa Anna at the battle of Buenavista and occupied the City of Mexico on September 14, 1847. After the defeat of Mexicans, a treaty was signed at Guadalupe Hidalgo.

Provisions of the Treaty of Guadalupe Hidalgo

(1) The provinces of Texas New Mexico and California were ceded to USA by Mexico.
(2) The boundary between the two countries was Rio Grande.
(3) USA agreed to pay a sum of $ 15 million to Mexico in return for the territoiy of Mexico. The claim of the American citizen against Mexico to the tune of $ 3 million was adjusted against this payment.
(4) The independence of Mexico was accepted by USA.

Results of the War

(1) The territory of America was expanded at the cost of a weaker neighbour. The expansion was completed with this war.
(2) The southern boundary was fixed at Rio Grande between America and Mexico.
(3) The annexation of California with America accelerated the settlement in the West.
(4) As a result of the war New States had been admitted with Union which led to problems between the existing states in the Congress. The northern states wanted that more free states had to be admitted while the southern states desired in favour of slave states to be admitted.
(5) As gold was available in plenty in California, means of transport was absolutely needed to this city and so the construction of transcontinental railway was undertaken.
(6) It provided an opportunity of construction of a canal across Panama.

16

The Compromise of 1850

The Question of Slavery

Towards the end of the Mexican War, the question of slavery extension raised its ugly head again in the history of U.S.A. The North and the South had opposite views on slavery. The Northerners considered slavery as an evil institution which should be condemned and prevented from expansion.

The Southerners, on the other hand, believed that slavery was a positive good and it entitled the protection of the Federal Government. The western farmers wanted to restrict it in the South alone to avoid competition and confrontation in the newly acquired territories. The Southerners wanted to keep slavery in all territories not only for its economic causes but also for establishing white supremacy. The Abolitionist Movement of the North alarmed the South and made them believe that their very existence was at stake.

The Problems of the Territories

The problems of slavery in the territories, temporarily settled by the division of the Louisiana purchase territory. Missouri compromise of 1820 was reopened during the Polk administration. In 1848 four newly acquired regions — Oregon, California, New Mexico, and Utah urgently needed legal Government. Polk suggested that the Missouri compromise line be extended to the Pacific, but this was not acceptable to the more extreme groups in either North or South. Before the end of Polk's administration, Oregon was organised as a territory without slavery, but no settlement could be made about the other areas. In these areas the question of slavery continued to be a thorny problem.

Zachary Taylor

In the 1848 election, both major parties sought support in each section and sedulously avoided any commitments about the slavery question. While the democrats nominated a Jacksonian from Michigan, Lewis Cass, the whigs adopted Zachary Taylor who had born bom in Virginia and owned a plantation in Lousinia. Taylor had never taken any intention in Lousinia. Taylor had never taken any interest in politics, but his war record made him an attractive candidate, and the Whig organisers, especially Thurlow Weed, had made overtures to him and won his support during the Mexican campaign. Meanwhile a small group of radical New York Jacksonians known as the "Burn-burnevi". (They were so called because according to their opponents they resembled a farmer who tried to get rid of rats by burning the barn.) The rival and more conservative faction among the New York Democratic were called "Hawkers" because they were said to Lusker after office bolted the Democratic Party and Joined forces with Birney and the abolitionists in a new Free Soil Party, which nominated ex-President Van Buren. Taylor won the election. He became the President of U.S.A. He proposed that both Californian and New Mexico be allowed to decide about the fate of slavery by themselves. In accepting the proposal California excluded slavery and became a free state in 1849. As the adoption of Taylor's proposal gave the North a majority in both Houses of the Congress, the southern owned its opposition to the northern domination.

Political Trends

The immediate impact of the sectional conflict was a change in the political trends of the country. The Northern Whig Party had split into two groups known as the "Conscience Whigs" and the "Cotton Whigs". The "Conscience Whigs" and the Jacksonian Democrats merged into a new political party in 1854 known as the — Republican Party. The Democratic Party remained to be the political instrument of the Southern planters. The Southern Democrats believed that the formation of a southern confederacy was inevitable to safeguard their peculiar political institutions. The question of the extension of slowing in the new territorial became the central point of discussion in the Congress. Henry Clay made a series of compromise proposals to satisfy both sections.

The Compromise of 1850

Henry Clay, assumed leadership in the talk of working out a settlement which would satisfy both sections and in January 1850 he made the following compromise proposals :

(1) California should be admitted as a Free State.
(2) New Mexico and Utah be organised as territorial without any reference to slavery.

(3) Texas should give up its claim to any part of New Mexico.
(4) The Federal Government should assume the public debt of Texas in return for its surrender of territorial claims .
(5) The slave trade should be abolished in the district of Columbia.
(6) As the new territories were unsuitable, for the growth of slavery, the North should not demand for its exclusion by law.
(7) A new Fugitive law be enacted providing for the capture and return of the escaped slaves to their owners. As there was something to please everybody in these proposals, still there was hope for a peaceful settlement. Daniel Webster supported Clay's proposals and pleaded for the preservation of the union. The Southerner demanded the legislation of the slavery in all territories.

The Compromise Accepted

Yet in spite of all the extremist oratory, it gradually became evident that majority opinion in both sections still favoured compromise solution. The northern businessmen preferred the preservation of the union for economic causes. The Southern extremists convened a conference at Nashville in Tennesse and decided to wait till the Congress decided on the compromise proposals. As President Taylor died in 1850, the Vice-President Millard Fillmore succeeded him to the Presidency. As the new President favoured a compromise, Clay's proposals were split into five separate bills and were passed by the Congress in 1850.

Importance of the Compromise of 1850

(1) The compromise provided for the establishment of legal governments in New Mexico and Utah.
(2) It provided for the salvation of slavery by popular sovereignty.
(3) It provided to reserve Oklahoma territory for the Indian tribes.
(4) The acceptance of the Fugitive Law by the North gave some relief to the southerners.
(5) The northerners believed that the Missouri compromise would remain in force for ever.

Causes for the Failure of the Compromise

It goes without saying that the compromise of 1850 was regarded as the greatest achievement of Henry Clay for his country. But it did not last long and failed to give peace and plenty due to the following reasons:

(1) Both the North and the South had a wrong notion that the question of slavery was a permanent feature of the land. But once again it spread war of hatred and animosity in the western lands.
(2) The Fugitive slave law denied the right of trial by jury according to the compromise. It was, therefore, considered as anti-christian

and anti-American ideals. As a result the Northerners began to help the run away slaves. This again inflamed the hatred and hostility.

(3) The Fugitive law paved the way for large scale corruption in judiciary.

(4) With the passing away of National Leaders like Clay, Webster and Calhoun hopes for a solution to the sectional dispute were lost.

(5) The North began to disobey the provisions of the compromise of 1850. So the militant extremists of the south desired secession and not piecemeal settlements.

(6) The rising of the inexperienced politicians at the national level brought only uncontrolled pride and passion.

(7) Gradually the south began to realise the Northern domination. So it began to break the compromise of 1850.

(8) The allies of south were gradually drifting towards the North. They were the middle western states. They formerly supported the South. Now it endangered the future prospects of the south.

(9) Most of the internal improvement schemes favoured only the development of the North. Hence, the compromise of 1850 failed to give peace and property to the nation.

17

The Kansas-Nebraska Act

The Revival of the Conflict

For three and a half years after the adoption of the compromise of 1850 most people tried to forget about slavery. This widespread desire for sectional harmony was very manifest during the election of 1852, The Democrats proclaimed their loyalty to the compromise; and after a deadlock among several of the party leaders, they gave their nomination to a dark-horse candidate, Franklin Pierce of New Hampshire. He won the election and became the President of America.

The great figure who dominated the Congress during this period was Stephen A. Douglas of Illinois. He was known to his admirers as the "Little Giant" (He was not much more than five feet tall). Douglas was the ablest and most aggressive debator in the Senate; and although he often showed a lack of moral sensitivity, his patriotism was unquestionable. He had no strong convictions about slavery, and believed primarily in advancing the unity and greatness of the country. It was Douglas, nevertheless, who was responsible for initiating the next phase in the sectional conflict.

A number of events led to the enactment of the Kansas-Nebraska Act in 1854 which in turn revived the old sectional conflict. The following were the chief causes for the passing of the Kansas-Nebraska Act :

(1) The middle western states had common economic interest with the Northern region. Hence, they became the allies of the North. But it was resented by the South.

(2) As population growth was rapid in the North and in the newly acquired territories, it threatened the political life of the southerners.

(3) The new immigrants from Europe, most of them being political refugees, had liberal convictions and it was natural for them to oppose slavery.

(4) Gradually the increased agricultural production of the middle western states was considered as a real challenge for the throne of 'king Cotton' the South.

(5) The expansion of the Free states alarmed the South. So it began to block federal aid for the internal improvements.

(6) The opposition of the South harmed the interest of the west. Hence, it joined with the North in the sectional conflict.

(7) The Cuban problem also paved the way for the passing of the Act of 1854. Slavery was legal in Cuba. The southerners desired to acquire the same. It was opposed by the North.

(8) The southerners were eager to acquire Mexico and Central America where new slave states may be created. But their aspirations were lashed to the ground due to the opposition in the North.

(9) The main issue before the country was the choice of a route for a transcontinental rail road. While Northerners wanted Chicago or St. Louis to be the eastern terminal, Southerners favoured a route running from New Orleans along the Mexican border to Los Angeles. Their strongest argument was that the line would be built across the territory of New Mexico, which had a government and some white inhabitants, whereas any northern line would run across country not yet opened for settlement and inhabited only by nomadic Indian tribes.

(10) The weakness and inefficiency of the Pierce administration helped for the escalation of the problems in the new territories.

The Kansas-Nebraska Act

The choice of a new route for a transcontinental rail road to link the west with the Gulf of Mexico became the feeding ground of a conflict.

The northerners wanted either Chicago or St. Louis to be linked with the gulf.

The Southerners favoured the route running from New Orienas along the Mexican border to Los Angles.

Stephen A. Douglas, the little giant from Illinois desired the line to be built from Chicago to San Francisco across the Rockies. As this proposed route had to pass through the Middle west which was not yet opened for settlement, Senator Douglas introduced a bill in 1854 authorising the creation of two new territories namely Kansas and Nebraska. In order to win the support of the south to his proposal he recommended the principle of 'popular sovereignty' be adopted in these two territories. He believed that popular sovereignty was the ideal solution to the problem. The following of the Kansas-Nebraska Bill proved to be great political blunder and its results were disastrous in the history of U.S.A. The act simply reopened the question of slavery to be settled in blood shed. Strongly backed by the Pierce administration the bill was passed by the Congress, but such a storm of indignation swept across the north that as Douglas remarked, he could have travelled from Boston to Chicago by the light of fires kindled to burn him in effigy. In short he failed to recognise the depth of the moral conviction now pervading Northern Society.

Nebraska

Of the two territories Nebraska was considered as unfit for slaves. The southern planters made no attempt to gain it for slavery. So Nebraska became a free soil without raising any problem. Kansas proved to be a trouble spot.

The Struggle for Kansas

At this juncture there was fate ambiguity in the theory of popular sovereignty. When and how the settlers should decide about slavery. The southerners thought that a decision would be made when the territory became a state. Others assumed that the territorial legislation would be given the power to decide about slavery. As slavery was prevalent in Missouri, the Missourians were eager to secure Kansas for slavery If it would become a free state, it would become a gate way for run away slaves.

In the meantime the anti-slavery groups in the North encouraged free-soilers to go to Kansas, with a view to winning the elections. The Missourians were determined in preventing Kansas becoming a free state at all costs. When the first elections were ordered for in 1855 the Missourians had paid a visit in large numbers and had taken part in the polls. As a result of this fraudulent voting the pre-slavery party did not accent the election results, convened a conference of its supporters and elected a legislature of its own. So there were now two rival governments in Kansas.

Confronting Kansas

There were now two rival governments in Kansas, and each of them was well supplied with weapons. Most slave-owners carried guns as a matter of course. The free-soilers received shipments of rifles from sympathisers in the North; these became known as "Beecher's Bibles" as a result of a statement by the Brooklyn Minister Henry Ward Beecher that a gun was "a greater moral Agency" in Kansas than a Bible. After casual shooting, organised violence began in May 1856, when a Federal Marshal, collected a posse of Missouri "border rufficans" and raided and ransacked the free soil headquarters Lawrence. In retaliation, John Brown a 56 year old abolitionist, of Connecticut ancestry raided a pro-slavery settlement at Pottawatomie and murdered five of its inhabitants in cold blood.

After this there was a period of open civil war, during which about two hundred people lost their lives. By the end of the year Federal troops succeeded to enforcing order; but the only legal legislature was still the pro-slavery legislature fraudulently elected by the Missourians, and the question of slavery in Kansas was still unsettled.

Formation of the Republican Party

Meanwhile, throughout the North indignation at the Kansas-Nebraska Act continued to increase. Many Northerners regarded the repeal of the Missouri compromise as a wanton repudiation of the Compromise of 1850 and as a proof that there was a southern conspiracy to spread slavery as widely as possible. This view was, of course, incorrect. The Kansas Nebraska Act had originated in Douglas desire for a northern rail road, not in a southern conspiracy in fact most southerners had been decidedly lukewarm about it. There was resurgence of anti-slavery sentiment in the place. It was greatly increased by the popularity of *Uncle Tom's Cabin* written by Harriet Beecher Stowe and first published in 1852. Her book was based on abolitionist propaganda.

In the spring of 1854 both the Whig and the democratic party began to hold joint meetings. It soon became evident that a permanent party organisation was required, and the name "Republican", with its Jeffersonian associations, was an obvious choice. A mass meeting at Jackson Michigan, in July 1854, which adopted this name, has often been regarded as the beginning of the new party Republicans organisations were not up in most of the Northern States in the course of the following year.

The Know-Nothing Movement

For a brief period the political scene was further confused by the growth of another new party, the Native Americans, generally known to their opponents as the Know-Nothing. This was the product of years of anti-catholic propaganda by protestant clergymen and journalists. A secret society, the order of the star spangled Banner, was formed about the year 1850 with a programme of restricting the rights of immigrants, and keeping America Protestant and Anglo-Saxon. It was directed chiefly against the Irish, who were now pouring into the country at the rate of nearly 100,000 a year.

The name "Know-Nothing" was derived from the fact that members were instructed, if asked about the society to assert that they know nothing about it. To gain influence in the country and for winning elections the

Know-Nothing organised a political party; in 1854 they won control of Massachussets and made big gains in other Northern states.

Fortunately, the movement died away even more rapidly than it had developed, once in office, the Know-Nothing did little except to demonstrate their lack of integrity. In Massachussets, for example, they appointed a committee to investigate nunneries. The committee men, toured the state and discovered nothing discreditable about the institutions they visited, but ran up an enormous expense account which the tax payers were required to pay. In 1855, moreover the national convention of the Know-Nothing voted to support the Kansas-Nebraska Act. After the party split into Northern and Southern groups, and most of the Northern Know-Nothing soon joined the Republicans.

The Elections of 1856

The voting during the elections indicated that unless the new administration conciliated the Northern element in Democratic Party by carrying out the promise of genuine popular sovereigns to Kansas, the Republicans might win all the free states in 1860.

President Buchanan and Kansas Question

In 1860 James Buchanan became the President. He showed the least interest in solving the Kansas problem. At first he evaded a decisive action and then pledged to establish a genuine popular government in Kansas. By this time the supreme court had to face the Dred Scott case.

The Dred Scott Decision

Dred Scott was a slave who had belonged to an army surgeon in Missouri. In 1834 he had been taken by his master for four years, first to the free state of Illinois and then to the free territory of Wisconisn, and then had been brought back to Missouri. A number of years later Scott said for his freedom on the ground that he had been taken to territory where slavery was prohibited. His suit was supported by individuals opposed to slavery who were hoping to receive judicial confirmation of their belief that a slave automatically became free when he was taken to free territory. The case eventually reached the Supreme Court by appeal from a circuit court. Of the nine Justices, seven were Democrats, and five of these (including Chief Justice Taney of Maryland now in his eightieth year) were southerners.

Six members of the court agreed that Scott's status was determined by the laws of the state in which he now resided in Missouri. This, of-course, was sufficient to settle the case. Toney, however, took the opportunity to make assertions of much more far reaching importance. Supported by two other Justices, he declared that scott had no right even to bring the suit, on the ground that no Negro could be a citizen of the United States. And with the support of the five other Justices, he went on to affirm that Congress had no power to prevent slave-owners from taking their slaves into any of the territories, because to do so would mean depriving citizens of their property without due process of law. In other words according to six members of the Supreme Court, the Missouri Compromise had been unconstitutional and slavery was legal in all territories even as far as north Oregan.

Toney had been a great Chief Justice and belonged to the old generation of southerners. He did not regard slavery as a positive good and had emancipated his own slaves. Yet he now gave judicial backing to the southern contention, that slavery could not constitutionally be excluded from any territory. Both his assertion that no Negro could be a citizen and his invalidation of the Missouri Compromise were based on faulty restoring. Toney, however, could claim that his denial to Congress of the power to exclude slavery from the territories was in conformity with the 1850 Compromise and the Kansas Nebraska Act, which had superseded the Missouri Compromise, and that many leaders of different shades of opinions had declared that the whole question should be settled by Judicial decision. In spite of this decision, the attempt to establish slavery in Kansas ended in failure.

In the meantime the Kansas was again invited to elect a new legislature in which the free soilers won control of the legislature. The proposal to admit Kansas as a slave state was rejected in the Congress. So Kansas decided to remain as a slave territory for the time being. Later on slavery was abolished in Kansas and it was admitted as a state in 1861.

Results

(1) Due to the Kansas Nebraska Act of 1854 once again the conflict between the North and the South was revived.
(2) The question of slavery led to a civil war in Kansas in which hundreds of people lost their lives.
(3) The sectional conflict helped for the formation of the Republican Party which stood for the abolition of slavery.
(4) The abolitionist movement gained momentum both in the North and the West.
(5) The theory of popular sovereignty proved that America would emerge as a land of the free soilers.
(6) It paved the way for the great civil war of 1861.
(7) Everybody realised that all regional differences would be settled only by a war.

18

John C. Calhoun

John C. Calhoun was born in South Carolina. He was a Scotch-Irish Calvinist by birth. He belonged only by marriage not by birth to the planter aristocracy of the state. He was the chief political figure in the state. Formerly a strong nationalist, he now changed into a champion of southern sectional interest, and in the course of time his theories as to the nature of the Federal Union were accepted through a large part of the south. In short, it was primally because of his capacity for uncompromising logic that he became the chief political spokesman of the cotton belt.

Calhoun was concerned with one of the permanent problems of government; and whatever one may think of the practical results of his logic, it should be recognised that the theoretical analysis which he presented in his *Exposition of Government* was a contribution to political theory of permanent importance.

The protection of minority rights had been one of the man's objectives of the American Constitution. The same problem in a different from confronted the men who drafted the charter of the United Nations, and resulted in the adoption of the veto power. A veto was also Calhoun solution. The powers of the Federal Government must be limited, and a minority section must be allowed to block action detrimental to its interests.

In his "South Carolina Exposition and Protest" of 1828 Calhoun adopted a states' rights theory of the constitution, arguing that sovereignty remained with the states and that any state could nullify an act of the Federal Government which it regarded as unconstitutional. In later years he favoured adoption of same system of concurrent majorities by which consent of both sections would be needed for Federal legislation. Calhoun was not an advocate of secession; on the contrary, his main objective as he saw it, was to make it unnecessary for the south to secede. But it is obvious that adoption of his proposals would have fatally weakened the Federal Union.

In so far as Calhoun's purposes were to protect agricultural interests and limit Federal powers, he was the successor of Jefferson and John Taylor. But he did not share Jefferson's liberalism. He defended slavery as a positive good. So he frankly repudiated the doctrine of human equality as expressed in the Declaration of Independence.

Calhoun was opposed to Federal power. He was against it only in so far as it worked to the detriment of the South. In the 1840's when he hoped to see the southern control of the Federal Government and the spending of Federal money on internal improvements beneficial to the South, he was willing to defend a loose construction of the Constitution.

Thus, under Calhoun's leadership, the South reacted to the threat of Northern domination by adopting a theory of the Federal Union which Northern and Western nationalists regarded as close to treason. After 1830 the sectional conflict was intensified by the divergence of attitudes towards slavery. The South became increasingly outspoken in the defence of her peculiar institution, while a militant abolitionist movement began to develop in parts of the North.

During Monroe's administration John C. Calhoun served as Secretary of War for some time. Before the election of 1824 Crawford's qualifications were weakened by a physical breakdown and believed that construction of internal improvements should as far as possible, be a state rather than a Federal responsibility.

The drive for expansion began to dominate national politics in 1843. When President Tyler and Secretary of State Upshur took up the Texas question. The admission of Texas, however, was delayed by sectional rivalry. Upshur was killed in an accident early in 1844, before the Texas negotiations had been completed, and was, succeeded by John C. Calhoun. Calhoun strengthened Northern opposition by indemnifying the movement for annexation with the cause of slavery. Later on it became the main issue in the forthcoming presidential election.

Calhoun thus rendered remarkable service for the southerners till his death in 1850.

Henry Clay

Henry Clay played a significant role in the history of U.S.A. He was born in Virginia and lived in Kontucky. He was by birth a frontier upper class man. Clay, although a Westerner was almost equally sympathetic to business interests and was opposed to the inflationary demands of the western farmers. His American System, confining a protective tariff with

Federal aid for the internal improvements needed for the development of the Mississipi Valley was an attempt to link the North with the Northwest and the border states in a programme of economic expansion. Through much of his career Clay seemed to be primarily a very supple politician. But he had an eloquence and personal charm which won him a large body of devoted adherents; and during times of crisis he could rise to real statesmanship.

While Clay represented the rising business class of the west, Benton was the voice of the farmers. He championed western expansion, demanded cheaper public land, and denounced the Eastern "money power". But unlike many other westerners, he was equally hostile to the state banks and insisted that specie was the only safe form of money; his speeches against the issuance of bank notes in any form won him the nick name "Old Bullion".

Western agrarian expansionism found expression in the elections of 1810 during the outbreak of the war of 1812. It sent to Congress a group of youngmen who quickly became known as the Warhawks. Having grown up since independence they displayed an aggressive and often boastful nationalism which had been unknown among the older generation. Their principle leader, Henry Clay, who was elected speaker of the House of Representatives, was more responsible than any other individual for pushing the somewhat reluctant Madison into war. As a result war was finally declared by Congress on June 18, 1812. The war of 1812 was, therefore, called "Mr. Madison's war" by his opponents. It begun on the Americans soil. The war came to an end by the Treaty of Ghent in 1814.

Henry Clay aroused the public sentiment through his speeches for the co-operation of the new sister republics. It greatly paved the way for unity and solidarity of the people.

During the "era of good feeling" the chief spokesman of the nationalist programme was Henry Clay. He was the advocate of the "American system". Older men, like Presidents Madison and Monroe, accepted it only with considerable misgivings. The measures advocated by Clay and other young republicans were similar to those originally advocated by Alexander Hamilton; but, unlike Hamilton they appealed to the mass of the American people, not merely to the upper class and sought the support of the agricultural south and west. He also actively participated in the revival of the sectional conflict along with Calhoun for the improvement of south and west. They did a lot for the improvement of the social conditions in those lands.

Henry Clay became a prominent political leader during this period. The most important development during Adam's Presidency was the amalgamation of the different political factions into two main groups. Adams had appointed Clay as Secretary of State, thereby causing the Jacksonians to accuse him of obtaining the presidency by means of "a corrupt bargain", and the followers of the two men began to call themselves the National Republicans.

Henry Clay gave proposals for a reduction of the tariff in the Congress. He was highly responsible for the drastic changes in the tariff reduction. Then in 1832 the National Republicans nominated him as their candidate for the post of President. But he was defeated in the election as against Jackson due to the renewal of the charter of the Bank of the United States. Further, in 1840 election the Whigs rejected Clay, Webster and then other outstanding leaders and gave their nomination to the elderly William Henry Harrison. But it cannot be denied that under Clay's leadership the Whigs succeeded in temporarily abolishing the Independent Treasury and raising the tariff, while the west obtained the Pre-emption Act it had long been seeking.

At the age of seventy, Henry Clay assumed the leadership in the task of working out a settlement which would satisfy both sections and in January 1850 he made a series of compromise proposals. He suggested that California be admitted as a state with its anti-slavery constitutions and that in the vast of the area acquired from Mexico, territorial governments be set up without any restriction about slavery. He made it plain that, in his opinion, slavery, would never actually be established in this area because the soil and climate were unsuitable; it was, therefore, unnecessary for the North to antagonize the South by demanding that it be excluded by law. Clay also proposed that northern public opinion be conciliated by the abolition of the slave trade in the district of Columbia. Further, he went on to urge to redress one of the main southern grievances by the enactment of a more stringent Fugitive slave-law. Daniel Webster, the powerful supporter of Clay gave his whole hearted cooperation. But the proposals were opposed by President Taylor and by the more extreme groups in both sections. After a long discussion the compromise of Clay was accepted. This was due to the dynamic leadership of the young democratic Senator from Illinois, Stephen A. Doughlas. Thus, Clay did a wonderful service to the southerners. Clay died in the year 1852. After his death, young people took up the task of Clay.

19

Social and Economic Conditions

Social Conditions

Many significant changes took place in the society during the 18th century. Particularly the 18th century is considered as the age of enlightenment in the history of the world. During this age of enlightenment many scientific inventions were made; many political philosophers advocated their ideas in the world. Among them John Locke came to the forefront. He advocated the three essential rights of man, *viz.*, liberty, right to property and right to life. These ideas greatly affected the people of America. They carefully followed liberty, equality and fraternity in their day to day life.

A far reaching development took place in the Americans Society. The European family had been patriarchal, characterised by the rule of the father over his wife and children. Wives had been denied the power to own property and deprived of other basic legal rights, while the power of a father over his children even included that of deed whom they should marry. The powers of the father decreased, and women and children acquired greater independence. The American family became less monarchial and more democratic. Women occupied a considerable position in the society. Education was given to them at par with men. The parents lost their control over their children in he society. However, they enjoyed full freedom. Unrestricted life paved the way for many love marriages. As a result of these love marriages, divorce, difference of opinion between husband and wife and other evils came into existence.

As the 19th century slowly advanced, a strong reaction began to develop against the brutalities of earlier days. The crusade against slavery came to overshadow all other reforms, to same extent it hampered them by attracting to much zeal to itself, yet gains were gradually achieved on many fronts.

Imprisonment for debt contained to be of rightwave, though its extent has been exaggerated. As late as 1830 hundreds of penniless persons were languishing in filthy holes, sometimes for owing less than one dollar. The poorer working classes were especially hard hit by this merciless practice. As the embattled labourer won the ballot and asserted himself, state legislatures gradually abolished debtors' prisons.

Criminal codes in the states were likewise being softened, in accordance with more enlightened European practices. The number of capital offences was being reduced and brutal punishments, such as whipping and branding were being slowly eliminated. Prisons were termed as "reformatories", "houses of correction" and "penitentiaries" (for penance).

During this period agitation for peace also gained some momentum. In 1828 the American Peace Society was formed with a ringing declaration of war on war.

Religion and morality both suffered from the surgical shock of separation from the mother country. Roaring revivals stirred the masses and huge camp meetings were held on the frontier. At these "religious fairs" as many as 25,000 persons would gather to drink the hell-five gospel, church attendance was a fairly regular ritual for about three-fourths of the 23,000,000 Americans in 1850, Congregationalism, Presbyterianism and Episcopalianism, as the older and more conservative faiths contained to flourish in the East. More popular in the West and South were the Methodists and Baptists. Religious diversity was accelerated by the disruptions of the churches over the slavery issue.

Many scientific achievements were made during this period. Thomas Jefferson, for example was a gifted amateur who won a gold medal for a new type of plan. Nathanial Bouditch, a great Mathematician, Mathew F. Maury an eminent oceanographer and Benjamin Silliman, a pioneer chemist made wonderful contributions during this period.

Education and Literature

Public education continued its upward climb during this period. The ideal of tax supported elementary schools adopted on a nationwide basis before the civil war, was still gathering its strength. Gradually education took a fair shape in the country.

It was during this period that foundations of the American Public School system were established and the belief that education ought to be free, universal and compulsory won general acceptance.

In 1800 many people in all parts of the country were illiterate. Some schools were maintained by the churches. Most of the northern states began to make appropriations for the support of education early in the 19th century. New York for instance took the initial step in 1812 largely through the efforts of De Witt Clinton. But, for a number of years, well-to-do parents were required to pay fees: and although the poor could have their children educated free, they were liable to be stigmatised pauper if they took advantage of this concession.

The first compulsory education law was passed in Massachusetts in 1852 and other States did not follow this example until after the Civil War. Horace Mann fought for universal education. By 1850 the nation had a total of 80,000 elementary schools, with nearly 3,500,000 pupils. Then colleges were established in the country for higher education.

Booker T. Washington took steps for the improvement of neglected Negro education, A graduate of Harvard Dr. W.E.R. Du Bois was the first black to receive the Ph.D. at that prestigious institution. The almost phenomenal growth of higher education owed much to the Morrill Act of 1862. Private philanthropy richly supplemented federal grants to higher education. Rockfeller died at 1837 after having given some 550 million dollars for philanthropic purposes. Sharp increase took place in professional and technical schools.

Books continued to be a major source of education and enjoyment, for both juveniles and adults. Best sellers of the 1880's were generally old favourites like David Copperfield and Ivanhoe. Well-stocked public libraries — the poorman's university were making encouraging progress, especially in Boston and New York.

Many literary luminaries lived during this period. They made wonderful contribution in the field of literature. General Lewis Wallace, Brot Harte, Mark Twain christened Samuel L. Clemens were some of the literary giants produced by America.

Economic Conditions

When George Washington first took the Presidential oath, the economic wheels of the South were cranking very badly. They were burdened with depressed prices, unmarketable products, over cropped lands and the deadweight of an unprofitable slave system. The South had remained entirely an agrarian while the north had become a centre for industries and commerce, irrigational facilities were made. The Erie canal which finally ribboned 363 miles was completed by sections. As a result the value of land along the route skyrocketed, and new cities — like Rochester and Syrrense sprouted up. Industry in the state boomed, as New York city expanded into the seaboard queen of the nation.

Other profound economic and political changes followed the completion of the canal. The price of potatoes in New York City was cut in half and many dispirited New England farmers, no longer able to face this ruinuous competition, abandoned their rocky holdings and went elsewhere. Thus, a significant change took place in the economic field during this period.

20

The Civil War

There was long drawn sectional conflict between the North and the South. It resulted in the secession of the South and the Civil war broke out in 1861. No single cause may be attributed for the outbreak of this terrible and horrible Civil War.

(1) The Political Causes.

(i) There was no national unity among the Americans. It was due to an amalgamation of various nationalities and races form Europe.

(ii) As most of the immigrants came to America as political refugees, political difference was its natural consequence.

(iii) As a result of the rapid development of industry and commerce, the principle of expansionism played its own role in politics.

(iv) The principle of political domination divided the country into two sections after independence.

(v) The Missourie Compromise of 1820 and the Compromise of 1850 were tentative in nature and they failed to settle the problem permanently.

(vi) The principle of popular sovereignty favoured the free sailers which was resented by the southerners.

(vii) The evergrowing population of the North was to determine the political future of the country.

(viii) Another reason for the war was the conflict of ideology. The North was democratic in its political ideals and ways of life whereas in the South the political power was in the hands of a few plantation owners. The democratic ideals were never allowed to flourish in the South.

(ix) As there were more educational opportunities in the North they became enlightened in their political attitude.

(x) The defeat of the South in the struggle for Kansas forced them to break away from the union.

(xi) Another political cause for the war was the increase of Free States in the Union which altered the balance of power in the Congress. So the South feared in this aspect.

(xii) The secession and the formation of a confederacy of the Southern States finally resulted in the outbreak of the Civil War.

(2) The Economic Causes

(i) The political conflict was based on the economic interests of the South and the North which had developed divergent economic systems.

(ii) The South had remained entirely an agrarian while the North had become a centre for industries and commerce.

(iii) The South favoured a low tariff whereas the North pleaded for a high protective tariff.

(iv) The banks and big Corporations, controlled by the northerners, began to exploit the southern agrarian economy.

(v) The South opposed Federal spending on internal improvements but the North interested in the Federal aid for internal improvements.

(vi) Really speaking the South was economically backward. It relied upon the business of the North for its exports and imports.

(vii) The combination of the Western farmers and the Northern businessman against slavery ruined the economic system of the South.

(viii) The loss of economic power forced them to break away from the Union.

(3) The Slavery

(i) The slavery greatly affected the morality of the people so they resented against it.

(ii) Slavery was a basic fixture of life in the South. The peculiar institution, called slavery, gave wealth and political power to the plantation owning aristocrats of the South.

(iii) The question of extension of slavery into the newly acquired territories revived the sectional conflict.

(iv) The Northerners were more politically influenced than the Southerners. In other words the northerners, as political opponents of the South, wanted to destroy slavery.

(v) As no new territory was available for the extension of slavery, the political future of the South was doomed.

(vi) The South desired to get all sorts of protection from the Federation for the extension of slavery in all territories. But the North desired the abolition of slavery by law. So it led to the Civil war.

(vii) The struggle for Kansas over the question of slavery ended in enmity between the confronting and conflicting sections.

(viii) The Abolitionist movements were highly responsible for the war.

(ix) The habitual practice of breaking the Fugitive law in the North widened the split.

(x) The Southerners believed that the destruction of slavery would affects their way of life. The Southerners, therefore, decided to secede from the Union.

(4) **Immediate Cause.** The immediate cause of the Civil war was the construction of the new railroads linked the West with the Northeast. The South was totally neglected in the railroad construction. The linking of the West with the Northeast led for closer economic ties and political affiliation. The South was politically isolated and neglected. In addition to this the emergence of the Republican Party greatly widened the gap between the North and the South. In the election of 1860, Abraham Lincoln, the ReRepublican Party candidate, was elected as the new President. The voting pattern clearly established the fact that no compromise was possible between the confronting groups.

The Formation of the Confederacy

Many Southern leaders had decided long before the election that they would not remain in the union under a Republican President. They began to take action as soon as the results were announced. The South Carolina legislature ordered the election of a State convention, which adopted an ordinance of secession on December 20. By an unanimous vote it declared that "the Union now subsisting between South Carolina and other States.. is hereby dissolved". Before the end of February 1861, similar action had been taken by six other States, all of them in the cotton belt : Mississippi, Florida, Alabama, Georgia, Louisiana and Texas. They formed a confederacy.

The confederacy announced that the nothern opposition to slavery and the violation of the rights of the Southerners by the North was the reason for secession. Jefferson Davis of Mississippi and Alexander Stephens of Georgia were chosen as President and Vice President of the Confederate States of America.

Under these circumstances the Federal Government took no action against the confederacy and actually a few Republican wanted the erring States to go in peace. After inauguration, President Lincoln proclaimed that the Southern States had no constitutional right to secede and that a peaceful secession was impossible. He also announced that the Union Government would not commit the first act of war.

Thus, Lincoln with no previous executive experience, assumed the presidency of the United states during the greatest crisis in its history.

Course of the Civil War

1. **The War Begins.** When the Federal Government sent reinforcements in defence of the Fort Sumter, it was attacked by the confederacy troops on April 12, 1861. It was done under the leadership of General Pierre G.T. Beauregard. Two days later the fort surrendered. At this juncture the firing on Fort Sumter provoked a burst of popular indignation. Lincoln, on his own responsibility called for 75,000 volunteers to enforce the laws of the United States and ordered a blockade of confederate seaports. Thus, war had begun.
2. **Resources of the Two Sides.** The struggle lasted for four years and more than 600,000 people lost their lives during this struggle.

   The North had greater potential strength. There were nearly 10 lakhs people in the nineteen free states and another 3 lakhs (including 4 lakhs slaves) in the four border states. The eleven states in the confederacy had only 6,500,000 white people along with 3,500,000 slaves. Nearly 2,000,000 soldiers served in the Northren army, as compared with only about 800,000 in the confederate army. In industrial equipment and transportation facilities the North had an overwhelming superiority.

   On the other hand, the confederacy had some strong initial advantages. She enjoyed the military advantage of possessing the inner lines; at the outset of the war she had much better generals; her citizens being more accustomed to outdoor life and to become shooting and horseback riding, required less training to become excellent soldiers; and her armies were fighting on their own territories in defence of their homes and their way of life. But as the struggle continued, the North was increasingly able to make her potential strength effective, while the confederacy could not replace her losses in manpower and supplies.

   The North won the War in the end partly because by controlling the army she was able to blockade confederate ports and impose an economic strangulation, and partly because her armies could afford to take much greater punishment in battle.

(3) **The Battle Grounds.** (a) *From Bull Run to Gettysburg*: At the beginning of the war the confederacy could count on the services of most of the ablest officers in the United States army, including particularly Robert E. Lee, who had universally been regarded as one of the greatest soldiers and noblest characters in American history. Lee was the first military adviser to Jaffarson Davis and then Commander of the armies in Virginia; he was not given command of all the confederate forces until almost the end of the war.

Lincoln, on the other hand, was very willing to give full authority to his generals, but could find able leaders only by a costly process of trial and error.

From a military point of view, the confederacy should probably have taken the offensive early in the war, while the North should have remained on the defensive until she had effectively mobilised her manpower and economic resources. Political considerations, however, made both these courses of action impossible.

The first of the attempts to invade Virginia was made in July 1861 under the leadership of General Irwin McDowell. The Northern army met confederate forces under Beauregard and Joseph Johnston at Bull Run. Both armies consisted mostly of raw recruits, and both of them were quickly thrown into complete confusion. The confederates, however, held their lines more successfully, largely owing to the firmness of a brigade commanded by Thomas J. Jackson, who earned here his title "Stone Wall", and the battle ended in a disorderly and panic stricken fight of the Union forces back to Washington.

In the meantime McDowell was replaced by George McClellan, who become in November General-in-Chief of all Union forces. He was a man of thirty-four years. McClellan had already served in the Mexican war and had afterwards become a railroad executive. His qualifications for military leadership were more open to question. He made many enemies, moreover, by his arrogance and outspoken contempt for all politicians.

Meanwhile, the North was establishing a blockade of the confederate coast which became steadily more effective. Almost the whole of the United States navy remained loyal to the Union, and during the war it was greatly enlarged. Northern military forces, moreover, helped to maintain the blockade by seizing a number of bases on island and headlands in confederate territory.

The Union army began its western campaigns in 1862, the army led by Ulysses Grant captured Fort Henry. A naval squadron under

Admiral Glalgon captured New Orleans, Chattanooga in Tennessee was captured and lost in 1863. There was bitter contest for Richmond, the Union armies were ultimately defeated by Lee. Then he marched northwards, won the battle of Manossas crossed the Potomac and the North was facing a decisive defeat.

The union army under George Mearde met Lee at Gettysburg in July 1863 and won a decisive victory. At the same time Grant captured Vicksburg after a fierce battle, Gettysburg and Vicksburg were the main turning points of the war. William Shevman, another commander of the union forces captured Atlausta in 1864 and begun his famous march through Georgia and also captured Savannah. Grant began his invasion of Virginia besiezed the city with a view to straving the armies of Lee. Now the confederate army realised that the war was lost, Rober Lee met Ulysses Grant at Appomattox on 9th April 1865 — and surrendered. On April 26, Johnston felt that further resistance was useless, surrendered to Sherman. Jefferson Davis, who had escaped into the mountains in the hope of continuing the war, was captured soon afterwards, and, the lost confederate forces in the field laid down their arms on May 26.

Lincoln did not live to see the end of the war. On April 14, while attending a performance at Ford's Theatre in Washington, he was assassinated by a demented confederated sympathiser, John Wilkes Booth.

Thus, the war ended in the victory of the North and the union was saved at a heavy cost.

Results of the Civil War

(1) It goes without saying that "the most important result of the civil war was the victory of the industrial capitalism over agrarian capitalism".

(2) It strengthened the forces of national unity and defeated the principle of states' rights.

(3) Another result of the war was the proclamation of Emancipation of the slaves. It paved the way for the abolition of a slavery.

(4) The union was saved at a heavy cost and the confederacy was destroyed.

(5) The war completely ruined the agrarian economy of the south.

(6) It wonderfully shaped the industrial policy of the Union.

(7) Moreover, it paved the way for Westward Movement. Due to this more lands were brought under cultivation.

(8) Scarcity of labour force in agriculture forced the farmers to seek technological assistance and also to adopt labour saving devices in agriculture.

(9) The scarcity of labour force in the industrial sector led for the increased use of machinery.

(10) Another result of the war was the inflation in the North. Moreover, the war accelerated the business growth in the north.

(11) Due to this civil war large corporations were benefited much by increased production.

(12) Many factories were established; so also a few mines were discovered.

(13) The war paved the way for the increase of taxes in the country. In addition to this the tariff was enhanced.

(14) The congress passed the Homestead Act in 1861 which provided the grant of free public land to all American Citizens.

(15) The proletarians suffered a lot from the inflation while the industrialists and big businessmen earned enormous profits.

(16) The Federal Government regularised the banking system.

(17) The interference of Emperor Nepolean II of France in their affairs was stopped by the civil war. The French army was defeated in the battle of Puebla. They were forced to leave Mexico by Monroe Doctrine.

(18) The Union Pacific and the Central Pacific were to be constructed as part of the transcontinental railroad.

(19) The ideas of Alexander Hamilton and Henry Clay had triumphed over the ideals of Jefferson and Jackson.

(20) It paved the way for rapid industrialisation.

(21) The British neutrality throughout the war helped to establish cordial relationship between U.S.A. and England.

(22) The civil war finally helped to change U.S.A. as a world power by the end of the 19th century.

The political leadership of the Union proved to be superior to that of the confederacy. President Lincoln, with his sense of humour and spirit of selflessness acted with courage and integrity and led his country on the road to victory. On the other hand, Jefferson Davis, President of Confederacy of the eleven states was a poor judge of men and lacked physical and emotional stamina required for good leadership.

The civil war broke out in April 1861 and ended in April 1861 and ended in April 1865. When Robert Lee, Commander of the Confederate Army surrendered to Ulysses Grant at Appomattox. The confronting armies met and fought in a number of battle fields such as Bull Run, Gettysburg, Vicksburg, Atlanta and Appomattox. The war ended in the victory of the North and its results were far reaching in the history of U.S.A. The following was the reasons for the victory of the North :

(i) The North had enormous population; but the South had lesser population. This manpower was highly responsible for the victory of the North in the civil war.

(ii) The northern army out-numbered the southern army which decided the fate of the war.

(iii) The northern army was well equipped and well-trained; but this was not in the case of southern army.

(iv) The Northern army had good transportation facilities in the North. It helped the army to move quickly and in time.

(v) As the west was linked with northeast by railroads, the combination of the western favouring economy and the northern industrial economy proved more than a match to that of the southern agricultural economy.

(vi) The north had entire control over sea. It was, therefore, very easy for them to blockade the confederate ports and imposed economic strangulation.

(vii) The financial condition of the south was very weak and meak. In addition to this its economy was ruined by the war.

(viii) The North increased its resources and improved its financial position by way of levying new taxes, raising tariffs, issuing of paper money and selling of war bonds.

(ix) Jefferson Davis never gave a free hand to the generals of the confederate army. On the other hand, Lincoln gave full freedom to his generals and was able to find more competent generals in course of the war.

(x) The Union fully analysed the various means of the success of war. It, therefore, started its offensive only after mobilising the manpower and economic resources.

(xi) The defensive tactics of the South paved the way for its doom and disaster.

(xii) The North was industrially well advanced and hence it offered everything for a long war; but the agricultural South could not offer much for a long war.

(xiii) As the North opposed slavery, it did not receive moral and material support from Europe.

(xiv) The expected help from Britain was not extended to the South. It remained neutral with some strong economic motivations.

To put it in a nutshell the victory of the North in the civil war may be regarded as the victory of the industrial capitalism over the agrarian capitalism. It was the triumph of Hamiltanism over that of Jeffersonism.

21

Abraham Lincoln

Abraham Lincoln was born in Kentucky in 1809. He was brought by his parents to Illinois at an early age. Lincoln had worked his way up from poverty and was now recognised as one of the ablest and most successful lawyers in the state. He had been one of the leaders of the Illinois Whigs. He served as a member in the House of Representatives for one term. A meditative and some what melancholy man with a great fondness for telling humorous stories, he had an innate kindliness and a lack of vanity which made people like and trust him; but he had not hitherto seemed to have declined for leadership outside his own community. Thus, Lincoln became a national figure.

Lincoln was always very clear in his speeches about slavery. He had arrived at definite conclusions and was able to state them lucidly, boldly and convincingly. As he declared in his speech accepting the senatorial nomination, he believed that "this government cannot endure permanently half slave and half free. Agitation would continue until a crisis had been reached and passed."

Hostile to the abolitionists, Lincoln did not propose to attack slavery in the South or repeal the Fugitive Slave Law. And although he insisted, that Negroes had a right to the life, liberty and pursuit of happiness promised to all men by the Declaration of Independence, he declared himself opposed to racial equality. The extinction of slavery, he believed, could only be a gradual and lengthy process; and if the North adopted an attitude of moral intolerance and condemnation toward the slave owners, the solution of the problem would become more difficult, Douglas' theory that it could be left to the people of each territory to decide for themselves was a more evasion of the issue.

Throughout the year 1859 the country was visibly drifting closer to the crisis which Lincoln had predicted. There was chaos and confusion in the country. It widened the gulf between North and South.

At this juncture the election of 1860 was considered as an important opportunity for Lincoln. He contested in the North where the race was mainly between Lincoln and Douglas. Lincoln run ahead in every state. He carried all the electoral votes of free states except New Jersey which gave three of its seven votes to Douglas. Lincoln had a clear majority of the electoral college. In the South the main contest was between Breckinridge and Bell. Some people voted for Bell. Thus, Lincoln had less than 40 per cent of the popular vote.

During the civil war Lincoln was the President of America. He did a wonderful service in the civil war. In his inaugural address Lincoln was careful not to slam the door against peaceful restoration of the Union. He asserted that the southern states had no constitutional right to secede. But he made it plain that the Union government should not commit the first act of war, and urged the southern states to change their mind before it was too late.

During the war Lincoln gave full authority to his generals. On September 22, 1862 Lincoln proclaimed in his capacity as Commander-in-Chief of the army, that gave emancipation to 1,50,000 Negroes who were enlisted in the Northern army.

During the time of the civil war Britain followed the policy of neutrality. It shows its diplomacy of the war that followed by Britain at this juncture.

On March 4, 1865, Lincoln began his second term, appealing to fellow countrymen in the immortal words of his Second Inaugural, "With malice towards none; with charity for all to do all which may achieve and cherish a just and lasting peace". It was obvious that the next few years would be largely occupied by conflict about reconstruction between the executive and the Congressional Radicals. Finally, Lincoln with his able and efficient commanders and with his excellent qualities achieved an astounding victory towards the end of the civil war. But he did not live to see the end of the war. On April 14, while attending a performance at Ford's Theatre in Washington, he was assassinated by a dissented confederate sympathiser, John Wilkes Booth. Thus, Lincoln, the saviour of Negroes was not able to save his life from the assassin's bullet and sacrificed his life not only for the poor Negroes but also for the welfare of the Americans.

PART II

1

Reconstruction and After

Abraham Lincoln was re-elected as President of the United States in the election of 1864. Republicans and war Democrats supported Lincoin but still a number of Republicans objected to Lincoln's leadership as he, they considered, showed a liberal attitude towards the South. The Radicals among the Republicans in the Congress criticised his conduct of war and his policy of post-war re-construction.

Believing that the purpose of the war was only to restore the Union, Lincoln wished the Southern States to regain their constitutional rights as quickly as possible. He wished that the reconstruction should be constrolled by the President, and not by Congress. The radicals wanted to wreak vengeance upon the South and impose drastic changes upon it in order to ensure loyalty.

The important problem was to determine the status of the seceded states of the confederacy. There was confusion whether this was within the realm of Congress as the President Lincoln held that the rebellious South was not legally seceded but their citizens had been misled by some dis-loyal citizens against the Federal authority. According to Lincoln the war was the act of the individuals and not of the states and he had to deal with the individals. Lincoln believed that he as the Presient and Commander-in-Chief of the Army and Navy had the power to pardon and had complete control over the situation.

Acting on this principle Lincoln proclaimed in 1863 that if any southern state with 10 per cent of the voters formed a Government loyal to the constitution and the union and obey the President and Congress laws that state would be recognised as a legal state. This was not acceptable to the Congress because it was under the impression that the President usurped the legislative powers. Though, Lincoln recognised some of the southern State Governments in Virginia, Arkansas, Tennessee, Louisiana but Congress refused to send the representatives and thus dispproved his action.

Some Republicans felt that the southern planters must be kept under Military rule. Others desired to give Negroes the right to vote immediately. In 1865 Congress proposed the 13th Amendment which abolished slavery and was ratified in December 1865.

There were conflicts about the reconstruction between the President an the Congress radicals. On April 14, 1865 Lincoln was assassinated.

Most southerners were willing to accept the supremacy of the federal Government and the abolition of slavery, and wanted to rebuild their economy. But their desire to forget the war was not reciprocated in the North which wanted to treat the South as a conquered territory. The hatred and antagonism lasted some years. It was only in 1877 that the union became acceptable to white southerners.

1. **The South After the Civil War.** The end of the civil war found the South utterly shattered. The confederate government had collapsed and law and order had crumbled and in some regions of the South freed Negroes, deserters from the two armies, criminals and looters terrorised the inhabitants. The Nothern army had laid waste the fairest lands of the South. Parts of many Southern towns were in ruin through siege or fire. Throughout the South, the crops had rafted in the fields and grass grown in the streets.

   The economic life of the South had cracked under the war. Trade war at a standstill, Factories were closed, Banks had shut their doors and rail roads were not able to work. The railway engines were dilapidated. "King cotton" was now a penniless beggar in rags. The huge cotton fields were chocked with weeds. The power of the rich planters had gone. The war had paralysed schools and churches. The political institutions were totally uprooted. Not a single political leader was there to lead and guide them. There were bitter quarrels among the Republicans regarding the reconstruction of the South.

2. **The Johnson Plan.** After the assassination of President Lincoln in 1865, Andrew Johnson became the President of U.S.A. He wanted to implement the liberal policies of his predecessor but had little skill in realising his scheme. To carry out his scheme of reconstruction :

   (1) He appointed provisional governors for the southern states.

   (2) He granted amnesty to all Southerners, except the political and military leaders of the confederacy, who were ready to take an oath of allegiance to the Federal Union.

   (3) The loyal southerners were required to invalidate the acts of recession, abolish slavery, repudiate the debts of the confederacy and ratify the constitution.

(4) The Federal Government had set up a Freed men's 'Bureau' in 1865 to provide food, shelter and medical attention to the free slaves. But it never planned to give them permanent relief.

3. **The Black Codes.** The New Southern Governments, established under the Johnson plan enacted a number of laws known as the "Black Codes". These codes gave the Negroes only a subordinate status in the Southern society. They were prevanted from voting, serving on Juries, carrying arms and appearing in public places. These codes only conferred them the rights of citizenship but denied all other democratic rights.

4. **The Radicals and the President.** The Radicals in the Congress led by Thaddeus Stevens opposed the Johnson's plan of Reconstruction in the South.

   (i) They thought that the black codes were anti-national and proved that the war had been fought in vain.

   (2) The confederacy should be considered as a conquerred territory and as such they needed more drastic conditions to be imposed for readmission in to the union.

   (3) They wanted to build a strong centre in the South for the Republican party.

   (4) The Speedy recovery of the South would pose a political problem in the country and would be detrimental to the interests of the northern businessmen.

   (5) The radicals refused to admit the representatives of the southern states in the Congress and decided to implement their own plan of reconstruction.

5. **The Radical's Plan.**

   (1) The Congress established a Joint committee on Reconstruction with fifteen members.

   (2) The Congress passed Freed men's Bureau Bill and a Civil Rights Bill to protect the life and the rights of the Negroes.

   (3) The Congress passed a Fourteenth Amendment to the Constitution in 1866. According to this amendment :

      (a) All persons born or naturalised in the United States were to be the citizens of the U.S.A.

      (b) No State shall make laws to abridgs the rights of the citizens.

      (c) No person shall be denied the equal protection of the laws.

(d) If any state denied the franchise to its citizens, its representation in the Congress should be proportionately reduced.

(e) No confederate official should hold official positin in the U.S.A.

(f) The debt of the confederacy was repudiated.

(g) All Southern States except Tennessee refused to ratify the Amendment as desired by the Radicals.

(4) After the congressional elections of 1866 the control of the Government was transferred to the Congress and the President remained a figure head.

(5) To restrict the powers of the President, the Congress passed a Tenure of Office Act which prohibited the President from dismissing any official without the consent of the Senate.

6. **Reconstruction Acts.** In 1867 the Congress passed a series of Reconstruction Acts, These acts declared that :

(a) No legal government existed in any part of the former confederacy.

(b) The conquerred territory was to be divided into five districts which were to be ruled by the army generals.

(c) The constitutional conventions elected by all, should frame constitutions the Fourteenth Amendment be ratified and then only apply for representation in the Congress.

7. As Johnson refused to accept the Reconstruction Acts of the Radicals, they wanted to remove Johnson by impeachment. The resolution failed in the Senate by the shortage of a single vote.

8. The Radicals also reduced the power of the Supreme Court to safeguard their reconstructional acts.

9. The Congress passed the Fifteenth Amendment which declared that the right to vote could not be denied or abridged on account of race or colour.

Results

(1) By 1870 all States ratified the Fifteenth Amendment and were back in the union.

(2) The Western South was reconstructed and reshaped on the lines of the Radicals Reconstruction Programme.

(3) The whites in the South re-established the White Supremacy.

(4) The southern conservatives known as "Bourbons" recaptured their lost political power.

(5) The whites adopted all means fair or foul to deny equality and freedom to the Negroes. The reconstruction was a tragic experience for the Negroes.

(6) The Reconstruction led for corruption in all walks of life.

(7) Public morals had deteriorated everywhere in all walks of life.

(8) The Southerners were determined in shaping a new South economically and politically well off.

2

Andrew Johnson (1865-1869)

Early Career

Andrew Johnson was born to improverished parents in North Carolina. He was the citizen of U.S.A. who had reached the white House from the humblest beginnings. He was orphaned in his early age and hence he never attended school but was apprenticed to a tailor at the age of ten. Since he was ambitious to get ahead, he taught himself to read and later his wife taught him to write and do simple arithmetic.

Political Career

He showed as an impassioned champion of the poor whites. When he was elected to the Congress he attracted much favourable attention in the North. In 1864 Andrew Johnson was elected as Vice President. He was intelligent, able, forceful and gifted with honesty. He became the Chief Executive of the Nation by virtue of the bullet that had killed Lincoln in April 14, 1865.

Lenient Johnson

The first and foremost duty of Johnson was the reconstruction of the South immediately after the civil war. He wanted to implement the liberal policies of his predecessor Abraham Lincoln. But he had very little skill in realising his schemes. To carry out his scheme of reconstruction :

(1) He appointed provisional governors for the southern States.

(2) He granted amnesty to all Southerners except the political and military leaders of the confederacy who were ready to take an oath of allegiance to the Federal Union.

(3) The Southern loyal people were required to invalidate the acts of recession, abolish slavery, repudiate the debts of the confederacy and ratify the constitution.

(4) The Federal government had set up a Freed men's Bureau in 1865 to provide food, shelter an medical attention to the freed slaves. But it never planned to give them permanent relief.

The Black Codes

The new southern governments, established under the Johnson plan enacted a number of laws known as the "Black Codes". These codes gave the Negro only a subordinate status in the southern society. There were considerable variation in the codes from State to State. Inspite of Johnson's suggestions Negroes were wholly prohibited from voting or serving as Juries, carrying arms and appearing in public places. These codes only conferred them the rights of citizenship but denied all democratic rights.

The Attitude of the Radicals

These Black Codes had shattered the hopes of the radials. They felt that no proper punishment was given to the confederate leaders of the South. They realised that Johnson's work of reconstruction was not complete.

The radicals thought that the confederacy should be considered as a conquered territory and as such they needed more drastic conditions to be imposed for re-admission into the union. They wanted to build a strong centre in the South for the Republican party. The radicals further thought that the speedy recovery of the South would pose a political problem in the country and would be detrimental to the interests of the northern businessmen.

When the Congress met in December 1865 under the able leadership of Thaddeus Stevens the radicals refused to admit the representatives of the reconstituted states of the South. Further, they decided to implement their own reconstruction.

The Radical Program

They established a joint committee on Reconstruction with fifteen members to investigate the whole problem. The Congress passed a Freed men's Bureau Bill and a Civil Rights Bill to protect the life and rights of the Negroes.

The Civil Rights Bill of 1865

The Bill has declared that Negroes should have the same rights as white people. It guaranteed protection to all the coloured people under the laws and decreed that cases arising under this Act should be tried in Federal Court.

Fourteenth Amendment

The Congress passed Fourteenth Amendment to the Constitution in 1866. According to this :

(a) All persons born or naturalised in the United States were to be the citizens of the U.S.A.
(b) No state shall make laws to abridge the rights of the citizens.
(c) No person shall be denied the equal protection of the laws.
(d) If any state denied the franchise to its citizens its representation in the Congress should be proportionately reduced.
(e) No former confederate official shall hold official position in the U.S.A. until pardoned by the Congress.
(f) The debt of the confederacy was repudiated.
(g) These measures had to be enforced by the Congress rather than by the President or by the courts.

All the Southern States except Tennesse refused to ratify the Amendment as desired by the Radicals. Congress, therefore, declared Tennessee to be back in the union but continued to deny recognition to the other Southern Governments.

The Election of 1866

In these elections the issue before the people was between the Presidential Reconstruction policy allowing the Southern people to shape their own institutions and the congressional reconstruction policy giving control over the South to the Congress. The radicals won a sweeping victory. They naturally interpreted this victory as a mandate for their programme.

The radicals first set out to deprive the powers of President Johnson. The Congress passed a Tenure of Office Act and Command of Army Act. These two Acts had reduced the President to mere figure head and complete control of government was transferred to the Congress.

Tenure of Office Act 1867

The President was prohibited from dismissing civil office holders without the consent of the Senate. Violation of the Act was declared to be a misdemeanour, punishable by fine and imprisonment.

Command of Army Act

By this Act, the President Johnson was deprived of his constitutional powers as Commander-in-Chief.

Johnson Walks the Impeacement Plank

As Johnson refused to accept the Reconstruction Acts of the Radicals they wanted to remove Johnson by impeachment. When Johnson tried to dismiss Stanton, Secretary of War, efforts for his impeachment were taken with most of the specific accusations being violation of the Tenure of Office Act in March 1868. The Radical influenced the House of

Representatives voted to impeach Johnson by a vote of 126 to 47 for high crimes and misdemeanours.

Then the Radical-led Senate set a court to try Johnson on the trumped up impeachment charges. The House conducted the prosecution. On May 16, 1868, the day for the first voting in the Senate, the tension was heavy. By a margin of only one vote the radicals failed to muster the two thirds majority for Johnson's removal.

Foreign Relations of Johnson's Government

Johnson's administration though largely reduced to a figure head achieved its most enduring success in the field of foreign relations. In 1867 United States signed a treaty with Russia by which Alaska was transferred to the United States for the bargain price of 7,200,00 dollars. The American Congress sanctioned this purchase because Russia had been conspicuously friendly to the North during the Civil War. Besides, the territory was rumoured to be teaming with furs, fish and gold.

3

Ulysses S. Grant (1869-1877)

Ulysses. S. Grant an adventurous military general of the civil war period was elected as the President of United States in 1868. At a time when an efficient administrator was required, Ulysses S. Grant who was a hopeless judge of men and totally ignorant of the problems of government was chosen and supported by the Republicans. A few men of ability and integrity served in his cabinet, his Secretary of State Hmilton Fish who provided the administration with the greatest efficiency was an extraordinary man with great simplicity of character, he retained much of the personal popularity with the mass of the voters. But as President he showed none of the energy, determination and clear headedness. Major questions of policy were now mostly decided by Congress rather than by the Executive.

Currency and Tariff Policies

During the civil war the Treasury had issued greenbacks to face the needs of the government as there was scarcity of gold. The Greenbacks were circulated along with the National Bank notes. Creditor and Debtor groups held sharply opposing views about monetary policy. Creditors wished to return to gold while the debtors favoured the continued use of greenback. In order to solve the financial crisis in the nation the Congress passed a Resumption Act in 1875 by which the green backs were paid by the Government at their face value after 1879.

Another financial question was tax reduction. The income and excise duties were abolished in 1872. A small temporary reduction in Tariff was alsa made in the same year.

The Treasury surplus was spent on many welfare schemes. Veterans were entitled to service-disability pensions. By 1889 there were nearly 500,000 pensioners who were receiving a total of 89,000,000 dollars a year. Besides this, the Federal government undertook a number of construction works. A number of post offices, Federal office buildings were constructed. Besides this, improvement works in rivers and harbours were also undertaken and congressmen supported each other in increasing the appropriations. This practice was known as "log rolling".

The Election of 1872

Grant won a sweeping victory supported by thirty one states. His rival Horace Greenlay got the support of seven states. Unable to tolerate the slanderous attacks Greeley died three weeks after the election.

Political Scandals

The next four years were filled chiefly with exposures of corruption of his administration. The first major scandal was the discovery of the distribution of stocks among a number of congress men by the organisers of the Credit Mobiliser. The Credit Mobiliser was a company formed by the directors of the Union Pacific Railroad to construct their own permanent way. They made immense profits by charging well over twice the real construction cost from the government and enriched themselves. This was done by extending bribes to the congressmen and others connected with the Governments.

Treasury Scandals

Afterward came exposures involving the Treasury and War Departments and exhibiting the total unfitness for high office of a number of men who had obtained the President confidence.

The biggest of the Treasury Scandals was the discovery of a "Whisky Ring". It was composed of tax collectors and distillers who had conspired to defraud the government of millions of dollars of excise duties. When the compiracy was known, quite a number of Grant's friends were caught. One among them was Orville E. Babcock, the Private Secretary of Grant. Babcock escaped punishment with the help of the President.

Scandals in the War Department

In the war department it was found that Indian post traders had obtained these very lucrative positions by bribing officials including secretary of war, William W. Belknap. Belknap escaped impeachment only because of Grant. With great regret he accepted his resignation.

Scandals in Other Departments

The above were only the major items in a series of revelations which showed that nearly every branch of the government was rampant with corruption. Customs collectors took bribes from importers, Navy department officials sold business to contractors, officials of the interior Department allowed speculators to obtain public lands without complying with the legal requirements and the American minister to Britain had actually used his official status to foist bogus mining stock on English investors. Thus, there was a great loss to the Government. And for all these reasons the administration of Ulysses. S. Grant was greatly criticised by the public and by the politicians.

Estimate

Yet Grant's "eight long years of Scandal" were not at all bad. The agony of reconstruction was nearing an end and the "bloody chasm" was being closed by amnesty. Substantial achievements were recorded in foreign affairs. The nation was expanding westward with marvellous rapidity and industry was on the verge of a great boom. The young republic was so big and powerful but the scandal spoiled the same during his time.

It is a curious fact that Grant, who put dishonest men into office, was an unconscious father of civil service reform. The scandals of his two terms goaded many citizens into action, and added to the popularity of spoilsmen sneerlingly dubbed "Snivel Service" reform.

4

Rutherford B. Hayes (1877-1881)

Rutherford B. Hayes succeeded Grant as the Republican candidate for presidentship. He was not a man of outstanding ability or colourful personality. But he had honest intentions and tried to re-establish the prestige and power of the President. He took drastic steps to remove scandals and corruption in the administration. He also tried to introduce the civil service reforms in order to remove the interference of the party leaders in appointments. But he lacked support.

Hayes began his presidency vigorously and impressively. He selected a top-flight cabinet and in fulfilment of his pre-election bargain with the South by withdrawing the Federal troops and appointing a Tennessee Democrat as Postmaster General, an office which meant control of considerable patronage.

Hayes-the idealist, reformer, and political purist parted company with the spoilsmongers. He believed that public office should not be a private property. He declared his intention of purging the civil service. He declared that the party leaders should have no more influence in appointments than other equally respectable citizens. No useless officer or employee should be retained. No officer should be required or permitted to take part in the management of political organisations, "Caucuses, conventions or election campaigns". This order struck at the root of the spoils system and led to a protracted struggle with Conkling and the stalwarts. Hayes enjoyed greater success in cleaning out the New York Custom House which had been hot bed of politics and a vital cog in Senator Conkling's political machine. But Hayes was not stronger and shrewd enough to bring about a thorough reform.

The Distress of the Debtor

Haye's period of Presidency was one of alarming unrest and turbulence due to the problem of the currency and also explosive atmosphere, largely a by product of the long years of depression and deflation following the panic of 1873. Labour disorders convulsed a number of the major cities in 1877. The paralyzing rail road strikes of that year verged on civil war in places like Baltimore. The new industrial age was gold standard, inspite of the bimetallic currency, and the value of money remained unchanged.

Foreign Frictions During Hayes Presidency

Economic unrest swept over California too by 1880, the Chinese immigrants in the Golden State was to the tune of 75,000. These Chinese immigrants offered cheap labour. In San Francisco, the native workingmen known as Kearneyites were violently aroused against the composition of cheap Chinese labour. Scores of harmless orientals were abused in various ways, including the forceable cutting off of precious pigtails offers were murdered outright. The present tense of thousands of coolies were regarded as a menace, the prospective millions as a calamity. Congress finally responded to all this uproar in 1879 by passing a bill severely restricting the influx of Chinese labourers. Hayes vetoed it on the ground that it violated the existing treaty with China. But in 1882 the Congress slammed the door on Chinese coolies for a period of ten years. Subsequently laws barred the door completely.

A serious problem developed over the prospective piercing of the Isthmus connecting the two Americas. A French company was organised under the dynamic leadership of Ferdinand de Lesseps, the conqueror of the Isthmus of Suez. Americans feared that the gigantic enterprise was but an entering wedge for the French government to violate the Monroe Doctrine. President Hayes sternly warned that any future canal would be virtually a part of the coast line of the United States. But the audacious undertaking bringing monopoly to business, injustice to labour and depression to the farmer.

Silver Problem

American money had originally consisted of both Silver and Gold, the ratio between them being fixed at 16 to 1. But since an ounce of silver was actually worth more than one sixteenth of an ounce of gold, people preferred to use silver for other purposes, and silver coins gradually dropped out of use. In 1873 Congress recognised this fact by voting to abandon the coinage of silver dollars. But when there was increase in production of silver, its value in relation to gold began to fall. This led to demands for a return to the coinage of silver, especially from the miners, who were hoping to obtain a higher price for it, and from agrarian debtor groups wanting to increase the quantity of money.

The Bland-Allison Act of 1878

A compromise was finally reached by Congress in the Bland-Allison Act of 1878. This law provided that the treasury, instead of coining all silver presented, would purchase from two to four million dollars worth of bullion a month and coin it into dollars then worthy of only 93 cents intrinsically. Hayes, a "Sound money" man vetoed the bill. But the Congress repassed it triumphantly. The Treasury bought only the minimum quantities of silver; and since it was at all times willing to change the silver dollars into gold, the country remained for all practical purposes era of the French was crippled by various obstacles. What Hayes could not prevent, nature did and, therefore, the company wound up its business.

Estimate

President Hayes, of course, not a great statesman, has been undeservedly belittled. Opposed by his party leaders and thwarted by Democratic majorities in Congress, he was able to secure little except routine legislation. He brought to his exalted office a high degree of patriotism, conscientiousness and devotion to duty. His single contribution was that he established the honesty of the Republicans.

5

Chester A. Arthur (1881-1885)

During the elections of 1880, James A. Garfield was nominated for the office of the Presidency. Chester A. Arthur was nominated for the post of the Vice President in order to conciliate the stalwarts. Both of them got elected. As soon as Garfield was inaugurated he became involved in the inevitable conflict with the party bosses about civil-service appointments. He antagonized Conkling by nominating his great rival, James G. Blaine as Secretary of State. Four months after assuming office, Garfield was assassinated by a disappointed office-seeker. This event did more than all the exposures of corruption to arouse public opinion to the need for reform.

Arthur Administration

Chester A. Arthur succeeded Garfield. Formerly a machine politician at the New York Customs House, he had been dismissed for purely political reasons by Hayes. His succession, seemed to most decent people to be a calamity. But Arthur was personally honest and did not lack ability. He surprised everybody by rising to the occasion and giving the nation perhaps its best administration since the civil war.

He supported civil-service reform and vigorously prosecuted the "star route" frauds in the post office. He reorganised his administration with a number of excellent appointments. He also tried to check Federal spending an unnecessary public works and to bring about a lower tariff but was over ruled on both issues by Congress. A tariff commission appointed in 1882 recommended reduction of many excessively high duties; but as a result of lobbying by industrialists and log-rolling by Congressmen, the so called "mongrel tariff" of 1883 was as high as the previous one.

Civil-Service Reforms

Agitation for cleansing the civil service meanwhile had became irresistible. Arthur commendably threw his influence behind the movement. The most important event of Arthur's administration was the enactment of the Pendleton Civil Service Act in 1883. It was called the Magna Carta of civil service reform. The spoils system was denounced and there was a clamour for the creation of a permanent civil service based on merit. The distribution of civil service jobs among politicians of the winning party led inevitably to incompetence, extravagance and corruption.

Pendleton Act of 1883

This Act instituted several desirable changes. It established a merit system-that is appointment to office on the basis of aptitude rather than "pull". It set up a civil service commission which was to administer open competitive examinations to applicants for posts in the "Classified" by the President were still the foot ball of politics. By 1884 he had classified nearly 14,000 federal offices or about 10% of the total. Succeeding Presidents added substantially to the classified group and by 1932, it included 79 per cent of all Federal Offices.

Of course, the reforms had ended some of the worst evils of the spoils system, but it had not abolished it. There were still many positions where political loyalty rather than merit continued to be the main criterion. Men of superior talents were not attracted to the American service because of low wages, little social prestige and also the examination system was designed to test specialised technical talents rather than general ability and education.

Naval Reforms

America's worm-eaten navy was in urgent need of modernisation. The civil war fleet had been allowed to rust and rot away as the nation concentrated on internal expansion. With only two iron ships, the navy was far inferior to the iron and steel navies of the major European powers, and in certain categories even to that of Chile.

In 1883 Congress appropriated money for four new ships, after a prolonged debate. This was a modest beginning, but a noteworthy one. Succeeding administrations added more and stronger warships. By the time the Spanish-American war broke out in 1898; the navy ranked about fifth among world navies.

Pan Americanism

James G. Blaire, the Secretary of State of Garfield was unable to get along with the Stalwart Arthur, and hence left the cabinet. Yet his brief term as Secretary of State had been marked by vigour and vision. He attempted to evidence the British to give up their joint rights to a future Isthmian Canal at Nicaragua or Panama, as guaranteed by the Clayton-Bulever treaty of

1850. Far more praise worthy and significant achievement was Blaines' dream of Pan-Americanism. Moving boldly, he had issued a call in 1881 to the Latin American nations for the first Pan-American conference in Washington, but his timid successor recalled the invitations.

Estimate

Chester A. Arthur's outstanding achievement of the Pendleton Act of 1883, formed the basis of Civil Service Reform. This Act enables the government to appoint men of ability in high position. In short, the achievements of Arthur were such that he fully merited a nomination "In his own right".

6

Rise of Big Business

The years between 1877-1891 were the greatest age of American expansion, when the people of the U.S.A. made their country the greatest agricultural and the greatest industrial nation on earth. No country has ever seen such material progress so great a scale in so short time as the U.S.A. made them.

The population, 31 million in 1860, had soared to 76 millions by 1900. In these forty years 14 million immigrants had arrived within the United States. The ceaseless move to the west had continued. Between 1861 to 1900 eleven new western states were admitted. The forming states of Kansas and Nebraska and the mining states of Nevada and Colorado were admitted during the sixties and seventies. Montana, North Dakota, South Dakota and Washington were admitted by the Omnibus Act of 1889; Idaho and Wyaming in 1890 and Utah in 1896. Historians have called this process of filling up the large empty spaces "the end of the frontier" in the sense that there was no longer any great part of the U.S.A. in which men had not settled. This phrase is true. But it does not mean that there was no longer any free land available. For many years after 1890, there was room for settlers in the west.

Homestead Act of 1862

This Act encouraged the westward flood. It gave 160 acres of land to a willing cultivators. After the Civil War many Southerners and army men settled there.

Growth of Cultivation

The invention of reapers, threshing machines, binders, rotary ploughs and the combined harvesters converted the northern part of the Great plains into a great grain producing region of the world. Thanks to these machines, wheat and maize farming was made possible on a colossal scale. In 1895, the U.S.A. grew three times as much of these two crops as in 1860. The State of Wyaming became the centre of the cattle lands. The rail roads took them to the slaughter houses of Chicago.

Minerals

The California Gold Rush of 1849 was the herald of later rushes. Silver was found in Nevada and gold in Colorado. Later finds included more gold in Idaho, Montana and Wyaming; more silver in Arizona, Idaho, Utah, Colarado, Montana and Wyaming. Thus, the Americans uncovered the mineral wealth of the whole length of the Rockies.

Growth in Railways

The rail road linked Atlantic and Pacific, brought the farmer his machinery, and took his grain to markets in the cities of the East; took the live cattle to the new city of Chicago and frozen meat (the first refrigerator car was on the rails in 1875) to the older cities of New York and Philadelphia; brought the miner the new engineering machinery without which he could not work and bore away the precious metals eastwards; and took the immigrants westward. In 1900 the rail-road mileage of the U.S.A. was 192,000. In Great Britain it was 20,000.

Effects of the Railroads

No one can measure the effects of the railroads in American History. They brought the frontier to an end, carrying millions of passengers to the Western States. They created cities like Omaha and Seattle where a generation before, there were empty spaces.

There were some evils also. The railroad companies saw the railroads not as an essential public service, but as a source of private profit. They did not obey the law of the States. Bribing the politicians wholesale they got the laws passed in their favour though the Government gave them extensive grants of lands alongside their tracts as well as huge loans.

The Growth of Industry

The rapid and extensive growth of railroads coincided with the growth of heavy industries, coal, mining, steel works and engineering. Between 1859 and 1899 the total value of American manufactured goods increased seven fold. By the end of the 19th century the U.S.A. made over twice as many as Great Britain. Thus, in the 40 years of the 19th century there was an enormous expansion of industry in the U.S.A. which became the world's leading Industrial nation.

The U.S.A. had great supplies of raw materials. The swift rise of her population created a huge and ever-expanding market. This market, offering the possibility of great profits, encouraged the discovery of coal, iron and oil, the building of factories, and the invention of mechanical devices. In these years vast new resources were exploited. They included the iron-fields around Lake-Superior, coal fields in Illinois and Ohio and in Alabama and oil well in California. Industry was not confined to the old cities of the East. Industry moved to the middle West, to the five great States of Ohio, Indiana, Illinois, Michigan, and Wisconsin. There great Industrial cities arose — Cincinnati, Indianapolis, Clevland, Milwaukee and above all Chicago. Yet the East still remained supreme. Pennsylvania, where oil was first struck in 1859 developed especially rapidly. Pittsburgh with its huge steelworks, was the central city of her growth. New York remained the financial metropolis of the country. The wealth of some citizens rose to astronomical figures.

Between 1860 and 1900 there were thousands of new inventions, ranging from the typewriter to the telephone and from the refrigerated rail car to the cash register Thomas A. Edison (1847-1931) invented the dynamo, the incandescent lamp, the moving picture and the electric train. The technique of mass production and the use of standardised parts grew up at this period. Mass production meant specialised labour.

Trusts

Great Corporation or Trusts developed in this period. A number of steel works or textile factories, instead of competing each other, combined with one another and sold their goods to the public at higher prices, often at whatever prices they chose. Thus, were born the great corporations, or trusts. They were huge alliances of firms in the same industry or trade. The railroad companies, the Standard Oil Company and the United States Steel Corporation were the trusts which dominated American industry towards the end of the 19th century.

A handful of men gained vast power and wealth. They were John Pierpoint, Margan the Banker, John D. Rockfeller of Standard Oil, P.D. Armour the Meat King and E.H. Harriman of Union, Southern Pacific Railroads and Andrew Carnegie the Steel King who were the real rulers of the U.S.A. in these years.

Trusts developed the industrial resources of the U.S.A. But they did great harm to American life. Trusts struck at all competitors and smashed small firm by cutting down their prices so as to under sell their rivals and forces them out of the market; bribed railroads to give them preferential freight rates; used police to break strikes; and bribed politicians, Congressmen, Senators and Government officials to attain their ends.

Americans found that their free land was in the hands of a few wealthy men and public opinion began to turn against the trusts. Laws were passed against them, in some of the States and in Congress. The most notable of these acts was the Sherman Anti-Trust Act of 1890, which forbade the combinations of trade. The aim of the act was to stop the growth of trusts and to break down those already formed.

It was one thing to pass laws; it was quite another to make them work. The opponents of Trusts came up against two strong forces — the American belief in free enterprise and the Supreme Court and its interpretation of the constitution. The 14th Amendment protected the Trusts against the State Laws. Any law passed by the States against the trusts were nullified by the decisions of the Supreme Court. Hence, no real control of the trusts was possible until the presidency of Theodore Roosevelt.

In general the Government, instead of stopping the growth of the Trusts, helped on their way by the methods of Tariffs. American manufacturers demanded tariffs to protect their infant industries against the long established British ones. This attitude continued even after the U.S.A. had became the world's largest industrial nation and when she could sell products cheaper than Britain. Though the tariff was unnecessary yet it remained only in order to keep up the prices of goods in America with a view to put an unjustified profit into the pockets of American manufactures.

Trade Unions

The last three decades of the 19th century saw the development of American Trade Unions. The rise of great Towns brought many thousands of workmen together. The manufacturers in their lust for huge profits reduced wages and increased hours of work.

For the following reasons trade Unions grew very slowly and suffered many set backs. The size of the country made a nationwide organisation difficult. The immigrants from Europe hindered the efforts of Trade Unions because the newcomers accepted low wages and kept the wages of Americans down. Americans believed in the right of every man to make his own way in the world without interference. The self made man was an American hero. Americans did not like trade unions. They did not support any movement for Government interference with industry or any proposals that the Federal or State Governments should regulate wages or hours of labour. Thus, the trade unions in the U.S.A. had a hard struggle against the employers. Trade unions had great difficulty in getting any laws made in their favour.

The years 1870 to 1900 were a period of continuous conflict between Masters and labourers in the U.S.A. The workmen did not get their fair share of the great increase in the national wealth. The invention of labour saving machines and over production threw men out of work. The great trusts fought the trade unions with the utmost violence with the help of Federal or State troops. Their great wealth and control of Government gave victory to the trusts.

7

Transportation, Industry and Labour

Industrial Revolution and Transport

After the adoption of agriculture as the way of life by the humanity, the dynamic and drastic changes that were brought in the processes of production were named as "Industrial Revolution". The cottage industries and handicrafts were converted into mechanised industries under the roofs of factories. Since the labourers swelled the Industries, Industrial cities came into existence. As a result of the industrial revolution, striking changes were introduced in the processes of production, transport vehicles and the agricultural production. The Industrial revolution that originated in England spread over to United States also. The fertility of the soil, stability of governments, Governmental patronage, economic growth and enterprising attitude of individuals provided congenial atmosphere in U.S.A. for the Industrial revolution and advancement of the economy to happen. Roads were laid throughout the length and breadth of the country employing the Steam Navigation, digging of canals, laying of railroads and establishment of weaving factories had contributed towards the development of economy and industry in U.S.A.

There was an outstanding development of American economy in the later part of the 19th century. More or less two lakhs of railway lines were laid. Capital investments exceeded one thousand crores dollars in the production sectors. More than 53 lakhs of labourers were employed in various industrial belts. Agricultural production also increased considerably.

Causes for the Development of Industries

(1) The soil was most fertile and contained mineral wealth in abundance.

(2) The natural wealth of the North Eastern regions combined with the European capital resulted in the mass production.

(3) The labour needs were satisfied by the natural growth of population in the American soil and also added by the pouring immigration of Europeans into U.S.A.

(4) The political unity brought about by the confederation and also the *laissez faire* policy helped the growth of Industries.

(5) U.S.A. was free from any strong adversary adjacent nation and hence the defence expenditures were very less. Such amount could be diverted to the developmental activities of the economy.

(6) American wages of life, customs, technical skill and above all the constitution of the Nation also contributed towards the development of the economy.

(7) Conquest of Nature was the prime duty of the people right from the beginning of colonisation of America. Galvinism advocated hard labour and the age of enlightenment encouraged individual freedom and rights. Hence, the welfare of both the individual and the Nation became the main mottos of life.

(8) Enterprising entrepreneurs with administrative talents, technocrats with the ambition of increasing the production combined with the technically qualified workers had caused for the abunding production in Industries.

(9) Industries themselves had their own research centres and the benefits of scientific inventions were able to be utilised by the industries.

(10) All the protective measures and aids were offered by the Federal Government.

(11) All the industrial concerns and business firms were allowed complete freedom of carrying on their activities throughout the Nation, by the constitutional provisions and the freedom was ratified by the judgements of Supreme Court in U.S.A.

(12) The protective tariffs of the Federal Government and the National Bank Act of 1863 also provided for the rapid growth of industry.

(13) The rights guaranteed in the American Constitution like Right of life, Freedom and Property rights had encouraged the individuals self efforts of improvement.

(14) Industrial Disputes Act and Welfare measure were not formulated in the initial stages of industrial development. Hence, with the hard labour and low wages for the labour, the proprietors were able to derive enormous profits. Such profits were ploughed back in the very same industry which helped the rapid growth of the Industrial Sector. Great Industrialists like Vanderbilt,

Andrew Carnegie John D. Rockefeller and J.P. Morgan had started from the scratch and reached the apex of glory in their sphere. They led their lives as multi millionaires possessing great wealth and prestige.

The Expansion of Railroads-Vanderbilt

The thirty years following the civil war may well be called the "railroad age" in America in 1860 in the North Eastern and Central Western regions. But the first large scale railroad was laid by Cornelius Vanderbilt in an outstanding manner. He was a New Yorker with semi-literacy. He brought the entire railroad traffic between New York and Chicago under his control and thereby was able to have 100,000,000 dollars earnings. Trans Continental Railways connecting the Pacific and Atlantic Oceans were about to be laid. Federal Government allotted 100 million acres of lands and the State Governments donated 50 million acres for that purpose.

Northern Railway connecting Tuluth and Seatle and North Pacific Railway connecting Chicago and Portland through St. Paul were laid. Besides, a number of railway tracks were laid throughout the country linking important metropolises. The first sleeping-car was built by George M. Pullman in 1864. As a result of the expansion of railroads in the country, railroad travel became quicker, cheaper, safer and more comfortable.

Steel Industry

High class anthracite coal, one of the raw materials for the production of Iron and Steel was abundantly available in Pennsylvania and Appalachean plateau lands. Iron ore was plentiful around the Lake Superior. Harnessing these two basic raw materials there emerged Iron and Steel industries in Pittsburgh and in the cities surrounding Pennsylvania. The production of pig. iron rose from 8 lakh tons to 14 million tons in 1900. Out of this 11 million tons of steel was manufactured. This million tons of steel was manufactured. This amount had exceeded the total production of the two countries namely Britain and Germany then.

Andrew Carnegie

The dominant figure in the growth of the American Steel industry was Andrew Carnegie brought to America from Scotland at the age of 13, he worked first in a cotton mill and then for the Pennsylvania Railroad and became an iron-manufacturer at Pittsburg in 1864. By 1900 the Carnegie Steel Company was making a quarter of all the steel in the United States. Carnegie's success was due primarily to his efficient business methods and driving energy and to his capacity for forming partnerships. In 1901, he amalgamated all his industrial firms with the name of "United States Steel Corporation".

Petroleum

After coal and iron, the most important mineral product was oil. It became indispensable when internal combustion engines came into general use. Petroleum was rich in the regions of California, Texas and Louisiana.

John D. Rockefeller

The greatest organiser of oil business was John D. Rockefeller who can be compared with Carnegie both as an industrial builder and a great philanthropist. During the early 1860's Rockefeller was a pretty driller at Cleveland in Ohio, but interested in oil business. Rockefeller left drilling to set up a refining company. He had well utilised his opportunities, adopted most efficient methods of production. By 1870 he had formed the Standard Oil Company of Ohio with his associates. He then formed alliances with refineries in other parts of the country and by the end of the decade his group controlled 90% of the oil business in U.S. In 1899 the various properties of the Rockefeller group were legally combined through the creation of a giant holding company, the Standard Oil Company of New Jersey.

Electricity

The growing use of electricity for power, light and communication was another notable feature of this period. Thomas Alva Edison had a genius for invention. He devised a satisfactory filament for bulbs in 1879. In 1882, he opened a power plant in New York City to supply current for electric lights. In the same year Frank J. Sprague worked out a practical method for using electrical power to provide transportation. The use of electricity for communication, which had already produced the telegraph, was further exemplified in 1876 with the invention of the telephone by Alexander Graham Bell. Competition in these public utilities meant waste and inconvenient duplication of equipments and hence there was a strong economic justification for the monopolistic tendencies. By 1900, 1,355,000 telephones were in use in the United States. All the Telegraph and Telephone industries were tied together by a single vast holing company, American Telephone and Telegraph Corporation.

Other Industries

Technological advance was producing equally revolutionary effects in many other human activities. A series of mechanical implements which transformed farming methods were devised. Business appliances like Typewriter, Adding machines and Cash registers were also invented. The making of clothes was mechanised by the Sewing Machines. Food habits were changed by the development of artificial refrigeration and of canning.

Formation of Trusts

Factories and large scale production were started only by the privateers in the United States. Such concerns of smaller sizes emerged in larger numbers. Soon, monopolistic tendencies began to operate, as a result of which combination of commercial firms called Trusts came into existence. The reasons were as follows :

(a) When there are unlimited number of firms and companies, they would enter into keen competition among themselves which would result in disaster and closure of a number of them. To avoid this, Trusts were preferred.

(b) Large scale production became possible by means of the inventions of new technical devices and machineries. Besides, new sources of energy like electricity and petroleum were also brought into industrial use. All these needed heavy capital investment which could not be provided by single individual. Hence, came the necessity of the formation of Trusts.

(c) Large scale production proved that regular supply of goods and cheaper rates for them would be possible.

(d) Problems pertaining the fixation of wages and serious problems connected with Trade Unions made the entrepreneurs to realise that Trust alone could solve such problems.

(e) Above all these things, the benefits of fixing up the prices according to their own whims and fancies, and earning undue profits by creating artificial scarcity, were possible only in Trusts.

Because of the above advantages a number of industrial and business firms put up all their resources in common and formed a single Trust under the leadership of single great entrepreneur. At one time, some 5,000 such independent firms got merged among themselves and formed 300 Trusts. Some such popular firms are given below :

(1) United States Steel Corporation : Andrew Carnegie
(2) Standard Oil Company of New Jersey : Rockefeller
(3) American Telephone and Telegraph Corporation
(4) McCornie Harvester Company, Chicago
(5) American Tobacco Company
(6) American Sugar Refining Company
(7) U.S. Rubber Company.

LABOUR MOVEMENT

The Conditions of the Labourers

(1) The Second half of the 19th century had not only seen the astonishing growth of American industry, but also the growth of American Labour movements.

(2) The Industrialisation process had transformed the skilled craftsmen into factory workers and thereby they lost their bargaining power.

(3) The movement of the American farmers into cities and the large scale immigration from Europe made the labour market cheaper.

(4) The Industrialists believed in the divine right of the capital and the relations between the capital and the labour were determined by the *laissez-faire* principles.

(5) The increased lust for profits reduced the wages and increased the working hours.

(6) Industrial accidents were frequent and the victims were not given any compensation.

(7) The workers had no job security and the new inventions increased the unemployment problem.

(8) Women and children were compelled to work for more than twelve hours a day.

(9) The workers were crowded into the slums which affected their health and life.

(10) The American public disliked trade unionism and the Government too favoured businessmen against the interests of the workers.

(11) Trade Unionism did not make much head way due to racial, linguistic and religious differences prevailing among the workers.

(12) The size of the country made it difficult to organise a nationwide trade union movement. Inspite of these hurdles there existed a few unions to safeguard the interests of the working class.

National Labour Union

William Sylvis was the first to make an earnest attempt to unite different unions into a single national union. He organised the National Labour Union in 1886 which claimed a membership of six lakhs. Its aims were:

(a) It demanded the establishment of a separate labour department in the Government.

(b) It wanted job security and the abolition of contract labour system.

(c) It desired an eight hour working day. As the union leaders took active part in politics, it resulted in the disappearance of the union by 1872.

The Knights of Labour

The garment cutters of Philadelphia organised the Knights of Labour under the leadership of Uriah Stephens in 1869. Its objectives were :

(a) They demanded a proper share of the production to the toilers.
(b) They wanted an eight hour working day.
(c) They preferred equal pay for equal work for both sexes.
(d) The child labour should be prohibited.
(e) Contract labour system should be abolished.
(f) They wanted enactment of Industrial Laws to safeguard safety and security of the working class.

Causes for Decline

The membership was opened to all workers of the Nation. It organised the producers' and consumers' co-operatives to accomplish its cherished ideals. It preferred industrial arbitration rather than strikes. It had a rapid growth under the leadership of Powderly of Pennsylvania. The union began to decline after 1886 due to the following causes :

(a) It involved in a series of unsuccessful strikes.
(b) The producers' co-operatives failed miserably due to mismanagement.
(c) The local units revolted against the control of the Central Union.
(d) The inefficiency and inability of union leaders to organise and guide the union in times of troubles. Finally, the Knights of Labour disappeared from the map of trade unionism.

The American Federation of Labour

The decline and disappearance of the Knights of Labour resulted in the formation of another trade union movement in 1886 by name, "The American Federation of Labour". Samuel Gampers, a cigar maker form New York launched this federation by uniting a number of labour unions. Its primary principles were :

(a) It believed in the capacity of the workers' collective bargaining.
(b) It made union membership a pre-requisite for working in a factory.
(c) It demanded reduction in working hours and restrictions on immigrants.
(d) It campaigned for legal benefits of the workers.
(e) It desired the prohibition of child labour

(f) It rejected the party policies as means to achieve their aims and goals.

(g) They wanted wage increase and compensation for industrial accidents.

Achievements

The American Federation of Labour stood for American system and accepted the capitalistic individualism in American Industry. It succeeded in the formation of strong national union for the workers. The establishment of eight hour working day was its chief accomplishment. It forced to recognize the right of collective bargaining of the working class. But the fact that both the Congress and the courts were unwilling to redress the grievances of the labourers should not be minimised or forgotten.

The Class Struggle

The Governments, the big Corporations and the courts were hostile to labour unions. To curb the activities of the unionists, the employer employed company police and private spies. They used "Yellow-dog", a document which prevented the worker from joining any union. They obtained injunctions (Court orders) to prevent strikes. The black listing of the union leaders and the importation of the contract labour resulted in labour unrest and nationwide strikes. The following were the notable industrial warfare of the 19th century U.S.A.

The Railroad Strike

The wage cuts implemented by the railroad in 1877 led to a nation wide strikes. Scores of workers were killed in the riots while considerable damage was done to the property. President Hayes utilised the services of the Federal troops to maintain law and order. The railroad strike failed miserably due to lack of proper organisation.

The Haymarket Riot

The working class launched series of strikes in 1886 demanding an eight hour working day. The workers in Chicago organised a demonstration at Hay market square in support of the worker's strike when the police attempted to break up the demonstration, a bomb exploded killing eleven people. Though the real culprit was not identified, eight workers were convicted and four others were hanged who were held responsible for the riots.

The Homestead Strike

When the Carnegie Steel at Homestead in Pennsylvania introduced wage cuts in 1892, the workers struck work and took possession of the factory.

There was a bitter battle between the workers and Pinkerton detectives employed by the company. Then the state millitia intervened and restored order.

The Pullman Strike

The Pullman palace car company at Chicago introduced wage cuts and sent out a number of workers on the grounds of economy in 1894 which led to a nation-wide strike. The American Railway union extended its support to the striking workers. The court prohibited the strike by an injunction. President Cleveland employed Federal troops to crush the strike.

Results

(1) The courts and legislatures combined together to prohibit strikes.

(2) The ever rising increase of the working class necessitated enacting of laws to maintain social security and economic Justice.

(3) The workers obtained wage increase and an eight hour working day.

(4) Individualism began to decline while the principle of collective bargaining received its recognition.

(5) Trade Unionism led for the organisation of a Socialist party in America.

(6) The economic power remained in the hands of big businessmen and in the large working class force.

(7) The class war against the capitalists never yielded the expected results.

8(a)

Agricultural Revolution

American economy developed by leaps and bounds especially after the civil war. Agriculture also contributed its mite for the rapid growth of the Nation. As there had been inventions in the Industrial Sector, so were the inventions in the Agricultural sphere and the Scientific methods of Cultivation. Hence, production increased. But the revenue of the farmers did not rise to that level. Since the Government was under the firm control of the Industrial magnates of the North Eastern States, it took steps to preserve the Agricultural Industry only belatedly. The frequent political uprisings, which broke out among the Agriculturists clearly reflected the impairment caused in the American society.

Mechanisation of Agriculture

New machineries and tools were invented in the Agricultural sphere of America as there had been innovations in the Technical and Technological field of Industrial Sector. The reaper and thresher, invented during the 1830's and 1840's first began to be widely used during the civil war. The later years of the 19th century saw a great variety of new appliances which mechanised the whole process of raising grain. In the 20th century the horse began to be replaced by the gasoline tractor and many of the daily farm house tasks were transformed by the use of electricity.

Westward Movement and the Agricultural Development

The fertile and virgin lands were abundantly available in the western regions and they helped in great deal for the Agricultural development. By the Act of 1862, sixty four hectares of land was freely given to every one who came forward to cultivate in the western regions. Two hundred million hectares of lands offered to the Agriculturists under this scheme. 3 ½ million hectares were utilised for establishing cattle farms. Since these lands were virgin most fertile and so far uncultivated the returns derived from them were manifold and far greater than the other lands in Europe. Hence, the nation need not depend upon other countries for their food.

Since new machines were utilized in Agriculture, it was enough to follow the extensive cultivation and not the intensive cultivation.

Scientific Improvements

The Congress had earmarked one thousand dollars for the introduction of Scientific improvements in 1839. A department of Agriculture was established in 1862, and its head was given cabinet rank in 1889. The two most important pieces of legislation for the improvement of agriculture were the Morrill Land Grant Act of 1862 which gave public land to the States for setting up agricultural colleges, and the Hatch Act of 1889, which provided for the creation of agricultural experiment stations in each of the States. Scientists did an immense amount of work in introducing new plants suited to the American soil and climate, creating valuable hybrids, devising methods for curing plant and animal diseases and checking insect pests, and evolving new methods of farming.

Farmer's Economic Problems

The Economic prosperity contributed by the farmers was not enjoyed by the farmers. They solved the problem of feeding of ever mounting population in Industrial cities satisfactorily. The farmers had to sell under strictly *laissez faire* conditions and there was a steady fall in farm prices. But the articles, the farmers bought, were sold at higher rates because they were controlled by trusts. In particular, the market for farm machinery was dominated by the McCormic Harvester Company of Chicago. While the industrial products were protected by the tariffs of the Government, the farm products languished under the severe competition on *laissez faire*. The fall in prices became worst under inflationary trends. More resentment was caused by the Elevator Companies which brought and stored the farmers' grain and the railroads which stripped it. Besides these two groups the Bankers and ship owners also joined in the exploitation of the farmers. Ultimately, the farmer was not able to determine the price for his own product.

The important items of farm products like grains, meat, cotton and tobacco procured foreign exchange from the European countries by means of their export. The foreign exchange earned in that way was utilised to pay the interest charges to be paid to the European Capitalists in America.

Of course, the cost of the cultivated lands had gone up in a very few years. Another consoling feature was that the farm labourers were raised to the status of the land owners. It was a great significant feat.

Important Agricultural Zones

Cotton was cultivated in the region ranging from North Carolina to Texas in South. It was exported as usual to the foreign countries expecially to the Great Britain. In general cotton cultivation was not profitable.

Grains were cultivated in the central Western States having Iowa as the centre. The grains produced thus were used for feeding the cattle and live stock.

Wheat was produced mostly in the Centre Atlantic States. It was cultivated in Kansas region during the winter season and North Dakota during the spring season.

Dairy farm products were concentrated in the States like New York, Michigan and Wisconsin. Vegetables and fruits were produced in the regions like California.

Rearing of Cattles

Vast meadows and grazing lands were helpful for rearing the cattles in regions ranging from Dakota in the North and Texas in the South in the years between 1870-80. The Cow Boy style of culture developed only in this area. 4 million cattles were driven to the Northern region. In course of time great cattle forms called "Ranches" came to be established in the States like Western Kansas, Nebraska, Dakotas, Colarado, Layamis, Montana. This kind of open Ranches slowly disappeared in the end of the century.

Effects

(1) The technological progress made possible an immense saving of labour. By the old methods each acre grown to wheat required 61 hours of labour, but as early as 1890 the use of machinery had reduced the time to 3 hours. Whereas the old-time wheat farmer could not plant more than 7 1/2 acres, since this was as much as he could reap during the limiting harvesting season, the farmer of 1890 could plant 135 acres.

(2) Mechanisation enabled the farmer to produce more. His life was easier than that of his grand-father. Agricultural farm products increased three fold in production while wheat alone increased six times. More and more lands were also brought under cultivation.

(3) The indiviual farmer did not benefit by the same amount of increase in production. Industrial development was upheld at the cost of Agrarian development. Lion's share of the gains accrued were squeezed out by the Industrial magnates. Hence, the resentment of the discontented and dissatisfied farmers got ventilated in the emergence of new political parties. Agricultural movements like Granges and populism were established and they bought about several changes in the American political field.

8(b)

Agrarian Movements

It is common that in all societies the rural agriculturists were inferior to the other sections of people in their societies. American society was not an exception to this. Hence, the conditions of farm labourers were lower in status and position to that of the Industrial labourers in the later of the 19th century in U.S.A. The revenue of the farmers did not increase to the level of the increase in production caused by the introduction of scientific methods, new machineries and farm implements. The causes were many. They were as follows :

1. **The Problem of Agricultural Debts.** Agriculturalists borrowed loans from the Bankers and warehouse owners for the purpose of cultivation. The loans were issued only on the forthcoming harvest. Generally the interest on these loans were exorbitant. Once the farmer had gone into debt, he usually found it impossible ever to extricate himself. The farmers had to necessarily sell their products only to their lenders who gave lesser prices. Hence, the farmers were not able to get profits in commensurate with the enormous work they had rendered in their production.
2. **Problem of Commercial Crops.** Money lenders forced the farmers to cultivate only the cash crops like tobacco and cotton some times. Since they were forced to cultivate the crops persistently, the lands lost the minerals needed for their cultivation in course of time. Some times, due to the abundance of production of the particular crop had caused stagnation in sales and thereby fall in prices.
3. **Competition from Foreign Countries.** Agricultural products were mostly exported to European countries. There they had to face the severe competition from the products which came from other countries like Canada, Argentina and Australia. Hence, drastic reduction of the prices became inevitable.

4. **Fixation of Prices.** The real producers of the agricultural products were not given any right in the fixation of their prices. On the other hand, the shipping and forwarding agencies, Banks in the Northern States and Commercial firms had taken the power of determining the prices of farm products. Hence, the farmers were completely squeezed of their profits.
5. **Hike in the Prices of Farm Implements.** Machines and Farm Implements' prices were soaring high because the manufacturers had formed Trusts among them, avoided unhealthy competition and thereby fixed up the prices at higher rates according to their own whims and fancies. For instance McCormic Harvester Company of Chicago had established its monopoly in the farm machinery. Thereby, the company was able to amass profits by fixing up high prices for the implements.
6. **Excessive Charges of Railroad Transports.** In most parts of the farm belt all the storage and transportation facilities were monopolised by single companies, which were able to dictate their own terms. The railroads demanded what seemed to the farmers to be excessive charges and particularly infuriated them by charging more for a short haul than for a long one. As a result heavy storage and transportation costs and other middlemen's charges, only a small part, probably not more than one-fifth, of the price paid for grain by the consumer actually went to the farmer who had produced it.
7. **Natural Disasters.** Farmers suffered very much due to the natural havocs like flood and drought. At the same time when the production increased the prices of the products automatically decreased. This sad state of affairs prevailed for a long period especially from 1890 onwards.
8. **Government's Policy of Currency.** The Government's policy of currency was prominently and primarily favourable to the rich trading class of people. When the peasants wanted liberal circulation of currency Eastern Commercial Organisations were against such circulation. Hence, it was clear that the Government was prejudicial against the farm labourers.
9. **Negligence of the Political Parties.** Both the leading political parties which were under the control of Industrial magnates of the Eastern states had completely ignored the problems of Agriculturists. They were not ready to show attention to the Farm works as they had bestowed their care to Industrial works. They showed great reluctance in introducing special Act for the protection and preservation of the Farm industry.

Thus, the rural Agrarian population was impoverished ultimately and had undergone untold hardships at the hands of Industrialists and middlemen. Hence, the farmers came to realise that they needed a separate political party to protect their interests. As a result of this Agrarian movements came into existence. They echoed the grievances of the farmers. The farmers began to enter into the arena of politics for solving their unsolved and long standing grievances.

Granger Movement

The volcanic grievances of the farmers took the shape of Granger movement. It gave the first expression of farm insurgency. In 1867 Oliver Hudson Kelley, a government clerk in Washington, had founded an organisation known as the patrons of Husbandry, but more frequently called the Grange. The original purpose of the Grange was to spread information about scientific agriculture, but it soon developed into a vehicle through which the farmers could voice their economic grievances, especially against the railroads. The Grangers put up candidates of their own, won control of several state legislatures, and enacted laws regulating the rates changed by railroads and elevator. The Grangers also set up a number of cooperatively owned factories, stores, and selling agencies, but most of these ventures turned out unsuccessfully as a result partly of mismanagement and partly of business opposition.

Greenback Party

The immediate heir of the Granger movement was the Greenback party, which was organised in 1876 in protest against the deflationary financial policies followed during the Grant administration. In 1878 the Greenbackers polled a million votes and elected 15 congress men. In the presidential election of 1880 their candidate James B. Weaver of Iowa, received only 300,000 votes and by 1888 the party was dead. Inflationists were now demanding unlimited coinage of silver and had lost interest in the Greenback question.

Federation of Farmers

Since the prices of Farm products had fallen down to the lowest level, agriculturists had to face serious repercussions. The peasants of central frontier states like Kansas, Nebraska, Minnesotta and Dakotas rose up in rebellion and as a result Federation of Farmers was founded. It absorbed the policies of the Granger movement and tried to redress the grievances of the peasants. It aimed at the Nationalisation of Railways, solving the deficiency of foreign exchange, closure of National Banks, reduction of Land Taxes. It appealed to the governments of all states to construct ware houses throughout the Nation and made arrangements for storing the grains and also loan facilities as per the date of application for the products stored in ware houses. This Federation also worked for the unity of Whites and Black men of America. But the then government simply discarded the appeals and the sufferings of the peasants became a continuing story.

Populist Party

Kindly refer Chapter 9.

Estimate

Of course the various agrarian movements that emerged as a result of the awakening of the peasants, had highlighted the exploitations of the capitalists in the various fields like political, economic and social conditions in America. The movements had insisted upon reform programme by means of which majority of the people could benefit. The demands deemed to be revolutionary in the initial stages but they became important policies which had to be implemented at any cost. But the then American Government had simply discarded them all despite their lofty ideologies. It indicated the victory of Hamiltonian policy over the Jeffersonians.

9

Populism

The last quarter of the 19th century had witnessed a farm insurgency which came to be known as the populist revolt. There were a number of causes for the rise of populist movement in U.S.A.

Causes for the Rise of Populist Movement

(1) As the political power was in the hands of the industrialist the very life of the farmers was in danger.
(2) American farmers believed that they were not receiving their due share of the national income for which they had contributed a lot.
(3) Most of the farmers were frontiers — men who were in isolation and often denied any convenience.
(4) Not only the farmers were ruined by natural calamities like heavy rain and drought but also they were exploited by urban people.
(5) The falling prices of grain, cotton and live stock and the ever increasing prices of machines and other implements naturally ruined the farmers.
(6) As the farmers had to pay high rate of interest, they were burdened with heavy debts to the bankers.
(7) They were exploited by the railroads and the trusts.
(8) Taxes on farmers were higher contrary to their ability to pay.
(9) The high tariff system mostly affected the western farmers.
(10) The numerous grievances of the farmers and workers resulted in the rise of populist movement in U.S.A.

Formation of New Parties

In 1867 Oliver Hudson Kelley had founded an organisation known as Grangers. The Grangers contested in the National and State elections and was in control of several state legislatures and enacted laws in favour of the farmers. The Grangers movement quickly disappeared from the political map of the country. In 1876 the Grangers movement was displaced by another organisation known as Greenbackers. The Greenbackers were represented by fifteen congressmen in 1878. In the presidential election of 1880 James Weaver contested as a candidate of the Greenbackers and polled only three lakhs votes. By 1888, it was a dead party. In addition to these parties, there were a number of minor parties such as the Farmer's Union, the Agricultural Wheel, the Northern Alliance, the Southern Alliance, and the National Farmer's Alliance. James Weaver, William Peffer, Jerry Simpson and Mary Elizabeth voiced the grievances of the farmers.

The Populists

The leaders of the various organisations of the farmers felt that the time was ripe for launching a new national political party. In may 1881, a new party was formed at Cincinnati and this people's party was later on came to be known as the populists. The populists platform demanded a number of reforms. Some of them were :

(1) Currency inflation.
(2) Unlimited silver and gold coins.
(3) Gradual income tax.
(4) Reduction of taxes.
(5) Government ownership of railroads, telegraphs and telephones.
(6) Prohibition of alien ownership of land.
(7) Establishment of a sub-treasury to help the farmers.
(8) Restriction of immigration.
(9) An eight hour day for government employees.
(10) Popular election of Senators and adoption of the initiative and referendum.

These proposals of the Populists, though seemed to be revolutionary in nature, were really Jeffersonism and Jacksonism.

Triumph of the Big Business

In the election of 1896 William McKinley, the Republican candidate defeated Bryan the Democratic Party candidate who was also a populist in name. There was a clear cut issue in the election and it was a conflict between capitalism and agrarianism. The victory of McKinley was interpreted as a victory of Hamiltonianism which favoured a capitalistic system. Most of the Republican Senators were millionaire businessmen. The industrialists themselves had grabbed the political power. The big business had achieved political power as well as economic dominance. Though, the populists failed to grab the political power, they had initiated a movement for the revitalization of democracy.

Causes for the Failure of the Populists

(1) No powerful organisation was ever formed to represent the farmers.

(2) Various organisations of the farmers were never united under one banner.

(3) Most Americans supported either the Republican or Democratic party and only a fraction of the population came under the populist banner.

(4) The policy of "raise less corn and mere hell" was never implemented. As new areas were annexed more production was the result.

(5) When the country was in depression, the populists programme seemed to be popular. As and when the American economy recovered, the populists lost ground.

(6) The farmers never revolted unitedly for their just causes.

(7) The Republican victory in the election of 1896 proved to be the grave yard of the populists.

(8) The big business scored a great victory over the agrarian ideals.

(9) The just demands of the populists were adopted both by the Republican and Democratic parties.

(10) America remained to be a capitalistic country.

(11) The expansion of the American empire in the Far East proved to be a vital point in the victory of big business.

(12) As American financiers had invested more money in foreign countries, it was essential for U.S.A. to remain as an industrial power.

10

Social, Economic and Cultural Development in U.S.A.

Alongside the industrial expansion of the post-war years in U.S.A. was occurring another transformation equally momentous and on an equally breath-taking scale; the settlement of the western half of the country. By the year 1860, the western most tier of states consisted of Minnesota, Iowa, Missouri, Arkansas and Texas only. Apart from the Spanish speaking inhabitants of New Mexico, the only well established white colony was Mormons in Utah. Yet by 1912 all parts of the western country had been organised into states and admitted into the union.

The Completion of Western Settlement

Across the country from the Dekotas down to the Texas stretched the Great plains, comprising almost one fifth of the area of the United States. The total lack of timber, the scarcity of water in this region became the settlement of Indian inhabitants. The desert plateaus between the Rockies and the Pacific range, became another region of their settlement. The Indians had to content themselves by living in such torrid and dry zones. The White Americans were not ready to tolerate the occupation of Indians even in these desert areas. Besides, Americans wanted to avenge the Indians because of their support to the southern states during the civil war.

The Conquest of the Indians

When the Indians were driven out from the East to the West, they had to enter into internecine war fare with the Indians who were already living there. In their mutual war thousands of Indians became victims of the suicidal war. The rest were easily wiped out by the White Americans.

During the civil war years there was savage fighting with the Apaches and Navaches in the South west and with the Arapaho and Cheyenne tribes in the Great plains. In 1867, the Congress passed a law providing for the removal of all the Indians to reserved areas of South Dekota and Oklahama. This was followed by nine years of war fare between Americans and Indiana. By 1875, the United States Army led by Sherman, Sheridan and other civil war veterans, had broken the back of Indian resistance. The Indian tribal people called Siowx under the leadership of Redcloud were defeated in 1867 and hence they were driven out from the South Dakota to the Black Hills. Sitting Bull, another Chief of the Indian tribes had slaughtered Colonel George Custer and his men in the battle of Little Big Horn. But Sitting Bull had surrendered in 1876. By 1890, all the uprisings of the Indians were easily suppressed. In other words, Indian resistance to the Whiteman's conquest of the continent war now ended. They were completely driven out to the dry zones reserved for them. The gold mines of California and Black Hills region of South Dakota had encouraged the westward movement of the Whites rapidly. Discovery of gold mines in Pikes peak of Colorado in 1858 and Comstock Lode in Nevada also had made these places thriving metropolis.

Indian Policy at a Later Period

The native Indians who were forced to live in the dry regions were also given citizenship right in 1924. The Indians living in the Oklahma region had absorbed the culture of the Americans and obtained Higher Education. The lands that belonged to the Indians were easily confiscated for the purpose of exhuming mineral mines, laying of Railway lines, or Roads and erection of beautiful parks. Thus, the Indian inhabitants had lost all their rights and properties.

Alaska

Alaska region situated in the Northwest of the American Continent was a colony of Russia. A Russian firm dealing in fur trade was administering the region. Snow bound Alaska region seemed to be a liability to Russia and an invasion from Great Britain was imminent. Hence, the Russian Tsar Alexander II decided to dispose of the region to the Americans for an amount of 72 Lakhs Dollars. It was useful both on strategic basis and economic basis. Hence, the Congress passed a resolution to effect the purchase of Alaska. With this the American territories were more or less exhausted of immigration.

Social Condition in America

The social and cultural conditions in America had undergone far reaching changes owing to the growth of the economy especially after the civil war. The American society had become urban and lost all its rural features due to the Industrial Revolution that took place there. Of cource, in some small cities, rural features appeared flagrantly. But some cities began to overflow with the population. New York, Chicago, Philadelphia, Boston, Detroit, Los Angles and Clevland had became great Industrial cities. The rapid development of the cities made the development of Public Health, Education, Police and so on as necessary corollaries to the cities growth. Contagious and epidemic diseases broke out in the congested areas of the cities for public health facilities were insufficient. Slums also developed simultaneously which caused the breakdown of law and order situations which resulted in turmoil. Vagabands and whores swelled the cities. The poverty in the slums and the violation of laws of the slum dwellers had made the voluntary service organisations to grow in number to alleviate the problem in the society.

Increasing Inflow of Labourers

The labourers were mostly the later immigrants from the Europe. The thriving economy and fastly developing transport facilities had made the inflow of working class increasing at a rapid rates. Such immigrations were abundant in cities like Michigan, New Jersey and Patterson. They came from the countries like England, Ireland, Germany and Scandinavia. Later immigrants came from Italy, Russia, Austria and Hungary. The early immigrants belonged to the wealthy civilized sections of their society whereas the later group belonged to the poor sections. Hence, the poor class of Chinese who migrated into USA and were ready to receive even low salaries, were despised by the Americans. As a result the immigration of Chinese was prohibited. It brought about radical changes in the American society. People belonging to diverse nations, religions, races and languages got themselves integrated together and formed one American Society. There was no place of honour for a single race and its cultural greatness. On the other hand, the American society had common goals and ideals for a prosperous future.

Economic Conditions

Agriculture was the prime occupation of the immigrants while the colonisation started in America. The Industrial development was realised to be essential for the growth of the economy after the war of Independence. Jefferson insisted upon the importance of agriculture while Hamilton pressed upon the industrial sector to be given priority in the nation. Jefferson's principles assured dominance from the times of Jackson till the Civil War. The Civil War appeared to be a war between conflicting ideologies of Agrarian Economy and Industrial Economy. The Industrial Revolution which originated in England spread over the entire European continent and reached the New world also. As a result the industrial production grew in greater magnitude. The European technicians and technocrats were employed in the Industries of America. Besides, Industrial entrepreneurs, capital and labour resources became amply available which ushered in the rapid flourishment of the Industrial Sector. The American Government also contributed towards the Industrial prosperity through its tariff policies. All these factors ultimately converted the American economy as an industrially based one. Of course, agriculture was concentrated in the Southern States. Yet a few industries sprouted these too. The *laissez faire* policy adopted in the commercial sector had encouraged a number of business firms to be started and flourished.

By 1880 it was realised that the freedom of action of the individuals could not help the development of the society. Hence, principles of co-operation and planned economy began to be eagerly adhered. Lesterward advocated this kind of new economic policy. He suggested that instead of surrendering before the powers of nature, man must plan his future with his power of reasoning. There are no natural bonds between the laws of nature and the development of humanity. The *Laissez Faire* doctrine of Adam Smith was opposed by people like Lawrence and Walker. Bellary advocated a National Socialist System. In 1875 Socialist Labour Party was established on the Mexican principles. Inspite of the emergence of a number of new economic doctrines, American society evolved only as a capitalistic one.

Development of Art, Literature and Culture

The reaction of many writers to the post war scene was to turn their backs to it. Regarding American Society as hopelessly vulgar and materialistic, they tried to escape into an ideal world of romantic imagery. The tendency to divorce art from daily life had already been manifest in the more conservative of the New England workers such as Longfellow and Lowell. They were considered to be exponents of a "Genteel Tradition". The literature of Mark Twain were the products of a man who plunged into American life, especially that of the new industrial cities, and set out to record what they experienced with few moral or aesthetic inhibitions. Mark Twain born in the Slave State of Missouri, spent a few years as a steam boat pilot on the Mississippi, served briefly in confederate regiment and then went out to the mining camps of Nevada. With all these experiences he gathered, he produced his literature with the American way of life as his base. *Tom Sawyer* and *Huckleyberry* were his masterpieces. Another popular writer of this period was

Henry James who eulogised the European culture and decried the wickedness and crudences of Americans in his literatures. Among his works, *The Portrait of a Lady*, *The Ambassadors*, *The Wings of the Dove* and *The Golden Bowl* were very popular. William Dean Howells had initiated a movement towards realism. Novelists like David Graham Philips, Upton Sinclair and Jack London dealt with social and economic problems on a relatively superficial level.

Painting, Architecture and Music

With the growth of national wealth, more money was available for the support of art. European influence, past and present were now predominant in this sphere. A rapidly increasing number of European masterpieces were shipped to the United States. The Metropolitan Museum of New York was founded in 1870. Artists of America founded organisations like "National Academy" and "The Society of American Artists" in 1877 for preserving their freedom. Robert Henry John, Sloan George Inness were the most popular artists of that period.

In the field of sculpture, American sculptors preferred to copy the Italian neo-classical school and produce allegeorical figures with flowing Roman robes in white marble. The greatest sculptor of America were Augustus Saint-Gaudems and Daniel Chester French.

In the sphere of architecture, aesthetic values were wholly ignored in the construction of factories and tenements. But the buildings of wealthy families were decorated with an incredible variety of cupolas, turrets, balconies and gables. Richardson and Stanford White were known for their artistic gifts and original creative power.

11

America as World Power

After Civil War of America, she continued her policy of isolation for a generation and during this period, she was busily engaged in improving her war broken economy, in building many industries and in settling the Negro problems which resulted in the transformation of the nation into an industrially advanced State. When America was involved in her internal affairs, the policies adopted by European countries turned the Americans' attention towards international affairs. There were a number of causes which diverted the American attention towards internationalism.

(1) Due to rapid industrial developments in America, she needed more markets for her industrial products. The American industrialist forced America to capture more colonies which led to international competition among the industrial nations.

(2) As more industries were started in America she required raw materials for which she had to end her policy of isolation and entered in the field of international politics.

(3) America wanted to control the Pacific Ocean so that she could get more markets in the Far East.

(4) The growth of trade competition and economic imperialism among the European countries made the world unsafe for a powerful life. As the world was drifting towards a global war, America felt that it could not remain as an isolated, unaffected country.

(5) As China was a weak nation, all the countries entered China and started business. So America wanted to follow the policy of Open Door in China so that she could send her goods to the Chinese market.

(6) Many European countries acquired colonies in foreign countries. So America decided to capture markets so that she could maintain her status and dignity on par with European countries.

(7) The American politicians and businessmen believed in manifest destiny and they were dreaming of world leadership in all fields.

(8) Technological development was drawing all parts of the world more closely together and making all countries more independent. So America could not remain an isolated country for long.

(9) The development of naval powers in America made her to assume the leadership of protecting the nations in the Latin American and Far Eastern countries This involvement of America in the affairs of Latin America and in the Far East made it to assume the role of a world power.

Overseas Expansion

1. **Alaska and Midway Islands (1867).** Seward, Secretary of State during the Andrew Johnson administration advocated that America should come out from her policy of isolation and should follow the Manifest Destiny. He stated that the growth of American powers should cross the Ex American hemisphere. He made a treaty with Russia in 1867 by which Alaska was purchased for $ 7,200,000 and in the same year he brought about the annexation of Midway Islands. The acquisition of these places was not recognised at that time but it was useful later on for America to become a world power.
2. **Samoan Islands.** America made up her mind to establish naval base in the pacific and she signed a treaty with Samoa by which she received the right to establish a naval base at Pago Pago. After this agreement, Germany and Britain were also interested to establish their control over Samoa which led to confrontation between the three powers. Then they agreed to have a joint control over the islands. Ten years later, the island was divided among the three powers and Tutuila which included Pago Pago became an American possession. The acquisition of Tutuila with its harbour Pago Pago was the important land mark of the new imperialistic policy of America.

Hawaii Island

The American citizens had been to Hawaii and had developed sugar and pineapple plantations. Consequently the American invested more money in the Hawaii soil which resulted America played a vital role in the economy and the administration of Hawaii. A new queen by name Liliuo Kalani came to power in 1891 and she tried to curtail the privileges enjoyed by Americans so for in the Hawaii soil. She declared that Hawaii was to be for the Hawaians which made the Americans to organise a revolution in January 1893. Consequently they seized power and asked the United States for assistance and annexation which was turned down by Cleveland, who opposed the imperialist expansion of America. In 1898, McKinley became the President of America after Cleveland and he accepted to annex the island of Hawaii. In July 1898 the Congress voted for annexation and it provided America the necessary naval base in the pacific. It also offered commercial expansion.

Pan-Americanism

America wanted to cultivate her relation with Latin American countries. She frequently interveted in a number of border disputes that arose among the Latin American countries and settled their problems amicably. The significant disputes were the boundary dispute between Argentina and Paraguay in 1876, between Mexico and Guatemala and between Columbia and Chile in 1880. After establishing her influence, she shifted her attention to control over Caribbean sea with a view to finding new markets for American industry and control over this region was absolutely necessary for security of America. To mobilise the support and cooperation of Latin American countries, a conference was finally held at Washington in 1889 which helped much for America to increase her trade relation with Latin American countries. This conference provided a clearing house to settle down the everlasting disputes among the countries and it was followed by a series of other conferences, mostly at five year intervals. These conferences helped to make trade alliances among the countries of the American hemisphere, to sort out and develop their unity and integration and to fix up the uniform tax system. In the long run the Pan-American policy served the political and economic interest of U.S.A. in the Southern Hemisphere.

The Venezuelan Boundary Dispute

The first assertion of American power in the Caribbean sea came in 1895 as a result of a boundary dispute between Venezuela and the British colony of Guiana. The American President Cleveland declared that the dispute should be settled through arbitration. This suggestion was not acceptable to Britain. So Secretary of State Olney declared that America would resort to war unless the British gave away its sovereignty over the entire hemisphere. He said, "Today the United States is practically sovereign on this continent, and its fiat is law upon the subjects to which it confines its interposition.... Its infinite source combined with its isolated position render it master of the situation and practically invulnerable as against any or all other powers". Britain was not willing to involve in the war with America because she had already involved in war with Africa and finally both countries accepted for arbitration. The Venezuelan boundary dispute gave an opportunity to U.S.A. to assert its power in the Caribbean.

The Spanish American War

The next step of American hegemony in the Caribbean sea was the Spanish American war. Spain had control over Cuba and Puerto Rico and she failed to introduce any reform there. So the Cubans started their revolt against the oppressive region of Spain and they were supported by Americans to obtain their independence. As a result of the war, America received Philippines, Puerto Rico and Guam from Spain (For details please see the next chapter). After this war, America became a colonial power and established its authority in the Caribbean sea.

Open Door Policy

After establishing American authority over Philippines, she wanted to control over the Far Eastern countries. So she started commercial relation with China and Indonesia. American missionaries had been sent to these countries and it found out that there was a good climate for setting up industries and establishing her authority in China. So America declared her policy of open door in China which became one of the guiding principles of American foreign policy.

China was a weak nation and considering her position, she could not send out the foreign people who were actively engaged in commercial interest. In the later part of the 19th century Britain, France, Russia and Japan annexed and assumed protectorate over a number of frontier areas of China, and Manchu the ruler of China was incompetent to exercise his authority. In this period John Hay, the American Secretary of State wanted to keep China open for the trade. He demanded commercial equality for citizens of all countries and the suggestion of open door policy in China was accepted by all the nations. As a result of this policy all the European countries entered China and performed their business without any fear which resulted in Chinese economy being exploited by these powers. The foreigners had more privileges rather than the native merchants and the indigenous industries in China were perished due to stiff competition. The Chinese who awoke from their slumber realised the gravity of the situation and put up a stiff fight with the foreign people in the name of "Boxer Rebellion". The Boxer killed the foreign people and a tense of terror prevailed everywhere in China and ultimately the upraising of the Boxer was ruthlessly crushed by a joint military force of all powers led by U.S.A.

The Panama Canal

The permission for digging this canal was obtained by France from the Republic of Colombia and France started construction of it. But it was stopped due to shortage of fund. As U.S.A. was badly in need of this canal for commercial purposes she purchased the right from France and offered an annual rent of 250,000 dollars to Columbia for the lease of a canal zone. When U.S.A. began to dig this canal, Columbia protected on the ground that the construction of this canal would not be benefit to Columbia. So U.S.A. instigated the people of Panama to revolt against Columbia and Panama was declared independent with the help of America and got permission from Panama for the construction of this canal. The construction was completed in the year 1914. Thus, America established her authority in the Panama Canal Zone.

Roosevelt Corollary

After the construction of the canal, it was necessary for U.S.A. to protect land control the Caribbean countries. The Europeans who lived in these countries invested money and controlled the countries. They constructed bases with the view to protect their citizens and properties. So the Caribbean countries suffered much from frequent revolutions which resulted American President Roosevelt introduced his policy of Corollary. According to the principles of Corollary, European countries should not have any relation with the countries in the American hemisphere and all relations of the European powers should be rooted through U.S.A. It also prevented the European powers from acquiring bases in Latin America and secured protection for American investment in South America. By the birth of 20th century the U.S.A. had grown into a world power and it played vital role in global wars.

12

Spanish American War of 1898

During the last decade of 19th Century there was keen competition among the European powers to establish their authority and colony in the Latin American and Far Eastern Countries. So USA also decided to involve in the affairs of the foreign countries. Spain which had control over the Latin American Countries lost her influence in all the countries except Cuba and Puerto Rico and a rule of Dictatorship was established in Cuba. The Cubans could not tolerate the autocratic reign of Spain and started revolutions which was supported by the Americans because the atrocities committed by the Spanish authority aroused public opinion in USA in favour of Cuba. Further, USA wanted to protect her subsentiment in USA in favour of war with Spain and the war started between the two countries.

Reasons for the War

(1) Cuba was under the control and protection of Spain and all the European Countries wanted to capture Cuba from Spain. If Cuba was to be captured by the other European powers, there would be danger to the protection and safety of the American people, so USA wanted to capture Cuba from Spain.

(2) Americans made financial investments in Cuba. As riots and revolutions were taking place on and off, the Americans could not perform the business peacefully and the American Capitalist lived in Cuba requested the mother country to set right their problems of protecting their investments and life.

(3) The ten year revolt of the Cubans form 1868 to 1878 against Spanish rule ended unsuccessfully.

(4) America helped to the rebels in Cuba and thereby instigated them to fight for the Cuban independence and Spain charged that America was aiding the rebels against a legal government. The

rebels who were expelled from Cuba went to America and made propaganda for Cuban independence.

(5) The Cubans revolted in 1895 which resulted there was heavy loss to the life and property of the Cubans. Further, the autocratic rule of Spain was intolerable and hence the people of Cuba did not like the rule and ready to fight for national independence.

(6) The Americans believed that a war with Spain would bring prosperity to the Americans in Cuba.

(7) Some assumed that the war would make USA as a global power.

(8) Spain imposed heavy taxes upon the Cubans and a duty of forty percentage on sugar was levied by Spain and these taxes were not liked by the people of Cuba. In 1895 a second rebellion broke out which was more serious than the previous one. The Cubans adopted guerilla war and it caused destruction to life and property on an unprecedented scale.

(9) As America wanted to become a global power, she was interested in the destruction of European Colonialism in Latin America so that she could extend her sphere of influence.

(10) 'The New York World', 'The New York Journal' and other magazines carried the atrocities of the Spanish rule which stirred the minds of the Americans and they clamoured for war with Spain.

(11) Dupley de Lome, a Spanish minister at Washington wrote a letter to his friend. The letter was stolen from the Post Office at Havana and published in the Newspapers. The letter stated that the President of America, Mr. McKinley was a tricky politician and he was always interested in Platitudes. These wordings inflamed the public feelings. So the relation between America and Spain was strained.

(12) In 1898 the American warship was sunk by an explosion at Havana. The reason for sinking this ship could not be found out and America accused that Spain was held responsible to this incident. The Americans and expelled rebels from Cuba made the slogan "Remember the Marine".

(13) When the Climate for the war was inevitable, President McKinley advised Spanish Government to make an armistice with the rebels of Cuba. The Queen of Spain accepted the term. Yet the American President sent a message to Congress requesting it to declare war with Spain. Congress adopted the Teller Amendment by which America declared that she would not acquire the Cuban territories. As soon as the Cuba was liberated, she would be returned to the inhabitants of the land. Thus, war was declared.

(14) As America wanted to erect naval base in the Pacific ocean, she had to involve in the Cuban crisis.

The Course of the War (1898) Capture of Phillipines

Theodore Roosevelt, Assistant Secretary of the Navy ordered Admiral Dewey to proceed to the Spanish Philippines. He sailed to Manila and destroyed the Spanish fleet. Then the American troops reached the islands. They were supported by the rebels of Philippines and with the help of the rebels and inhabitants, the Americans captured Manila without much Spanish resistance. When Philippines was conquered, most Americans including the president did not know where the islands were.

Conquest of Cuba

Admiral Sampson sailed his fleet and blockaded the Coast of Cuba. The Spanish navy was destroyed near Santiago and cleared the way for the landing of an American army on the Cuban soil. There was a fierce fight between the armies of the two countries in Cuba. The American army was helped by the rebels and inhabitants of Cuba. The American land forces suffered terribly for want of adequate preparations. Yet they won the battle. Another, under General Miles invaded the territory of Puerto Rico and it was captured very easily. The conquest of Puerto Rico was described as moon light victory.

The naval strength of the two powers were equal. But the United States had better equipped war ships and well trained soldiers. So America was able to win over the war easily.

Treaty of Paris 1898

After the war, the French ambassador in Washington, acting on behalf of Spain signed a peace treaty at Paris on 12th August, 1898. The basic clauses of this treaty were :

(1) Spain agreed to give up her claim on Cuba.
(2) Spain agreed to cede Puerto Rico, Philippines, and a Pacific island to USA.
(3) Spain accepted to assume the entire Cuban debts.
(4) America agreed to pay to Spain twenty million dollars for the loss of Philippines.

Results of the War

(1) Spain lost her colonies in the new world.
(2) America became a global power.

(3) The war contributed a close relation between USA and UK. During the war, the German fleet went to Manila to help the Spanish warship. But the advancement of the German fleet was blockaded by Britain and thus the friendship between UK and USA was cemented.

(4) USA acquired many valuable islands and developed Asiatic interest. The acquisition of Philippines in Asia made USA to promote her trade with many countries in Asia.

(5) As USA had control over the Atlantic and Pacific Oceans, she decided to dig a canal across the Central America which led to the Panama crisis and construction of Panama Canal.

13

Progressivism in U.S.A.

The birth of the twentieth century had witnessed many progressive reforms and all the reforms were advocated by the leaders like Theodore Roosevelt, Taft, Wilson, Tom Johnson and La Follelte. The reforms were based upon the ideals of democratic movement, protection to private property, individual freedom and rule of law. It hated the class distinction and paved the way for ethical, moral and humanitarian concepts. Progressivism was the movement of middle class people, small businessmen, farmers, advocates and journalists.

Aims of Progressivism

(1) Progressivism aimed to root out the political corruption and privileges enjoyed by the wealthy people.

(2) It insisted that the will of the majority of the people must be effective and implemented and make official more responsible to the electorate rather than politicians.

(3) Progressivism insisted the destruction of the invisible government of bosses and machines.

(4) It demanded to impose control over monopoly.

(5) It wanted to ban the exploitation of the farmers and working class by the wealthy people and politicians.

(6) It advocated for regulation of big business and legislation that would protect the people from exploitation.

In the Progressive movement there were two groups called Progressive Democrats and Progressive Republicans. Some leaders wished to promote the welfare of the people. They were called as Jeffersonian and others who wished the Government to assume more responsibilities were called as Hamiltonian.

The Problem of Monopoly

Monopoly was the main problem in the development of the small business. The growth of monopoly in big business crushed the existence of small scale industries. They fixed up an abnormal prices for the commodities and earned huge profit and at the same time they eliminated the small business men in the markets. So the reformers considered the growth of these monopoly as the chief economic problems and they demanded protection to the small business against the monopolistic atrocities. They insisted that the Government should come forward to curb the growth of monopoly. As a result of the demands of the reformers, President Roosevelt desired to have a fundamental change in the economic system. The idea of removing monopoly in American enterprises was openly written in the book entitled "The Promise of American Life" by Herbert Croly. This book mentioned about the individual freedom and liberty to form trade unions. It exposed the corruption of the politicians and drawbacks of the monopoly. It argued that economic injustice should be ended not by dissolving the trusts but by extending the powers of the Government to control the monopoly.

Muckrakers

A group of journalist known as Muckrakers exposed the fraud and draft with emphasis on the corrupt connections between business and politics. They published an analysis of political corruption which made the people to know the political corruption and unhuman atrocities of the big business people. So the writing of Muckrakers made the people vigilant and awareness to the current problems.

City Reformers

The reformers advocated many reforms such as city planning, pure administrative system in municipalities, health programme for slums, more funds for schools, parks, playgrounds, and other improvements. The main enemies of the people in implementing reforms were the powerful street car and the public utility corporation that had obtained special privileges by corrupt methods. The corruption of the politicians and unfair methods of big businesses were hated by the reformers. Tom Johnson implemented a number of reforms in the administrative structure of Cleveland City Government. A new plan was introduced in the cities and as per the plan many commissions were appointed to look after the various municipal functions. The traditional form of government in the cities were abolished and an attempt was made to put an end to the corrupt practices of the politicians.

State Reforms

Robert Marion La Follette of Wisconsin was the outstanding figure among the state reformers who fought for democratic ideals. He was the Governor of Wisconsin and he introduced a series of laws known as Wisconsin idea. It included taxation of the railroads, fixation of railroad rates, income and inheritance taxes, regulation of banks and insurance companies, limitation of hours of work for women and children, implementation of the workmen compensation law and creation of the forest reserve. These reforms were implemented in many states in USA.

Natural Reforms

(1) All the members of the party must be present when the selection of the party candidate was made.

(2) Delegates to the national nominating conventions were to be directly elected.

(3) The Seventh Amendment advocated that the members of the Senate should be directly elected by the people.

(4) The initiative, by which five per cent of the electorate could ask the legislature to consider the particular proposal.

(5) The elected legislator could be removed by a measure called 'the recall'.

(6) A measure called 'referendum' was made to submit any proposal for popular vote.

(7) American Women Suffrage Association led by Catt and Shaw was started with the idea of fighting for more freedom to women. Some states granted more freedom and voting rights to women. It was decided to bring a constitutional amendment for this purpose. In 1920 Congress passed the Nineteenth Amendment which granted women's suffrage.

(8) To curb the monopoly and business corporations many commissions were set up to regulate the prices and rates of railways and public utilities.

(9) Bribery of the politicians and state officials were diminished by enacting Anti Corrupt laws and modifying the civil service rules.

(10) Workmen's Compensation Acts were adopted to provide risk allowance and compulsory insurance for the benefit of the injured workers.

(11) A series of laws were enacted to limit the working hours of the labourers, and fix minimum wages. By 1923, minimum-wage laws for women had been adopted in fifteen states and also in the district of Columbia.

(12) Another important reform was the introduction of total prohibition in the country. The Methodist, Beptist and Presbyterian Churches strongly advocated and made pressure on the politicians to bring a legislation for the total legislation.

So the Eighteenth Amendment adopted in 1919, provided for the implementation of total prohibition in the country. But this measure proved to be a total failure.

Many reforms were brought in USA for the benefit and welfare of the middle class people. The important reforms of fixing up the wages for the labourers, regulating the prices and rates of railways, rooting out the corrupt practices of the politicians, eliminating the monopoly of the big business, executing many reforms in the banks and Life Insurance Corporations and so on were held responsible for the implementation of a number of welfare measures. As these measures largely benefited the middle class men, progressivism was considered as a great middle class movement.

14

Progressive Era

In 1900 on the assassination of President Mc Kinley, Vice-President Theodore Roosevelt assumed the presidency. An extraordinary character in many respects his rise to eminence was spectacular.

As President he implemented a series of successful social welfare schemes and pursued a vigorous foreign policy.

Now, let us discuss about the progressive movement of U.S.A.

The Progressive Movement

The birth of the twentieth century had witnessed the rise of a movement of reform known as Progressivism. This new movement was represented by Theodore Roosevelt, Taft, Wilson, Tom Johnson and La Follette in national and state politics. Progressivism believed in the American ideals of democratic movement, individual liberty, the rule of law and protection of private property. The leaders of the Progressive Movement stood for ethical, humanitarian and religious values and disliked class hatreds. In fact Progressivism was a great middle class movement because it derived the support of small businessmen, farmers, lawyers and Journalists. It also had only middle class objectives.

Purposes of Progressivism

The reformers had a number of grievances which prompted them to start this new movement.

(1) The growth of political corruption alarmed the reformers.

(2) They wanted to abolish the special privileges granted to the wealthy class.

(3) They insisted that a good government should reflect the wishes of the people.

(4) They demanded the destruction of the invisible government of bosses and machines.

(5) They wanted to impose some control over monopoly.

(6) They dissented to the exploitation of the farmers and the working class.

(7) They advocated for the regulation of big business and protection of weaker sections in the society.

Both the progressive Republicans and progressive Democrats had found a place in the Progressive Movement. Some leaders who believed in Jeffersonian principles wished to promote the welfare of the people while others who believed in Hamiltonian principles wished the government to assume more responsibilities.

Problem of Monopoly

The reformers considered the growth of monopoly as the chief economic problem of the country. They desired the prohibition of monopoly protection of small businessmen and enforcement of effective competition. The government should assume broader economic responsibilities to curb the growth of monopoly. They also advocated for a strong trade union movement. President Roosevelt also desired to have a fundamental change in the economic system and believed in the principle of government supremacy over big business.

City Reforms

The reformers attacked the structure and administrative system of city governments. The Progressives fought for corrupt-free administrative system, city-planning, health programme for slums, and more money for schools, parks, playgrounds and other improvements. Not only the corrupt politicians, but also powerful street-car and corporations were found to be the enemies of people. Tom Johnson implemented a number of reforms in the administrative structure of Cleveland city government. A new plan called commission plan was introduced in a number of cities. According to this plan the municipal functions were vested with small commissions. In some other cities administrative functions were vested with city mangers. The effects of these reforms were really unimpressive.

State Reforms

La Follette of Wisconsin was the greatest of all the progressives who fought for democratic ideals. He became a staunch enemy of machine politicians. As the governor of Wisconisin, he had implemented a number of reforms which included taxation of the railroads. Fixation of railroads rates, regulation of banks and insurance companies, fixation of working hours for women and children, workers' compensation law and primary election system. These reforms were known as Wisconsin idea and this idea was shared by Charles Evans Hughes a future Secretary of State and Woodrow Wilson, the President of U.S.A.

National Reforms

Efforts were taken to diminish the influence of political bosses. There were :

(1) Adoption of primary system allowing popular choice of party candidates.

(2) Delegates to the national nominating conventions were to be directly elected.

(3) The Seventeenth Amendment adopted in 1913, established direct popular election of Senators.

(4) A measure called "Initiative" by which a five per cent of the citizens of a state could ask a legislature to consider a particular proposal.

(5) Another measure called "referendum" could make a proposal to be submitted for popular vote.

(6) The elected or appointed officials could be removed by a measure called "the recall". A number of States had adopted these measures, but the results were disappointing to the reforms.

(7) The National American Women Suffrage Association led by Catt and Shaw became more active seeking women's suffrage. Only a few States had granted the voting right to women. Many believed that a constitutional amendment was essential for women's suffrage. In 1930, Congress passed the Nineteenth Amendment which granted women's suffrage.

(8) There was also a drive for total prohibition. The Eighteenth Amendment, adopted in 1919, provided for the implemention of total prohibition in the country. But this measure proved to be a total failure.

The progressives were mainly responsible for the implementation of a number of welfare measures. A number of states enacted laws regulating wages, working hours, worker's compensation and health programmes. Though political bossism was eradicated to some extent, the influence of big businessmen in politics could not be eradicated. The extension of women's suffrage was really a leap forward towards democracy. As these measures largely benefited the middle class men, progressivism was considered as a great middle class movement.

T. Roosevelt (The New President)

Theodore Roosevelt became the President of U.S.A. by accident. He had already spent one term as a legislator in New York, served as a member of the United States Civil Service Commission, played a vital role as Assistant Secretary of the Navy and commanded the "Rough Riders" in the Cuban War of 1898 which made him a national hero. After serving a term as Governor of New York, he became the Vice-president of U.S.A.

in 1900. When President Mckinley was assassinated by an anarchist in 1901, Roosevelt succeeded to the Presidency. In 1904, he was re-elected as President.

Domestic Policies

When Theodore Roosevelt became the President of U.S.A., the nation needed a number of reforms. His policies may be considered as a blueprint of far-reaching reforms. They were:

(1) He wanted government control over big business.
(2) He desired to grant more authority for the interstate commerce commission.
(3) He favoured conservation of natural resources.
(4) He desired the extension of the merit system in the civil service. After the civil war he was the first President to assert strong executive leadership. He introduced a new spirit into Federal policies.

The Coal Strike

The rapid growth of industries was accompanied by a number of industrial problems. The miners in the anthracite areas of Pennsylvania were exploited by mine-owners for many years. Their problems were:

(a) Long hours of work for low wages.
(b) Forced to live in the company houses.
(c) Compelled to trade at company stores.
(d) Refusal of Union recognition and collective bargaining.

To achieve these just goals the miners, under the dynamic leadership of John Mitchell went on strike in 1902. As the coal became scare, the Federal Government was forced to intervene. The policy of the President was "a square deal" for all-capital, labour and the public. The President intervened in the coal strike in order to bring about a settlement by negotiation. As the mine-owners refused to negotiate with Mitchell, Roosevelt forced them to accept arbitration by a government commission. Finally, the miners received higher wages and nine-hour day.

Enforcement of the Sherman Act

Roosevelt began his trust-busting campaign in 1902. He ordered the Attorney General to file a suit under the Sherman Act against the Northern Securities Company. This Company controlled the Northern Pacific, the Great Northern, the Chicago and Quincy rail roads. The President announced that the big business should be compelled to obey the law. The Supreme Court rule was in favour of the government. The Federal Government attacked a number of other trusts including Standard Oil Company. Roosevelt's trustbusting crusade aroused great popular enthusiasm throughout the country. But a number of trusts had made informal "Community of interest" agreements for stabilizing prices and production. As the trust-busting crusade failed to yield good results, Roosevelt announced that he wanted to draw only line against misconduct and not against wealth.

Strengthening I.C.C.

Roosevelt proposed to strengthen the Interstate Commerce Commission. The Elkins Act of 1903 prohibited the practice of secret rebates granted by the railroads. This act was directed against big corporations like Standard Oil Company which had obtained rebates from the railroads. In 1906, the Congress passed the Hepburn Act which conferred a number of powers upon the interstate Commerce Commission. The act authorised the commission to reduce unreasonable rates. It placed the burden of proof upon the railroads and no longer upon the commission. It empowered the commission to prescribe a uniform system of book-keeping for all railroads.

Conservation

Roosevelt's campaign for the conservation of natural resources may be regarded as the most important contribution to national welfare. Realising the vital importance of conservation, he aroused the public interest on safeguarding the natural resources. The transfer of public lands to private ownership resulted in wasteful exploitation of natural resources. Large areas of forests were reserved and people were prohibited from entering into these forest reserves.

Irrigation

The Newlands Act of 1902 authorised the Federal Government to establish irrigation projects in various parts of the country. It also authorised to create a Reclamation Service to Supervise the projects. By 1907 twenty-eight projects were undertaken in fourteen states.

Waterways

The internal waterways established by the Federal Government facilitated transportation, promoted irrigation projects and helped to develop water-power sites.

Other Reforms

The Congress passed the Meat Inspection Act and the pure Food And Drug Act in 1906. The Meat Inspection Act Provided for federal inspection of factories packing meat for inter state commerce. The Pure Food and Drug Act prohibited the sale of harmful food materials. It also ordered to label correctly the medicines containing dangerous drugs. But this act failed to purify the drug industry.

The Muckrakers

A group of popular writers who brought out the scandalous conditions in business and politics were named as "Muckrakers" by Roosevelt. Their works exerted a powerful influence in stirring public opinion. The President's crusade for social justice was aided by a number of writers such as Upton Sinclair (*The Jungle*), Ida Tarbell (*History of the Standard Oil Company*), Raybaker (*The Railroads on Trial*) and Frank Norriswho had written the *Octopus*.

Estimate

Roosevelt is one of the most controversial characters in the history of U.S.A. Though he was responsible for implementing a number of reforms, his achievements in domestic affairs were in fact meagre. He was the first progressive President who introduced a new spirit into federal politics. He had no real desire to make total changes in the existing economic system. His campaign against rich miserably failed. He was not successful in his reforms because the conservatives in the Congress opposed him. As he had no sympathy for socialism, he was always ready for a compromise. He opened the gates of national politics to the reformers and gave the progressive movement a chance to flourish.

Big Stick Policy

President Theodore Roosevelt took the United States into world affairs. His aggressive policy increased the influence and prestige of the United States as a world power. He proclaimed his policy by saying "speak softly, and carry a big stick, and you will go far". By his big stick policy he placed the United States deeply involved in the affairs of Latin America.

The Roosevelt Corollary

Most of the Carribbean and Central American Republics were ruled by dictators. As there occurred frequent revolutions in these countries, they were unable to repay their national debts. To collect their debts, France, Italy, Belgium and other European powers threatened to use force in order to safeguard the rights of their citizens. The international law too permitted such interventions. The danger of European intervention forced President Roosevelt to pronounce his Caribbean policy on the basis of Monroe Doctrine which became to be known as "The Roosevelt Corollary". He announced that "chronic wrong doing or an importance which results in a general loosening of the ties of civilized society, may in America, compel the United States to exercise an international policy power". The President had three reasons for proclaiming his policy.

(a) He wanted to prevent European powers from acquiring bases in the American hemisphere.

(b) He desired to protect the interest of American bankers and businessmen.

(c) He earnestly wished to enhance the American influence in the Caribbean region. The big stick policy, the Latin Americans feared, may lead to imperialistic activities of U.S.A.

Application of the Roosevelt Corollary

The principle of Roosevelt corollary was first applied in the Dominican Republic in 1905. It was unable to repay its debts. When the European powers were about to intervene in the affairs of Dominican Republic, President Roosevelt restrained them from armed intervention. The U.S.A. took charge of the finances of the country, collected the taxes, and repaid the foreign debts. In Venezuela too, President Roosevelt intervened and the foreign debt was settled by arbitration. In 1906, there were revolutionary activities in Cuba. The American administration landed its army on Cuban soil, crushed the revolutionary disturbances and remained there until 1909.

Panama Canal

The United States had deep interest in the Panama Canal project. The seizure of the Panama Canal Zone stood as the supreme example for the big stick policy of Roosevelt. He claimed that he had taken Panama in his own way. The growth of American empire across the pacific necessitated a canal across the Central America. Before 1903, Panama was a part of the Republic of Colombia. A French canal company got permission from Colombia... dug a canal in 1878. The French company could not complete the canal work due to landslides and fever. A new Panama canal Company acquired the rights from the French company and was ready to sell it to the United States. The Hay Herran Treaty of 1903, provided Colombia to grant the Panama Zone for lease. But the Colombian Senate refused to ratify the treaty for want of better terms.

The irritated Americans and the Panamanians hatched a plot to establish an independent Panama State. In 1903 the revolutionaries in Panama proclaimed its independence. The American war ships prevented the Colombian army from landing in Panama. The new Panama government signed a treaty with U.S.A. and granted the lease of land for constructing the Panama canal. The treaty also gave U.S.A. the right of maintaining order in the canal zone. Construction of the Panama canal was completed in 1914 which essentially served the interests of U.S.A. The whole Panama affair gave a severe shock to the Latin Americans.

The Far East

The Russo-Japanese War of 1904 ended in the victory of Japan. As U.S.A. regarded Russia as a dangerous power, extended its diplomatic support to Japan. In 1905, Roosevelt acted as mediator and convened a peace conference at Portsmouth in New Hampshire. The warring nations ended their war by signing the Treaty of Portsmouth in 1905. As Roosevelt was responsible for the successful conclusion of peace talks, he was awarded the Nobel Peace Prize.

The peace treaty was followed by a conflict between America and Japan. Now U.S.A. regarded Japan as a real threat to her interests in the Pacific area. The Americans began to talk of the imagined "Yellow peril" and began to practise racial discrimination in its national life. The Gentlemen's Agreement of 1908 gave a satisfactory solution to the confronting powers. The Root-Takahira Agreement of 1908 finally settled the differences. Both countries agreed to uphold the existing territorial possessions and maintain the *status quo* in the Pacific area.

Relations with Europe

Roosevelt kept on good relations with Britain. He played a vital role in settling disputes between the powers. He intervened in the Franco-German conflict over Morocco and forced them to agree for an international conference in 1906. His activities as an arbitrator towards peace may also to be commended.

William Taft

A student of law, William Howard Taft who succeeded Roosevelt in the Presidency was a native of Ohio and a graduate from Cincinnati. He served as Governor General in the Philippines and as Federal Judge and as Secretary of War. He contested in the 1908 elections as Republican candidate. He defeated his Democratic rival William Bryan and became President. He was polished and cautious; he was aristocratic in nature. So he did not prove himself as successful President. Yet his administration was noted for a series of measures taken against the trusts and in support of dollar diplomacy.

Dollar Diplomacy

In the Presidential election of 1908, William Taft, the Republican party candidate defeated his opponent Bryan and became President. The

President and his Secretary of State Philander Knox used the enormous American economy to achieve diplomatic objectives. This policy of using economic means to active political goals is known as "Dollar Diplomacy".

(1) The dollar diplomacy would give the American businessmen a free hand to act.
(2) It would help the American financiers to earn more profits from the debtor countries.
(3) It would serve American strategic and financial interests.
(4) It would promote order and prosperity in the Caribbean.
(5) The American administration believed that the American dollar alone could safeguard the interests of the American financiers.

The real intention of the American administration was to extend the American influence in foreign countries and attain rapid economic development.

The Economic Imperialism

The dollar diplomacy encouraged the American capitalists to invest more in foreign countries. The President described his policy only as an effort to increase American trade. He believed that American dollars would help to maintain the balance of power in the Far East. It would safeguard his "open door policy" and the territorial integrity of China. As the American investment followed the same pattern as that of European financiers, the dollar diplomacy attempted to increase the American economic imperialism. As Knox, the Secretary of State, was not very tactful in implementing this policy, it miserably failed to achieve the desired goals.

The Implementation of Dollar Diplomacy

The American administration followed tactless and uncivilized means to implement the dollar diplomacy.

(a) If a weak country did not support the American cause, then there would be internal conflicts with the aid of American officials.
(b) American arms would be freely utilised to topple any established government.
(c) A revolutionary government would be recognized only on the condition of granting more economic concessions to the American financiers.
(d) If a dictator would act as the shadow of American administration, he would be allowed to remain in power at all costs.
(e) Sometimes force was used to threaten the inhabitants. American navy was always ready to strike against enemies of American interests.

(f) American army was stationed in a few countries to safeguard the American citizens.

(g) No country could get aid from other European powers as it would violate the principles of Monroe Doctrine. The dollar diplomacy stood as a concrete example for American imperialism.

Intervention in Caribbean Countries

As most of the Caribbean countries were in a chaotic condition it invariably helped U.S.A. to intervene frequently. During the Taft and Knox regime U.S.A. intervened in the affairs of Nicaragua in 1909. Nicaragua is situated in a strategic position. President Jose Zelaya of Nicaragua wanted to construct a canal across the country with the aid of a few foreign powers. As the new canal would not serve the American interests, American officials induced the rebels to revolt against Jose Zelaya. The rebels were aided with arms and ammunitions. The President was removed and a new government was set up. The new regime was recognized only after the grant of more economic concessions to the American financiers. When the American bankers took charge of the country's finances in 1911, the people revolted against the new imperialism. The revolution was crushed by the American Marines in 1912, and the country was virtually in the hands of Mariners for the next twenty years. American officials decided in advance who should win in the elections if they were held. Rulers friendly to U.S.A. alone were kept in power. Nicaragua which was under the grip of the American navy never witnessed a free election. American influence became a permanent factor in the country's political life. In addition to these economic concessions, the Taft administration was allowed to establish naval bases in the islands of Great Corn and Little Corn.

In Honduras also the Taft administration intervened and forced it to fall in line with the dollar diplomacy. As it was unable to repay its debts, the American bankers took charge of the country's finances. A number of Latin American countries were forced to purchase warships from U.S.A. alone. It helped the American shipping industry to flourish.

The Chinese Consortium

The dollar diplomacy had its impact in the Far East also. The American businessmen believed that there were immense opportunities for profit, power and idealistic enterprises in China. They believed that American influence may be increased in the Far East by investing more capital. Knox, Secretary of State, persuaded American financiers to join with British, French and German bankers in a consortium in the construction of Hukuang Railroad in China. To destroy the Japanese and European influence in China, American financiers vainly tried to purchase the existing railroads from Japan and Russia. Then the President offered a big loan to the Chinese Government by inviting it to purchase these railroads. In his endeavour to construct a new railroad in China, Knox miserably failed.

Causes for the Failure of Dollar Diplomacy

(1) As the dollar diplomacy attempted to establish an American economic imperialism, most South American countries opposed economic intervention.

(2) Though the dollar diplomacy of Taft was essentially different from the Big Stick Policy of Roosevelt, there was no change in its political motives.

(3) The new policy tried to safeguard only the interests of American financiers and took least interest in the welfare of other nations.

(4) As U.S.A. wanted to increase its political power through economic intervention, it was bound to fail.

(5) Both Russia and Japan opposed the open door policy as it curtailed their wide economic activities. So the failure of dollar diplomacy in the Far East was not a surprise one.

(6) The dollar diplomacy attempted to support the dictators of various Latin American countries against democratic ideals.

(7) As most countries of the globe realised the real impact of this economic intervention, they opposed it tooth and nail. Hence, the dollar diplomacy failed to yield good results in the history of U.S.A.

Woodrow Wilson (1913-1921)

In the 1912 presidential election, Thomas Woodrow Wilson, the candidate of the Democratic Party defeated the other contestants, William Taft and Theodore Roosevelt. His father was a Presbyterian preacher. He began his career as a lawyer. He served as professor of political economy in Princeton University. For sometime he served as Governor of New Jersey. As governor he gained a reputation for his programme called New Freedom — freedom for small businessman against monopolistic control of trusts. The common people welcomed the programme and elected school master Wilson with a large majority. He was assisted by Colonel House and Bryan to implement a series of progressive reforms at home and followed a forward policy abroad.

New Freedom

(i) *Economic Reforms*: In his inaugural address he outlined his programme. He promoted the growth of trade through a reduction of tariff. The Underwood Tariff Act of 1913 enacted accordingly, provided substantial cut in the tariff rates, widened the free list and reduced the duties on numerous items (iron, steel, cotton and woolen goods).

Congress framed laws for the regulation of trusts.

To regulate commerce between states and with foreign countries two acts were framed *viz.*, the Clayton Anti-Trust Act and the Trade Commission Act of 1914. The former was intended to eradicate the evils which were associated with trusts, railroad and labour. The latter empowered to prevent persons and corporations from drifting into unfair methods of competition.

The Adamcon Act of 1916 provided for an eight hour day for all employees in railways, engaged in inter-state commerce and extra pay for overtime work.

The Federal Reserve Act (1913) aimed at the reorganisations of banking and currency. Accordingly a Federal Reserve Board was set up to supervise the entire federal banking system. The country was divided into 12 banking districts and at the financial centre of each district, a federal bank was established. The Board was authorised to issue notes.

The financial houses of Wall Street were brought under control.

The President took measures for promoting the welfare of peasants and workers.

Like Jefferson, Wilson claimed himself as the champion of the right of the common people.

(ii) *Constitutional Changes*: In 1920 two amendments were incorporated in the constitution. The 18th amendment introduced nation wide prohibition. The 19th amendment was carried into effect for granting suffrage to women. In most of the states the women were not eligible to vote. There was a movement in favour of the extension of franchise but while one organisation of women agitated for vote, an other equally powerful organisation of women opposed it. Yet in consideration of services rendered by women during the World Wart public opinion turned in favour of the reform. The Nineteenth Amendment stated: "the right of citizens of the United States to vote shall not be deprived by the United States or by any State on account of sex." Since then women took a more serious interest in politics than what they did in the past.

Woodrow Wilson's Foreign Policy

President Woodrow Wilson's foreign policy was basically a departure from the policy of his predecessors-Roosevelt and Taft. He was an avowed enemy of imperialism. Repudiating the policy of his predecessors, in a speech at Mobile in October 1913, he declared that the United States would never again seek one additional foot of territory by conquest and that its foreign policy should not be determined by "material interest". But inspite of these noble declarations, his administration was responsible for more intervention than those of Roosevelt and Taft. It is very difficult to explain the difference between principle and practice. Perhaps it might have been largely due to the outbreak of World War I. The diplomatic history of the U.S.A. can be studied under various headings.

Wilson's Caribbean Policy

A considerable change in the American Caribbean policy was made due to the increasing American interest in the Caribbean region. Instead of merely watching the entire region from being intervened by foreigners, Wilson decided to give a strong protection to the American bankers in these republics. Whenever internal disturbances occurred in these islands, American troops were sent there to provide protection to the American settlers. Thus, America had to interfere in the affairs of Haiti, Nicaragua, Dominican Republic and Mexico.

Haiti

Natives of the island Haiti in West Indies broke out a revolution opposing the presence of American traders in 1915. Fearing the intervention of other European countries, Wilson rushed American troops to Haiti and insurrection was suppressed. Yet the Haitian Government was allowed to function under the surveillance of America till 1934.

Dominican Republic

The conflicts between the American officials and the native Government led to a deadlock; the marines then took control of the country in 1916 and stayed until 1924. In 1917 Cuba too was occupied and she was under American control till 1922.

Nicaragua

In 1916, United States forced the native Government which was already under her control to sign the Bryan-Chamorro Treaty by which the U.S. got certain important naval bases along with a right to construct a canal in Nicaragua. When the natives resented at it, the policy of suppression was followed and the land was occupied.

After the First World War, the U.S.A. abandoned interventionism and began to move more friendly with Latin America.

The Mexican Revolution

Mexican dictator Diaz (1876-1911) had allowed foreign capital into Mexico. American capital was invested in railroads, mines, plantations and oil fields. Mexico attained economic growth which only benefited the upper class. Labourers and low class people were exploited. So the discontented Mexican thought that foreigners took away their national wealth.

In 1913, Huerta seized power and became Mexican President. Britain and American businessmen who controlled majority of Mexican mines; oil-wells and plantations supported Huerta. Wilson refused to recognise his government.

The Mexican constitutionalists wanted to bring about land and labour reforms. The Mexican President of Huerta opposed this. Wilson sided with the constitutionalist and allowed them to buy ammunitions in the U.S.A. German merchant ship carried arms for the Mexican President Huerta. It was about to land in Veracruz To avert German involvement in Mexican affairs Wilson ordered to seize Veracruz. Mexican blood was shed. Wilson's intention was to help the constitutionalists. He has to do much to repair the damage done to Mexico, by arranging a conference of the representatives of the South American countries to deal with Mexican problem. It was a step to good neighbour policy.

During and after Huerta's regime disorder prevailed in the country. During the Presidency of Carranza, Mexican bandits attacked Americans as a result of which many Americans lost their lives and property. One bandit Panchovilla, led raids into New Mexico. In 1916 an American army invaded Mexico to catch Panchovilla. Since the U.S.A. was engaged in European affairs she had to give up the attempt of catching Panchovilla. Wilson managed to maintain peace with Mexico inspite of Mexican worst Government, the provocation offered by Mexican bandits and the desire of many Americans to go to war with Mexico.

Relations with Japan

When the First World War broke out, Japan entered the war as an ally of Britain. This gave a free hand to Japan to seize a number of territories in China under the pretext of expelling the German from the Far East. But her intention was to dominate the entire China. So, she presented her twenty one demands to China in 1915. If these demands were to be accepted the entire China would come under the control of Japan. That means disregarding the Open Door policy. Immediately United States vehemently protested against the Japanese attitude towards China, but in vain. Afterwards, as the United States also entered the war on the side of the Allies, friendly understanding were re-established between Japan and America. In 1917, the Japanese diplomat Ishii came to Washington, and signed the Lausing-Ishii agreement with the American Government. This treaty again assured the Open Door and the territorial integrity in China. Thus, everytime, whenever Japan violated the terms signed earlier with America; American Presidents repeated the same paper. However, after the First World War, she paid less interest towards the affairs of China.

Wilson and the First World War

The First World War broke out in August 1914. It immediately created problems for the American people and for Wilson. Wilson proclaimed neutrality at the outset and every one in the U.S.A. supported him. Several times he mediated between the Allies and the Central Powers to see whether peace could be made. He was unsuccessful in this, but he remained very firm in his neutrality. Americans including Wilson, were more sympathetic towards the Allies than towards the Central powers. There were many reasons for this.

(1) The most obvious of these were language and tradition.

(2) The second factor was the propaganda to capture American opinion by lectures, press articles, rumors and stories of atrocities.

(3) The third factor was the trade between the U.S.A. and the Allies. The trade rose steadily. As against total exports of 824,000,000 dollars in 1914, it rose to 3,214,000,000 dollars in 1916.

(4) After 1915, enormous loans were floated in U.S.A. by the Allies to pay for the American goods and ammunition. The Americans were worried that the Allies would stop buying American goods, which would plunge the economy back into depression. These were some of the reasons which made America to enter the war.

Besides, during the early February 1916, Germany had begun the submarine warfare sinking many ships without warning in which many Americans lost their lives. British vessel Lusitania was drowned without warning on May 7,1915. It resulted in the loss of 1198 lives of whom 128 were Americans. This shocking event caused a burst of indignation. In addition to this the first American ship was sunk on March 12, 1916 and during the next three weeks five more ships were drowned with the loss of 25 American lives.

The last and most provoking reason for U.S. to enter war was the Zimmermann note of February 1917, intercepted and decoded by Britain and sent to U.S. It contained an offer from Germany to Mexico that in the event of the German victory in a war with the U.S.A. Mexico should have Texas. On 2nd April 1917, Wilson appeared before the Congress and asked for a declaration of a state of war. Congress responded and the U.S. entered war on Good Friday, April 6, 1917.

The United States at War 1917-18

The U.S.A. played considerable and decisive part in the First World War. Her direct contribution was two fold. First she loaned the Allies vast sums of money, ten thousand millions of dollars. Secondly, she contributed man power. The U.S. Government conscripted men for the army, took over the railroad controlled American industry, shut down non-essential industries and controlled food supply. Wilson declared from the beginning that their fight was not with the German people but with their tyrannous and autocratic government. With the entry of U.S., Germany was defeated on all fronts and the war came to an end by the end of 1918.

The Peace Conference at Paris

After the overthrow of Germany, Turkey and Austria-Hungary, the peace conference met in Paris on 18th January 1919 to decide the future map of Europe. The major decisions of the conference were thrashed out by a council of four, consisting of Wilson, Clemenceau of France, Lloyd George of Britain and Orlando of Italy. Each one of the European nations attended with certain selfish motives of taking revenge against the defeated. But Woodrow Wilson sponsored moderate peace terms. His purpose was justice rather than vengeance and he wished "to make the world safe for democracy". In January, 1918, Wilson expressed his broad ideals in Fourteen Points which he believed would make world peace. These Fourteen Points may be summarised as follows :

(1) An open treaty not a secret one decided by diplomatists among themselves.
(2) Freedom of the seas for all shipping.
(3) Equality of trade between nations (removal of economic barriers between nations.)
(4) Reduction of armaments to the lowest consistent with domestic safety.
(5) Impartial settlements of colonial claims (A setlement of colonial problems, paying attention to the peoples of the colonies).
(6) The evacuation of Russian, territory by Germany.
(7) Self-determination for the peoples of Austria, Hungary and Turkey.
(8) The independence of Poland with free access to the sea.
(9) The establishment of a general association of nations in order to safeguard the independence of each nation.

(10) Evacuation and Restoration of Belgium.

(11) Evacuation and restoration of France.

(12) Readjustment of Italian frontiers along her recognizable times of nationality.

(13) Evacuation and restoration of Serbia and an outlet to the sea for Serbia.

(14) Securing of sovereignity for the Turkish portion and ottonman Empire.

This statement was highly important since it offered the hope of new world free from the threat of war. German people accepted the fourteen points and asked for peace terms on the basis of these fourteen points.

The biennial election to Congress held in November 1918 gave Wilson's opponents, the Republicans a majority in both Houses and there was a steady growth of popular feeling against Wilson for his leniency of treatment to Germans.

The Treaty of Versailles and the League of Nations

Wilson himself headed the U.S. delegation and thus became the first American President to go overseas on a diplomatic mission. There was difference of opinion between France and the U.S.A. regarding the settlement. Wilson was always for a just settlement to satisfy the claims of both sides and desirous of preventing any future war. The French view was that Germany would not accept any settlement since she (Germany) wanted to dominate Europe. Hence, the conference should weaken Germany and strengthen France.

As a result the peace signed at Paris has been described as a "Dictated Peace". According to Lansingh, the terms of peace were immeasurably harsh and humiliating.

Wilson was victorious in establishing the League of Nations. He being the principal author of the League covenant, its main principle was that all nations should settle their disputes peacefully.

But alas! when the treaty was submitted to the U.S. Senate, in July 1919, the Republican led Senate objected to the ratification of the treaty just to humiliate Wilson. Wilson in his attempt to appeal to the people was affected with paralytic stroke and so the cause of the League was left without effective leadership. Besides, by refusing to assume commitments of the treaty, the USA led to division of the World into two hostile alliances. The unjust and humiliating treats had become the seed fon the Global War II in 1939.

15

Era of Prosperity and Depression

Prosperity

Herbert Hoover was elected in 1928 as Republican candidate. He rode to the presidency on the crest of a prosperity wave. Prior to this he was a successful engineer and businessman with a distinguished record in public service. With this he put the prevailing prosperity on durable foundations. There was rapid expansion of production. Trade increased, economy experienced a boom prosperity came to the land, banks gave attractive dividends to the shareholders.

The application of new scientific inventions, new sources of power and new techniques for promoting efficiency resulted in the rapid economic development during the 1920's. The rapid economic progress witnessed the rapid growth of service, distribution and white-collar occupations. But due to the introduction of improved productive methods, the number of industrial workers employed in various industries actually decreased. The introduction of standardization and the division of labour helped to cut the costs, higher wages increased the purchasing power and mass production resulted in the low prices of the commodities. By and large Americans became a people on wheels. The age of coal and steam was replaced by an age of oil and electricity. This era of abundance enriched the lives of the average citizen and it offered a high standard of living for everybody. Unfortunately this period of prosperity was followed by the great depression of 1930's.

Causes of the Depression

After the inauguration of Herbert Hoover as President in March, 1929, there came the crash and depression. A number of causes were responsible for the economic depression of 1930's.

1. **Result of the First World War.** The economic depression was a delayed result of the first global war which affected the entire world.

2. **Mass Production.** The high profits of the period of prosperity encouraged the American manufactures to produce more goods. The depression forced diem to produce less by dismissing thousands of workers. The result was unemployment, less production and more starvation.
3. **Distribution of Income.** The profits made by the industry was not evenly distributed among the population. As the profits went to a very small proportion of the population (0.3 per cent), the purchasing power of the people considerably decreased.
4. **Savings and Purchasing Power.** A large part of the population, especially workers in depressed occupation such as textile workers and the miners and most of the farmers had no share in the prosperity. They saved little to purchase in the domestic market. As most of the big corporations were accumulating savings instead of distributing their profits to stock-holders, it reduced the purchasing power of the general public.
5. **Growth of Debt.** There was a rapid increase in private debts. Average Americans had debt in the form of instalment buying. Small businessmen were borrowing heavily for expansion. As private debts increased day by day, everybody seemed to be in debt. When depression came the whole structure collapsed like a house of cards. There was also considerable increase in the public debt.
6. **Foreign Investment.** The First World War changed U.S.A. from a debtor country to a creditor country. American bankers and businessmen invested their capital in foreign countries. More money was offered to the dictators of Latin America. More goods were exported and no goods were imported. By 1929, the debtor countries were unable to repay their loans. It contributed a major cause for the great depression.
7. **Growth of Speculation.** The rapid increase in the number of stock holders made U.S.A. a country of capitalists. People bought stocks not because they wanted sound investment, but to make fortunes by gambling on the prices of the stocks. As millions of Americans engaged in speculation, stock prices went on rising. In October 1929, suddenly the prices began to fall. There was none to purchase any stock. Companies went bankrupt and many stock-holders were ruined.
8. **Monopoly.** Big corporations controlled transportation and public utilities. To maintain uniform prices, they followed the path of a price leader. When depression came, these corporations cut their

production in order to maintain the high prices and this price rigidity was found to be major weakness in the economic system.

9. **Prosperity.** The prosperity depends upon the confidence of the businessmen. When depression came, this confidence disappeared and businessmen were not ready to take any risks.

The Course of the Depression

The most terrible result of the depression was unemployment. About sixteen million (¼th of labour force) workers had become unemployed by 1933. The national income decreased by fifty per cent. Production was dropped by 37 per cent. Exports and imports were also considerably affected. In 1929 corporations had earned good profits whereas they had incurred a heavy loss in 1932. Farm production dropped by only 6 per cent but prices fell by 63 per cent. This grim situation was unequalled in American history.

Many assumed that the economy would quickly recover. The unemployed were forced to depend on private charity. Thousands of people had become homeless migrants and wandering aimlessly in the country. Thousands of people were living on the pavements. Half a million workers had returned to agriculture, Still the victims of the depression displayed their remarkable patience. They displayed an extraordinary respect for law and order and the rights of property. The country had witnessed only a few organised agitations by farmers.

The Impact of the Depression

The depression struck a fatal blow at liberalism, democracy and capitalism. The starving people turned to communism which promised a classless society and a planned economy. In Germany the Fascists won a great victory by stirring up racial and religions hatreds. Only Soviet Union alone remained unaffected by the depression. Many professors, writers, religious leaders and students turned their attention towards socialism and communism They demanded redistribution of the wealth, demanded inflation, denounced bankers and advocated isolationism.

Government and the Depression

Many conservatives believed that the economic system was basically sound and regarded the crisis as the effects of war and the post-war debt. They insisted that the Federal government should take positive steps to restore prosperity. A few blamed the government for the depression. President Hoover believed that the depression would be overcome by the determined Americans. He opposed government control of industry and never departed from his belief in "rugged individualism". The government made some feeble attempts to deal with the problems of depression. A Reconstruction Finance Corporation was established to help the banks and industries. Private charities were encouraged. But there was not a revolutionary plan to conquer depression.

Calvin Coolidge

In 1920 Warren G. Harding was elected to the presidency. His administration ended in 1923 with his death in office. Calvin Coolidge, the Vice-President, succeeded in the presidency and in 1924 he was elected for a regular term.

Calvin Coolidge had good virtues of honesty, morality, and frugality. He seemed to be a crystallization of the common place. A painfully shy individual of average height (5 feet 10"). He was blessed with only mediocre powers of leadership. He would occasionally flash a dry wit in private; but his speeches delivered in New England were invariably boring. He believed that "the men who builds a factory builds a temple".

The Harding-Coolidge era spanned the craziest years of the so called "Gin and Jazz age" of the "Roaring Twenties". Materialism was an unlovely offspring of synicism. An obsession with sex accompanied the materialistic urge. Spiritual life seemed to be retreating before materialism in this "Era of wonderful nonsense".

Novelists, like F. Scott Fitzerald and Theodore Ireisar lived during this period. Despite the moon of saxophones, high quality poetry was still being written. Among them Edwin A. Robinson, Ezra Pound and T.S. Eliot was a Missourian and later became a British Subject.

Even architecture married itself to the new-materialism and functionalism.

Moral decay in the 1920's was vastly accelerated by prohibition.

Hailed as a strong silent man (and really neither), Coolidge was the clear choice of the Republican when they met at Cleveland, in June 1924. Although he had been in office less than a year, he had brought responsibility to his scandal besmirched party.

Gradually under Presidents Coolidge and Hoover the Republic began to side toward the back door. Americans participated as consultants in the non-political functions of the League, such as conferences to control opium and prostitution.

Good Neighbourism

Despite current anti-war sentiment the United States was reluctantly forced to adopt war like measures in Latin America. Disorders in Nicaragua had jeopardized American lives and prosperity and in 1927

President Coolidge despatched over 5000 troops to this troubled land. His political foes accused him of "waging a private war".

Mexican friction, at the same time came to a boil over oil. The government in Mexico City was attempting to wrest from American petroleum companies the private properties which, under the new constitution of 1917, were now legally vested in the Mexican nation. Relations between the two neighbour republics deteriorated alarmingly.

In 1927, Coolidge adopted the happy suggestion and sent his ambassador Dwight W. Morrow, a Wall Street banker. By a combination of tact and charm, Morrow succeeded where others had failed. He was conspicuously aided by the goodwill tour of aviator Charles A. Lindbergh, hero-conqueror of the Atlantics who on this trip met his future bride, Morrow's daughter. So successful was Lindbergh as "Ambassasor of the Air" that one American newspaper suggested as a new variant of an old floras theme "Say it with fliers".

Under such promising auspices, Morrow finally worked out a temporary acceptable compromise. The American oil companies were permitted to retain the rights they had secured prior to the Constitution of 1917, but not those obtained later. Thus, the Coolidge years ended with a bright new day dawning in relations with Latin America.

Hoover

Herbert Hoover was elected in 1928 as Republican candidate and rode to the presidency on the crest of a prosperity wave.

Chubby-faced and ruddy-complexioned Herbert Hoover, a living example of the American success story was an intriguing mixture of two centuries. As a poor orphan boy who had worked his way through Stanford University, he had absorbed the 19th century copy book maxims of industry, thrift and self-reliance. He was a successful mining engineer and a brilliant businessman. He had adopted to a high degree the efficiency-expertice of the 20th century.

Even before entering the White House, Hoover had become world-famous as the "Great Humanitarian". He was a dignified politician. He was clam and cool in nature. A millionaire in his own right, he found that his conservative instincts recoiled from anything suggesting socialism, paternalism or "planned economy".

The Heyday of Bootleggers and Kidnappers

President Hoover was a darling of the days. He had referred the prohibition in 1928 as a "far reaching" experiment, noble in motive" — hence the popular expression the "noble experiment". Yet lofty though its purposes might be, prohibition was sinking to the ignoble level of lawlessness and gangsterism.

Early in his administration Hoover attempted to grapple with crime and the liquor problem by appointing the Wickersham investigating commission. There were 11 members. After two years of probing, they submitted a report in 1931. They recommended that the experiment be continued with modifications.

Lawlessness spawned by prohibition and bootleggers manifested itself further in the "snatch racker" — or kidnapping for ransom.

Farmers

Herbert Hoover did a wonderful service to the lot of the farmers. The Agricultural Marketing Act passed by Congress in June, 1929, was designed to help themselves, largely through producers' cooperatives. It set up a Federal Farm Board with a revolving fund of half a billion dollars at its disposal. Money was lent generously to farm organisations seeking to buy, sell and store agricultural surpluses.

Besides, there were Grand Stabilisation Corporation and the Cotton Stabilication Corporation.

Tariff

Hoover made certain changes in the tariff to give relief to the farmers. It was a fairly reasonable protective measure, designed to assist the farmers. The average duty on non-free goods was raised from 38.5% as established by the Fordney-Mccomber Act of 1922 to nearly 60%. There arose controversy over the bill. However, he defended the bill and signed the same.

During the time of Hoover motor industry developed to a greater extent. New industries spurted forth; older ones grew sickly. Really speaking gasoline age witnessed a tremendous progress.

Movies eclipsed all other new forms of amusements in the phenomenol growth of their popularity.

Herbert Hoover Forerunner of the New Deal

Most imposing of the public enterprises was the gigantic Hoover Dam — originally called Bowlder Dam on the Colorado River. It was completed in 1936 after a period of 6 years. The work was started by Hoover in 1930. It was completed in 1936 under Roosevelt. It was highly useful for irrigation, flood control and electric power.

But Hoover sternly fought all schemes that he regarded as "socialistic". His administration also provided some indirect benefits for labour. After stormy debate, Congress passed the Norris-La Guardia Anti-Injunction Act in 1932 and Hoover signed it.

Hoover—Pioneer for the Good Neighbour Policy

Shortly after his election in 1928 he had undertaken a goodwill tour of Latin America on an American battleship. After depression, economic imperialism of the United States became much less popular.

As an advocate of international goodwill, Hoover strove to abandon the interventionist twist given to the Monroe Doctrine by Theodore Roosevelt.

Herbert Hoover, the Engineer in politics, thus happily engineered the foundation stones of the "Good Neighbour Policy". Upon them rose an imposing edifice in the days of his successor, Franklin Roosevelt.

16

F.D. Roosevelt

Franklin D. Roosevelt became the President of America on the 4th of March 1933. It was a critical time in the history of the United States. Most of the banks had been closed; many of the business firms were working with losses and millions of workers were unemployed. Though he had no peaceful domestic life because of his secret love affairs, he gave strong executive leadership to the country.

A distant cousin of Theodore Roosevelt, he served in the New York State legislature and as Assistant Secretary of the Navy under President Wilson. Twice he was elected Governor of New York with large majority.

In the election of 1932 he contested for the presidency as candidate of the Democratic party, promising 'a new deal' to eradicate the problems that confronted the nation.

With progressivism as his ideology, Roosevelt became the symbol of dynamic leadership.

NEW DEAL

Good Neighbour Policy

Under F.D. Roosevelt the New Deal period witnessed changes in the American foreign policy. Particularly it witnessed a great change in the Latin American states. He pursued a friendly policy towards Latin America.

The Republican administration of the post war period made earnest attempts towards the improvement of relations with the neighbouring countries. In Mexico the Americans owned extensive lands and held oil rights. But in the case of nationalisation of foreign assets strained relations began. President Harding even threatened war. However, it was settled by Morrow as mentioned earlier.

President Hoover took steps to cultivate cordial relations with Latin America. He undertook a tour for cementing the relations.

Under President F.D. Roosevelt this attitude of equality and amity was consolidated into what was called the good neighbour policy.

In his inaugural address in March 1933, he stated thus, "I would dedicate this Nation to the policy of the good neighbour who resolutely respects himself and because he does so respects the rights of others". Again in December 1933 he observed, "The definite policy of the United States from now on is opposed to armed intervention".

In 1933 Secretary of State, Cordell Hull signed a convention at the conference of American states at Montevideo, declaring "No State has the right to intervene in the internal or external affairs of another".

The good neighbour policy was applied towards the Philippines also. In 1934 the Tydings Me Duffie Act provided the complete independence after a ten year period.

The Roosevelt administration did much to undo what the previous Presidents did in the Caribbean. A treaty already signed with Cuba and it provided intervention for the United States. In the same year all troops were withdrawn from Haiti. A treaty with Panama in 1936 stated that the United States would have no right of intervention in that state.

Mexico nationalised foreign oil interests valued at forty crores of dollars.

Reciprocal trade agreements concluded with Latin American states, contributed to the expansion of trade.

No doubt the good neighbour policy had its rewards. They are:

(1) It paved the way for collective security.
(2) It helped the promotion of co-operation in the political and commercial fields.
(3) It created a sense of fearless among the Latin American states.
(4) The American administration became more realistic.
(5) Roosevelt maintained cordial relations with Soviet Russia.

The Roosevelt-Lituvania Agreement signed at Washington on the 16th of November 1936 provided for a settlement. It extended recognition to the Soviet government. In return Russia consented to discontinue communist propaganda against the United States.

New Deal

The New Deal is the name given to the great series of actions undertaken by Franklin D. Roosevelt's administration to lift the American people out of depression and to lead them to a new future. All these were mainly guided by three principles — Relief, Recovery and Reform. Relief was the first. Millions of Americans who were in desperate need of food and cash had to be helped. Recovery was the second. Government had to lead the country out of depression. Reform was third. Glaring wrongs had to be set right in order that the U.S.A. might go forward to a new future.

Roosevelt wanted to help the poor as well as the poverty stricken industries. He wanted to attack rich employers and financiers, and to help the workmen to organise themselves into trade unions in order to be enabled to bargain fairly with their employers. He wanted to help industry by enabling the ordinary American to buy more from the business firms. He wanted to stop American natural resources — her oil and land — in order to keep them for future Americans.

Methods of Execution

The Methods were bold and skilful.

(1) He made it clear that the New deal was his personal policy and not the policy of the Democratic Party.

(2) He used his full powers which the Constitution allowed him. No previous American President wielded such great power in peace time.

(3) He made full use of expert advises, for which he relied on college Professors, experts in Finances and Economics, Writers, Scholars, Lawyers and Social Workers. This group of advisers known as "Brain Trust" entered the White House and planned many of the details of the New Deal. To administer the New Deal legislation men of a similar type were brought into the lower level of Government service. These people were New Dealers rather than Democrats, who gave unique flavour to his administration.

(4) Franklin D. Roosevelt cleverly used his own genius for winning popularity in order to gain popular support for his policy. His quick answers, his great friendliness and his willingness to crack jokes won him popularity among the pressmen.

The New Deal in Operation

It had become customary to talk of two "New Deals" not one. The "First New Deal" lasted from 1933 to 1935, its main aims being to restore the banking system, to provide jobs for the unemployed, to raise agricultural prices in order to help farmers and to set industries on their feet again.

The "Second New Deal" from 1935 to 1938 brought more measures of lasting reforms. Franklin D. Roosevelt took a stronger action against the depression. Congress effected the programme by enacting a series of laws. Everyone supported him and hailed him as a great national leader.

Enemies of the New Deal critised it as socialistic.

The aim of the New Deal was to check deflation and bankruptcy, and to restore business by increasing the prices, wages, and the purchasing power of the consumer.

He argued that economy had fallen out of balance and it should be rectified by government action. Hence, he should maintain balance between agriculture and industry, balance between the wage earner, the employer and the consumer.

The New Deal not only lent money to business and saving property owners but also adopted new measures to aid different groups in the community.

The National Industrial Recovery Act was intended to stabilise industrial prices and to raise wages. The Agricultural Adjustment Act was to raise farm prices. There were measures for reforming banking and financial practices.

Congress appropriated large sums for direct relief and ambitious public work programme. Appropriation for relief was the most significant feature of the "New Deal". If people were starving and no help was available from other sources, the Federal Government ought to assume responsibilities.

The Supreme Court struck down the N.I.R.A. (The National Industrial Recovery Act) and A.A.A. (Agricultural Adjustment Administration) in 1935 and 1936. The Supreme Court upto 1937 was a conservative body and ruled out numerous New Deal measures as unconstitutional. Hence, during his second and third terms, Roosevelt appointed eight new judges and this changed the character of the Supreme Court. Franklin D. Roosevelt adopted the Keynesian theory of Government spending and asked Congress for large new appropriations for relief and public works.

NEW DEAL LEGISLATION

1. **Industry and Labour.** The National Industrial Recovery Act of 1933 aimed at the recovery of America from the depression, by enabling people back to work, to earn wages again, and to buy more. It also aims at stablising prices, and restricting competition to protect business. Further it aimed at raising wages and lowering hours of work, but getting rid of child labour and making trade unions legal.

   The National Industrial Recovery Act set up a Public Works Administration (P.W.A.) and National Recovery Administration (N.R.A.). The P.W.A. encouraged building of public works of all kinds. The Federal Government employed many men on building Dams, Aerodromes, Warships, Post Offices and various Government Offices. The Federal Government both gave and lent money to states and cities for public works... Schools, Hospitals, Roads, Bridges, etc. The P.W.A. provided work for millions of men.

The N.R.A. had to draft rules or codes to govern industries. These codes would have the force of a law. These codes abolished child labour, shortened hours of work, fixed a minimum wage and stopped unfair competitive price cutting. These codes gave labourers to bargain collectively through their representatives.

The National Industrial Recovery Act was not successful for three reasons:

(1) The enforcement of codes was not possible.

(2) "Big Business" raised prices, and disliked Government control and labourers' right to bargain collectively.

(3) In 1935, the Supreme Court voided the Act on the ground that the legislative power had been transferred to the Executive and its scope had been extended beyond the inter-state commerce.

(4) The Wagner Act of 1935 gave labourers the right of collective bargaining. It was criticised on the ground that it protected only the rights of businessmen. The citrics further remarked that the Wagner Act made a class discrimination.

2. **Agriculture. The Farmers Relief Act (1933) and the A.A.A.** Even in the period of prosperity American farmers had gained nothing. During the depression they had suffered a lot. The prices of farm products fell beyond the cost price. They could not sell their farm products overseas due to tariff retaliation by foreign countries against American goods.

   Franklin D. Roosevelt did much to help farmers. The Farmers Relief Act of 1933 created the Agricultural Adjustment Administration known as A.A.A. The A.A.A. encouraged co-operative marketing of farm products and reduced the acreage. To reduce the acreage the Federal Government paid cash to farmers. The money needed to pay farmers was got through the levy of excise taxes.

Criticism

To pay farmers for producing less according to the enemies of Franklin D. Roosevelt, showed the economic insanity of his Government. The Supreme Court held it void on the ground that the A.A.A. had impaired the states' Rights and the excise taxes were unconstitutional.

3. **Currency, Banking and Finance.** When Franklin D. Roosevelt came to office all the banks in the U.S.A. had closed their doors. His first task was to make the National Financial System work again. Within a week of entering office he got Congress to pass an Emergency Banking Act, giving him control over the banks and power to re-open these banks which he considered solvent.

The Banking Act of 1933 established stricter control of the banks. A Federal Deposit Insurance Corporation was set up. This Corporation guaranteed deposits in banks and safeguarded depositors against losing their money in a time of panic. Confidence was restored, banks were reopened and people began to deposit their money in them again. Making use of Federal Reserve banking system created by Wilson, Roosevelt encouraged banks to lend money at lower rates of interest.

The Securities Act (1933) regulated the stock exchanges. It stopped the formation of fraudulent companies. It forbade the buying of stocks on margin less than 55 per cent.

The Federal Government withdraw gold and silver from circulation, bought them and stored them. The paper Dollar was devalued to less than 60 per cent of its former value. These increased the quantity of money in circulation.

4. **The Tennessee Valley Authority.** During the First World War the Government had built at Muscle Shoals on the Tennessee River a dam to provide power, and a Nitrate Factory. Senator Norris of Nebraska had twice got through Congress bills which would have enabled the Federal Government to use the Muscle Shoals Dam for the benefit of the inhabitants of the Tennessee Valley. But Presidents Coolidge and Hoover had vetoed them.

   Franklin D. Roosevelt took up Norris scheme and extended it. In 1933 the Tennessee Valley Authority (T.V.A.) was created. Through the T.V.A., Roosevelt planned the welfare of the whole Tennessee Valley, a region consisting of 41,000 square miles covering parts of seven states. The T.V.A. took over the Muscle Shoals Dam and built other Dams. It set up hydroelectric stations and solo electricity direct to industry and farmers, at rates far below those charged by private companies. It undertook schemes of flood control, built navigation channels in the Tennessee River; stopped soil erosion by planting trees; aided farmers by developing new fertilizers and built model villages. Cheap electricity brought great changes in the lives of the farmers in the valley. It also attracted industry. T.V.A. meant something more than the business of selling electricity. The Government replanned the whole life of the valley by using its natural resources for the benefit of its inhabitants.

Criticism

The private companies criticised the T.V.A. yardstick in fixing rates for the supply of electricity. They pointed out that Government money carried no interest, and that the Government had no taxes to pay. Congressmen resented the political independence of the T.V.A. and prevented any extension of the idea to other parts.

5. **Social Security.** Before 1933, the U.S.A. had no national scheme of unemployment or health insurance or of old age pension. The Social Security Act (1935) was very important of all New Deal Laws. The Act established a scheme of old age pensions, created a plan of unemployment insurance and provided Federal grants to States to help the blind and to care for children's health.

   Down to 1940 Franklin D. Roosevelt administration spent about 16,000 million dollars on relief measures. Every year it spent more than it took in. National debt increased from 22, 000 million dollars to 44, 000 million dollars.

6. **Soil Conservation.** A Soil Conservation Service set up in 1934, set out to persuade farmers to adopt terraced farming and other conservation practices. The government added extensively to its forest reserves and restricted the grazing of cattle on public land.
7. **Civilian Conservation Corps.** This was set up in 1933, to provide temporary work for boys between the ages of 18 and 25. By 1940 the C.C.C. had employed a total of 2,000,000 boys, mainly on reforestation and other activities.
8. **Shipping and Housing.** The maritime commission undertook to build fifty ships and handed them over to private companies. Cheap houses for low income people were constructed.
9. **The Works Progress Administration.** It gave jobs to millions of men and women. The government gave them wages enough to keep them alive. The W.P.A. built roads, dams, airports, schools, hospitals, playgrounds, swimming pools etc.
10. **Control over Drought and Dust.** In the years 1933-35 the great plains were hit by a serious drought and there was a danger that the region might become a desert. To tackle the problem Congress provided funds by which seeds and livestocks were to be provided to the farmers. 190 million trees were also planted to reduce the velocity of the wind and to retain the moisture.

Results of the New Deal

It was not revolutionary as there was no change in the ownership. Big corporations become bigger. It gave the Federal Government broader responsibilities to regulate the movement of economy to provide security and to protect the unprivileged groups.

The opponents of the New Deal remarked that it attacked private enterprise, imposed bureaucratic regulations, increased the national debt., and gave privilege to labour. The supporters of the New Deal argued that the falling of private enterprises was inevitable in a mature economy. Public money should be spent in such things which would add to the National wealth, so that budget deficit and increase in the national debt would not cause alarm. An unrestricted private enterprise of the 1920's could not promote general welfare. The Republicans accepted the basic New Deal Legislation.

Although the New Deal could not restore prosperity, it introduced a new spirit — a change of the outlook of many millions of Americans. Many of the ideas the New Deal put into practice — collective bargaining between employers and employees, the regulation of the stock exchange, the control of the output of crops, the restiction of hours of work — are now accepted part of the normal pattern of American life. Franklin D. Roosevelt made Americans realise that the vast resources of the United States should be used by means of National Planning for the benefit of all and not merely for the private profit of a few. Americans began to feel that the Federal Government, representing all the people, should look after the unemployed and the poor. Thus, Roosevelt achieved without the introduction of socialism.

The satisfactory achievements of the New Deal are the Dams built on the Western States, rural electrification, the promotion of soil conservation and the construction by the P.W.A. of Roads, Bridges, Schools, Hospitals and Works of art. By its forward-looking and adventurous attitude, it restored American morale.

World War II

As President Roosevelt was enacting an enlightened foreign policy towards Latin America and United States dependencies, storm clouds were gathering in far off places. While the Axis powers started ravaging Europe, the United States, steeped in isolationism, proclaimed its neutrality. But as war continued unabated, America became increasingly unneutral in thought and deed. With the infamous Japanese attack on Pearl Harbour, America plunged into headlong war and helped to bring it to a successful conclusion.

The Neutrality Acts

In 1935, the Italian dictator Beni'o Mussolini pushed his normally pacific citizens into a brutal war of aggression against the Empire of Abyssinia. The reaction of the U.S. was the passage of the Neutrality Act of 1935, which enabled the President to declare the existence of war and then to prohibit the export of arms to belligerents. In 1937, provisions were added to prohibit any financial aid to belligerents.

Amendments of Neutrality Act

For nearly two years before the actual outbreak, Roosevelt and Cardel Hull, the Secretary of State had been looking for ways of checking the drift towards war. They saw the futility of appeasement. It was Neville Chamberlain who insisted that if Hitler was sufficiently appeased, he would finally settle down. His illusion was finally shattered by the seizure of prague. In July, after Chamberlain had finally dropped appeasement, Roosevelt asked Senate leaders of both parties to consider revising the neutrality legislation but it failed. But when the war came, the America sentiment immediately changed. Congress passed a new Neutrality Act in November allowing the sale of munitions to the beligerents. under cash and carry rules. While at the same time, American merchantships were forbidden to enter the combat zone. It was followed by a curiously quite winter in Europe-which was called the "phony war" by Senator Borah.

Fall of France

In the spring of 1940 German forces seized Denmark and Norway, in April overran Holland and Belgium and in May quickly inflicted a crushing defeat in the French army. German forces crushed the entire British army at Dunkirk — American opinion veered sharply in support of the British and the President shipped surplus arms and planes to them. The German forces continued their stunning successes and France was capitulated on June 22, 1940. A majority of the people felt that defeating Hitler was more important than staying out of war.

Battle of Britain

The fall of France was followed by aerial warfare, now named the "Battle of Britain" in which the Royal Airforce beat back the German Luftwaffe destroying enemy planes at a rate of two German for one British. In October the Germans and Italians moved into the Balkans. The British countered by landings on Crete and other Greek islands and beginning in November, punished the Italian Navy and pulvertized the Italian army in North Africa.

Panama Declaration

A Conference was held at Panama with a view to keep the war out of the Western hemisphere on October 3, 1939 in which a warning to the belligerent nations to keep off the Neutrality zone was issued.

The Act of Havana

Another conference of the ministers at Havana in 1940 passed the Act of Havana by which transfer of any European colony in American to non-Americans was forbidden. In August 1940, Roosevelt signed the Ogdenburg agreement with the Canadian Prime Minister which provided for joint defence of the two countries.

American Policy

As opinion crystallized the administration became firmer. In May 1940 Aviation industry was expanded to the level of producing 50,000 war planes a year. By October, Congress appropriated no less than 17,692,000,000 for defence. In September 1940, the Congress passed the Conscription Act and Selective Service Act which required the registration of all men between twenty one and thirty five years of age. Later the laws were made more stiff and the age range was extended between 18 and 45 years. The period of training was also increased to 18 months.

Hostility with Japan

United States had its own peculiar problems in its relations with Japan. In the spring of 1940, Secretary of State Cordel Hull had cautioned the world against tinkering with the Dutch East Indies. In September, he made a similar statement about French Indo-China directly to Japan, which was even then on the verge of formal military alliance with Germany and Italy. Roosevelt forbade the shipment of oil or scrap iron outside the Western hemisphere, except to Britain. This prohibition caused profound indignation of Japan against U.S.

The Election of 1940

Under this tumultuous context, the American people went through a presidential campaign. The Democrats violating tradition nominated Roosevelt for a third term. Roosevelt reiterated in a number of speeches that American boys were "not going to be sent into any foreign wars". In the end, Roosevelt was re-elected though by a reduced majority. The Americans were afraid that if Britain was conquered by Hitler, United States would have to fight the Axis powers, without any powerful ally. Probably the chief reason for Roosevelt's victory was the feeling of many independent voters that it was wise to keep an experienced man in office in a time of crisis and that his defeat would be regarded as a repudiation of his foreign policy.

Land-Lease Act of March 1941

Roosevelt interpreted the election result as a mandate for all out support of Britain. In a speech on December 29, he declared that "the Axis powers are not going to win this war" and that the United States "must be the great arsenal of democracy". Since the British needed supplies far in excess of what they could pay for and transport. In order to solve the financial problems, Roosevelt devised the land lease programme by which he proposed that goods rather than money be lent to Britain, with the understanding that repayment be made in kind after the war. The

Congress approved it in March 1941 and authorised President to lend goods to any country whose defence is vital to the defence of the U.S. Henry Simson, the Secretary of War described this as a declaration of economic war and it was only a matter of time before Germany and U.S. were involved in armed conflict.

Undeclared Naval War

As German submarines were deeply engaged in sinking British freighters, U.S. herself undertook to transport war material. American naval and Air patrols in the North Atlantic were alerted. Soon shooting followed. In September the destroyer Gheer was attacked by a submarine and in October one of the two attacked destroyers, Reuben James was only Congress swept away what was left of the Neutrality Act. Even merchant vessels were armed. This was probably as close to the full belligerency as it was possible to go without taking the final plunge.

Atlantic Charter

All these events had made United States and Britain to become more intimate. Roosevelt and Chunchil held a conference on a battleship near the coast of Newfoundland in August 1941. Their main purpose was to discuss Britain's need for supplies and they issued an eight point statement of war aims which became known as the Atlantic Charter. It called for a peace which would give all men security and freedom from fear and want aid for the disarmament of aggressor nations.

Far East Rumble

Nazi victories gave Japan a free hand in the Far East. Japanese forces began to infiltrate into Indo-China and the Japanese leaders made it plain that the "new order" of the "Japanese coprosperity sphere" was to include Indonesia as well as China and Manchuko. The American Government retaliated it by giving further credits to China and restricting sales of scrap iron to Japan. After sometime when the troop movements of Japan made obvious of its preparation for attack, gasoline shipments were stopped and Japanese assets in the U.S. were forzen. Subsequently the compromise talks between Japanese ambassador Kichisaburo Nomura and Secretary Hull held in Washington broke down before the end of November.

Pearl Harbour

A Japanese carrier force was noted absent from its home base by American intelligence. The best American guess was that it was headed for Singapore or Philippines. But instead, having decided to cripple the American fleet, it attacked the Pearl Harbour naval base of Hawaii on Sunday morning December 7, 1941. In this attack 2403 persons were killed and over 1000 injured. Nearly 150 aeroplanes were destroyed and six battleships were sunk or severely damaged. The following day Congress declared war on Japan and three days later the Axis Powers declared war on the United States. On January 1, 1942 representatives of U.S., Britain, Soviet Union, China and Twenty two other countries signed a Declaration of the U.N. by which they accepted the Atlantic Charter and pledged themselves not to make peace until the enemy had been defeated.

17

American Domestic and Foreign Policy–1950's

Under Truman

After coming to power, Truman announced his determination to continue the social welfare legislation. The Congress voted for a sharp reduction in war time taxes and gave relief to the tax payers. These measures gave a welcome end to the New Deal.

The Congress enacted the Taft — Hartley Act in 1947 and this law defined the unfair practice of the trade unions and banned jurisdictional strikes, sympathetic strikes, secondary boycotts and contribution to political parties.

The workers received wage increase and pension benefits.

A National Housing Act provided for the allotment of federal funds for slum clearance and house building for low income group.

An agricultural Act extended price support to farm products.

After the end of World War II steps were taken for reconstruction.

Under Truman it was decided to assist the backward countries with scientific and technological data so as to render them less vulnerable to communist influence. So effective were these ventures that Russia found it risky to extend her influence to the West.

Eisenhower

The administration of Eisenhower was a period of economic boom. Great encouragement was given to private enterprises. It came in for favourable treatment. Production continued to expand, workers received higher wages and price controls disappeared. The old age and retirement benefits were not only increased but were given wider application.

Large amounts were allotted for undertaking house and road building programmes.

Alaska and Hawaii were admitted as states into the union.

The increased farm production created large surpluses leading to the downward trend in prices. This affected the standard of living of the peasants.

The Agricultural Act of 1956 brought to give relief to the cultivators. It introduced the soil bank to pay compensation to the farmers for removing marginal lands form cultivation and raised the price support to farm produce.

The Landrum Griffen Act of 1959 required labour unions to report their membership and finances to the government and banned secondary boycotts and picketing. As a true democrat Eisenhower promoted civil liberties and sought to undo social segregation.

Foreign Policy After World War II

Dulles decided to rely upon a policy of "containment" of communism. In accordance with this policy the administration interfered in Guatemala and entered into entangling alliances with amenable powers of Europe and Asia.

Even before the end of World War II, it became obvious for the United States that Soviet co-operation could not he enlisted for the establishment of a new world order. Hence, these two nations started drifting towards opposite directions. Soviet Unions launched an expansionist policy while U.S.A. took active strides in the achievement of free society, freedom of individual enterprise, orderly development in the inland and its foreign policy too aimed at the establishment of the same in other countries along with the policies of Economic Reconstruction, freeing the enslaved nations and maintaining their national integrity. These features were conspicuously obvious in its foreign policy after World War II.

Foreign Policy of Harry S. Truman (1945-53)

His foreign policy was chiefly moulded by the Cold War with Russia and it was a fact that the World War II had thrust world leadership upon the United States and in the post World War II period. United States accepted the leadership for the sake of her own security. Soviet Union, so long an ally of U.S.A. had now turned a rival due to the mutual distrust and jealousy caused during the World War II and the hostility between them came to be called as Cold War — a condition of neither peace nor war. In the negotiations of peace treaties Soviet Union adopted dilatory tactics and was aiming at the establishment of its regime in Poland, Rumania and Bulgaria. Soviet Russia turned Eastern Germany into a communist puppet as against Potsdam Agreement of 1945. All these iron curtain conspiracies made U.S.A. to retard through its policy of containment.

Truman Doctrine

He followed the policy of combating the communist danger by checking its ever increasing intervention in Greece and Turkey which, when liberated after World War II, were to fall a victim to Russian Bear. Truman advocated his famous doctrine in the Congress in March 19, 1947 and sought sanction of money to the tune of 400,000,000 dollars for economic and military assistance to Greece and Turkey.

Marshall Plan

George C. Marshall the U.S. Secretary of State announced a plan of American aid in reviving the economies of the war desolated nations. Countries like Italy, France and Western Germany were suffering from economic depression and deprivation which could easily become a prey to communists and hence they had to safeguard through economic restoration. In November 1947, Truman requested Congress, seventeen billion dollars. It was certain that the "Marshall Plan" officially known as the "European Recovery Programme" not only hampered the growth of communist parties in the nations of Western Europe, but also enabled those countries in a short time to regain their pre-war level of Agricultural and Industrial production.

North Atlantic Treaty

The logical sequel to economic co-operation was military alliance. U.S. affirmed its support for regional security pacts like Brussels Pact of 1948. With this encouragement the State department sponsored negotiations for the expansion of the Brussels Pact which led to the formation in 1949, of the North Atlantic Treaty Organisation. It combined every principal North Atlantic, Baltic and Mediterranean Nation that dared to join a Military Alliance of joint defence against Russia. The organisation was given substance by the establishment of an international army. General Eisenhover was its first Supreme Allied Commander in Europe. This epoch making agreement was the first permanent Military Alliance ever entered into by the U.S.

The Berlin Airlift

In April 1948 Russian relations with Western Europe worsened as the Soviets attempted to starve the allies out of occupied Berlin by closing of all ground communications. The Allies supplied Berlin by Air for eleven months and refused to flinch at the prospect of Russian aerial attack. In the end the baffled Russian backed down at a considerable cost of prestige in Europe.

TRUMAN AND THE FAR EAST

China

Nationalist Government of Chiang-Kai-Shek had its catastrophic fall in its bitter civil war with the communists. This was attributed to the lack of effective half hearted and inconsistent assistance of United States. Truman administration was severely critisized for this.

Japan

Allied council under the leadership of Mac Arthur had taken up the administration of Japan after its surrender. A constitution was drawn by the elected Diet in 1946, in which a bill of rights was incorporated. An efficient administration was offered to Japan to the extent that the services of Mac Arthur in his own words "carried to the land of our vanquished foe the solace and hope and faith of Christian morals".

Korean Volcano Erupts

The principal test of the United Nations was the defence of South Korea against the aggression of North Korea and Communist China. As the richest and strongest of the sincere members of the U.N., most of the burden of the Korean "police action" was carried by the United States. At the end of World War II, Korea, North of 38 degree parallel was occupied by communist troops; South of that line, by United States and Allied forces. The temporary line gradually became a semi permanent boundary as each group insisted, it had the right to organise the whole. Free elections were held under the supervision of U.N. in 1948, following which the Republic of Korea was established under President Syngman Rhee. In 1949 American troops were withdrawn.

In June 1950, the North Koreans using Russian equipment, invaded South Korea. President Truman ordered American forces into Korea under the command of Mac Arthur. Though American forces initially suffered defeats, in September, a perfectly executed amphibious operation was performed at Inchom and within ten days the capital of the Republic Seoul was liberated. While the troops proceeded further to Manchurian border, Chinese communists troops entered and drove the U.N. forces back to thirty-eight parallel. Armistice negotiations began in July 1951 and dragged on inconclusively till late 1952. By this police action-communist aggression by direct attack appeared to be stopped. Thus, Truman's primary purpose was achieved.

Dwight D. Eisenhower's Foreign Policy (1953-1961)

Eisenhower in his inaugural address promised to follow the policy of Internationalism and pledged American co-operation with other powers to wipe out causes of mutual fear and distrust among nations. His Secretary of State John, Foster Dulles discontented with containment policy advocated for more dynamism in Foreign policy.

Korean Armistice

In compliance with his electoral pledge, Eisenhover went to Korea to get the stalled armistice talks in motion in December 1952 and negotiations were renewed. Finally, in July 1953 an armistice was arrived at with North Korean and Chinese Communists and the two parties agreed to exchange the prisoners of war. The proposal of unification of Korea in Geneva Conference 1954 was defeated by Communist opposition.

Indo-China and S.E.A.T.O.

When the Communist led National movements conquered France in Indo-China, a conference was held at Geneva in 1954. Indo-China was divided into three parts — Loas, Cambodia and Vietnam. Vietnam was to be divided at the 17th parallel. When South Vietnam and North Vietnam struggled to achieve a stable regime, Americans assisted South Vietnam and North Vietnam was supported by Russia and China. At this context United States took the lead in setting up the South East Asia Treaty Organisation in 1954, a defence alliance of all friendly Nations who agreed to mutual economic co-operation and protection against subversion or aggression.

Formosa

Tension became so acute in the Far East when Chinese Communists boosted up the military preparations for the attack on Chiang Kai-Shek in Formosa in 1955. Eisenhover took an unparalleled step of asking the Congress for a advance authorisation to use armed forces to repel a communist assault on Formasa. Besides, U.S. continued to deny recognition to Red China and block her entry into the United Nations.

Europe and Middle East Crises

Next to Korea, the most troublesome part of the world from an American point of view was that known as the Near East or Middle East which lies between India and the Mediterranean. There was a power vacuum when British abandoned its policing policy in this part of the world. After World War II the new State of Israel was founded there mostly financed by American private gifts. Neighbouring Arab States dedicated themselves to its extermination. At the same time Western Europe became increasingly dependent on Near Eastern petroleum which came via the Suez Canal. In October 1956, Colonel Nasser nationalised the canal and barred Israeli shipping. Israel, Britain and France in succession attacked Egypt. In the Suez crisis the U.S. found herself in an odd situation of joining with Soviet Union in condemning the aggressive activities of England and France and these two countries withdrew their forces within a week.

In March 1957, the Congress adopted a formal military policy, at the request of President Eisenhover, concerning the Near East called the "Eisenhower Doctrine" according to which the President was authorised to use armed force to assist any nation which asked for help against the aggressive attack of a communist country.

Russo-American Relations

Nikita Khruschev succeeded Joseph Stalin and eased the political tension in Soviet Russia. A cordial relationship between America and Russia was expected but the pubble of hope was pricked when the Russians had exploded "Hydrogen bomb" in 1954, the most lethal weapon. Besides, both these nations entered into a mad race for more sophisticated weapons like Inter continental Ballistic Missiles. Soon Russia launched the first artificial satellite called Sputnik in October 1957 which staggered the Americans. U.S.A. also retaliated it by its Explorer I and the race gathered more momentum. To put an end to this unhealthy race, United Nations convened a Disarmament Commission in London but in vain. A summit meeting was arranged on May 16, 1960 in Paris but turned out to be an incredible fiasco due to V2 reconnoiter incident. Eisenhower assumed personal responsibility for it. So the conference collapsed and Russians no more trusted Eisenhower.

Cuba's Castroism Spells Communism

Latin American countries received very limited assistance from U.S.A., after World War II. In 1954, Eisenhover sent military help to overthrow communist assisted Gautemalan Government. In 1959, Fidel Castro, a young student leader toppled the British regime in Cuba with the sufferance of U.S.A. but soon he alienated American sympathy by nationalising the properties owned by U.S. Soon Russians' help was sought by Castro. Eisenhower applied Monroe Doctrine and declared to meet any interference with force and broke of diplomatic relations with Cuba in 1961.

Foreign Policy of John Fitzgerald Kennedy (1961-63)

In foreign policy Kennedy's record was much more positive and eventful. Changes in world affairs were making not only new methods necessary but also a fundamental revaluation of the aims of American policy. With the increased flexibility in international affairs, it became possible for the U.S. and the Soviet Union to negotiate a settlement instead of remaining forzen in attitudes of mutual fear and hostility. In July 1963, in the hope of providing for security against possible atomic mis-understanding a "hot line" telephone was installed between Moscow and Washington.

Latin American Problems

As soon as Kennedy assumed office, he had to bear the discredit of the blunder committed by the Central Intelligence Agency in Cuba. 14,000 Cuban refugees armed and trained by U.S. launched an attack on Cuba at the Bay of Pigs, expecting popular uprising and the result was complete fiasco. Realisting the situations in Latin America, an alliance for progress was outlined in 1961 by U.S. Dominican Republic was saved from subversion by Trujillo. Kennedy visited Venezuela, Columbia and Mexico to maintain cordiality. Another disappointment for U.S. was the lack of support for Latin American countries for sanctions against Castro eventhough a declaration to the effect that Castro's regime was incompatible with the principles of the Organisation of American States was obtained at the Second punta del Este Conference.

Cuban Episode

In July 1963, the U.S. became aware that Soviet missiles were being shipped to Cuba and placed in sites where they could threaten the U.S. Kennedy took a firm stand by insisting that the Russian missiles must be shipped back to Russia and implying that the alternative would be atomic warfare. At the same time Kennedy was careful to leave the Russians dignified way of retreat which would give the impression that there had been a notation between equals. After thirty six hours of tension and anxiety, the good news that the Russians were going to withdraw their missiles became public.

Policy in Laos

When a civil war broke out, a settlement was negotiated according to which a tripartite regime consisting of the representatives of western, neutralists and communist factions.

Congo Problem

When Belgium evacuated Congo in June 1960, due to lack of proper leadership, anarchy prevailed there. U.N. security forces intervened at the instance of the Congo Government. Even then Left Wing leader Patrice Lumumba was assassinated and U.N. General Secretary Dag

Hammarskjold died in the cause of Congo peace. Kennedy gave every possible help to the United Nations.

Nuclear Test Ban Treaty

A treaty to prevent the pollution of the planet by atomic fall out from atmospheric or oceanic tests of nuclear devices was signed in Moscow by the United States, Great Britain and the Soviet Union in September 1963. If President Kennedy is remembered as a great President, the test ban may be his principal monument.

Berlin Wall

In 1961, When Khruschev met Kennedy at Vienna, he threatened to turn the whole Berlin city over to the Communist East Germans, with all the explosive possibilities of World War III. But Kennedy munted up the armed forces to thwart the attempts of Russians. This time the Russians backed off. Their response was Berlin Wall, constructed of barbed wire and concrete. It was designed to prevent the drain of population from the East German "Paradise" to West Germany. Kennedy felt that wall was not worth a war and avoided an all out conflict with Russia on the Berlin issue.

Foreign Policy of Lyndon Baines Johnson (1963-69)

The foreign policy of Johnson was marked by the feature of Interventionism. While the relations with Soviet Union showed definite improvement under his leadership, the U.S. used its armed forces against communism in Latin America and the Far East. The first example of Johnsonian interventionism was in the Dominican Republic in April 1965.

Dominican Republic

When the leftist group professing to be the followers to Juan Boxh, the deposed President of the Republic, revolted against the conservative leadership fearing communist instigation, Johnson sent 20,000 troops, to protect the American lives and properties in the Republic. With the assistence of other Latin American countries order and peace was restored. In the free elections held in 1965 Balaguer was elected President.

The Vietnam War

Johnson had to take active praticipation in South Vietnam to save it from the communists. Tonkin Gulf became the centre of Naval battles. Following assault on the American camp at Pleiku by the Vietcong, the American troops resorted to Air attack and full scale use of American troops. More than half a million American men were committed to this war. As the war dragged on for a number of years, Johnson's popularity too considerably declined.

Foreign Policy of Richard Nixon

Nixon's foreign policy embodied in Nixon Doctrine was outlined by himself in July 1969. "United States will participate in the defence and development of allies and friends but we will help where it makes of real difference and is considered in our interest".

Policy in Vietnam

Nixon wanted to bring peace to South Vietnam and honour to America by following a policy of parallel tracks of Negotiation and Vietnamization. By Vietnamization he wanted to make South Vietnam to stand on its own. After negotiation for four years, an agreement was signed in Paris on January 27, 1973 by U.S. and three Vietnamese Parties "The Agreement on ending the war and the Restoring peace in Vietnam".

Nixon opened a new chapter by re-establishing relations with China. Dr. Kissinger, the Secretary of State visited China in July 1971 and paved the way for Nixon's visit of China in February 1972. Since 1971, the relations between U.S. and China have been constantly improving. Not only the commercial but also cultural and scientific contact between them are also on the increase.

Relations with Soviet Russia

The first two years of Nixon's administration showed a clear trend towards greater understanding between Soviet Union and U.S. This trend was interrupted by the tension which arose as a result of the Soviet role in the violation of cease-fire in the Middle East by Egypt. But the strategic Arms Limitations Treaty in May 1971 agreed by the two countries based on a link between offensive and defensive limitations is a remarkable achievement. The two countries had agreed to co-operate in a very extensive field. Henry Alfred Kissinger, the Secretary of State of Nixon had played a vital role in designing the foreign policy of U.S. and became one of the indispensable members of Nixon's administration.

Importance of Truman Administration

President Truman remained in power from 1945 to 1952. A Democrat from Missouri, he was elected to the Senate in 1934 and to Vice Presidency in 1944. Upon the death of Roosevelt in office, he became President. A close follower of Roosevelt's policy, he sought to continue the New Deal and to conciliate Russia. But difficulties appeared formidable. The post war-country did not welcome continued progressivism and the consequent expansion of federal control. There came a conservative reaction under Republican leadership.

The transition from war to peace demanded changes — social, political and economic. Soviet Russia seemed determined to extend the sphere of her influence, for which she wanted disorganised Europe. This awakened the administration to the perils ahead. In his attempt to check the rising tide of international communism he not only did formulate aid-programmes but did fight a major war in Korea.

Reaction Against New Deal

The implementation of the New Deal legislations and the conduct of war were attended with the imposition of vexatious controls upon the life of the people. At the end of war, the inhabitants rallied to the Republican Party for the recovery of their rights. In the Congressional election of 1946 the Republicans wrested control of both the houses of Congress. President Truman announced his determination to continue the social welfare legislation and consequent imposition of governmental regulation, but the Congress dominated the Republicans proceeded to liquidate the agencies of the New Deal and social control. Thus, it rejected funds for the working of the National Resources Planning Board, turned over the Employment Service to State governments, cut down allotments made for the Interior and Agriculture Departments and terminated the Farm Security Administration. It also voted for a sharp reduction in war time taxes and gave relief to the tax payers. These measures gave a welcome end to the New Deal.

Having achieved these, the Republicans decided to deprive the labour of the gains it wrested during the New deal and World War periods so as to strengthen the capitalistic order. In 1947 Congress enacted the Taft Hartley Act and carried it over Truman's veto. This law defined the unfair labour practices of the trade unions and banned jurisdictional strikes, sympathetic strikes, secondary boycotts and contribution to political parties. The unions were required to abide by a sixty day cooling off period before launching a strike so as to give opportunity to the athorities to seek a settlement of disputes. The union leaders were directed to swear that they were not communists. Only those unions which submitted financial accounts and declared that their officers did not belong to or support any organisation that advocated the overthrow of government by force, could have their cases heard by the Labour Board. The closed shops or unions which forbade the employment of non-union workers were outlawed. And the employers were permitted to due the unions for broken contracts and seek damages. Because of these restrictions, the labour condemned the law as a slave bill. Despite this, the workers received wage increase and pension benefits.

A National Housing Act provided for the allotment of federal funds for slum clearance and house building for low income groups. An agricultural Act extended price support to farm products.

The Reorganisation Act of 1946 improved the working and procedure of Congress. The bureaus and agencies were consolidated and Congressmen were given more of financial privileges. The Twenty Second Amendment to the Constitution (1915) restricted the term of the President to two. A new Department of Defence and another for Air Force were created. Because of the development of atomic energy, Congress set up an Atomic Energy Commission and a Joint Congressional Committee on Atomic Energy.

Settlements

In 1945 Truman, Stalin and Attlee met in a conference at Potsdam near Berlin to consider the post war issues. They decided to entrust the administration of defeated Germany to an Allied Control Council and to settle peace treaties with the defeated powers. A council of the foreign ministers of Britain, France, Russia and the United States called a peace conference at Paris in 1946 and concluded peace treaties with Italy, Hungary, Bulgaria, Rumania and Finland. These settlements took away territories from these countries, imposed upon them heavy war indemnity and deprived them of their war machine. However, differences with Russia prevented conclusion of peace treaties with Japan and Germany.

The United States played an effective role in bringing about the trial and execution of war criminals and military occupation of Japan and Germany. As the Allied Control Council could not agree on the administration of Germany due to ideological differences, the United States, France and Britain in 1946 united their three zones into a single territorial unit called Trizonia. Russia retained the independent control of the Eastern zone. However, the location of West Berlin in the communist held East Germany created problems in the context of the Cold War. In 1948 Russia ordered a blockade of Berlin but the Allies faced the situation squarely and arranged for an airlift of supplies to the city. In the next year the Allied powers agreed to discuss the issue and the blockade was lifted. The people of the three Allied zones, as agreed by their conquerors, decided to reorganise Trizonia into a federal democratic republic with provision to admit states from the Russian zone. In 1949 the Federal Republic of Germany with Bonn as capital was created. Russia organised her occupation zone into a Democratic Germany under communist rule. These developments divided Germany into two states and left her reunification at the mercy of big power politics.

Rejection of Isolationism

After the end of World War II, the United States made no attempt to retreat to isolationism. With seven per cent of the world's population but thirty per cent of its estimated income, the country found it no difficult a task to emerge as a arbiter of destiny of the international community. She controlled the Atlantic as well as the Pacific and influenced the developments else where. In accordance with her new status, the country accepted the United Nations Organisation, wrote off the loans given to the Allied Powers for economic recovery and allotted huge amounts for promoting the reconstruction of the war-torn and backward countries.

The Russian communism and its concept of world revolution presented a powerful challenge to American expansionism and its capitalistic order. Russia not only annexed the Baltic states and set up communist governments in eastern Europe but also supported revolutionary movements in other regions. It appeared that both Greece anc Turkey would fall to communism and Russia would extend her influence to the Mediterranean. Therefore, in 1947 in his address to Congress, Trunan demanded extension of American aid to any country whose freedom and independence were threatened through aggression from within or without. In response to what was called Truman Doctrine; Congress voted forty crores of dollars for furnishing arms and provisions to Greece and Turkey and assisting them with naval and military commissions. These enabled the two countries to reorganise their armed forces and thwart communist threat.

This was followed by the Marshall Plan or European Recovery Programme. In 1947 George Marshall, Secretary of State declared that if the countries of Europe would reach an agreement on their needs to cover the cost of reconstruction of the programme. He also made it clear that it was not directed against hunger, poverty, desperation and chaos. The European countries welcomed this announcement. However, Foreign Minister Molotov of U.S.S.R. suggested that instead of collective aid, individual help with each nation as a unit should be granted, for organising Europe under her control. As this suggestion proved unacceptable, Russia withdrew her support to the plan. Nevertheless, sixteen European countries joined together to draw up plans for recovery and the United States furnished funds for implementation. Recovery was slow yet the lure of money induced the people to reject communist overtures. In fact both the Truman Doctrine and the Marshall plan were related programmes, aimed at safeguarding American interests in Europe and as such they represented a part of the strategy of containing Russia.

Rightly, the Soviets considered them as manoeuvres intended for gaining advantages in the Cold war.

In 1948 Congress authorized Truman to initiate steps for promoting collective security with the co-operation of friendly powers. Accordingly, the President opened negotiations with countries, which were opposed to communism, leading to the settlement of the North Atlantic Treaty in 1948 and creation of the North Atlantic Treaty Organisation in 1950. The twelve nations which joined this defensive alliance, pledged to maintain the security of Northern Atlantic region by use of force and to consider any threat to any one of them as a threat to the security of all. Apart from these, Congress made appropriations to assist the backward countries with scientific and technological data so as to render them less vulnerable to communist influence. So effective were these ventures, that Russia found it risky to extend her influence to the west.

The Korean War

The Korean War that broke out on 25 June, 1950 marked a violent confrontation between the American bloc and the Soviet bloc and an extension of the Cold War into a hot war. The hostilities began, when the troops of the Soviet backed North Korea crossed the 38th parallel and attacked the American backed South Korea. At the instance of the United States, the United Nations Organisation condemned the aggression and called upon North Korea to withdaw her forces. But as North Korea rejected the call, the Security Council authorised military action and permitted the United States to organise a united command of the United Nations forces in Korea.

Truman appointed General Mac Arthur in command of the operations. Yet the communist offensive continued unabated and the South Korean forces were pushed to Pusan in the extreme South. With the arrival of reinforcements the American forces launched a counter-offensive, drove the North Koreans back across the border and occupied their capital Pyongyang. It appeared that the communist forces were defeated, but China came to the rescue of North Korea and threw into the arena her powerful army. Encountered by a major offensive by the Chinese, the Americans retreated. There followed a stage of attack and counter-attack and advance and retreat until the war reached a stalemate, with the line of battle settled just north of the old boundary.

The two sides opened a negotiation in their bid to seek settlement. For more than a year they talked in vain, for no agreement could be reached over the issue of repatriation of prisoners of war. The communists demanded the return of all prisoners irrespective of individual desires.

The United States did not agree for fear that those who rejected communism would be killed as traitors, but insisted upon voluntary repatriation. The alignment of boundary between two Koreas too causes differences. Dissatisfied with the talks, Mac Arthur demanded authority to reinvade North Korea and carry the war to China. For fear that it would lead the country to major war, Truman removed Mac Arthur form command. As no settlement could be found, the United States broke off the negotiations. However, after the death of Stalin in 1953, Malenkov, who became Premier, accepted a Chinese proposal that all prisoners who insisted on repatriation should be returned, while others should be handed over to a neutral country. Accordingly in July 1953 after Eisenhower assumed the presidency, the United States, China and North Korea signed a cease fire and accepted a settlement on prisoners. Korea remained divided as before.

Despite the localised charater of the Korean War, it had a powerful impact upon the country. As it threatened the possibility of a major war, wartime atmosphere together with its armament production and political restriction returned to the land. The war convinced the Americans of the necessity of strengthening the defences against international communism. Therefore, it appeared essential to transform Japan into an ally. Accordingly a peace conference was convened at San Francisco and a treaty with Japan was signed in 1951 recognising the sovereignty of Japan over her home islands. Another treaty permitted the United States to retain bases and troops in Japan under pretension of safeguarding Japanese security. This arrangement was strengthened by a mutual defence pact signed by the United States with Japan, New Zealand and Australia. These settlements made Japan the centre of American defence system against Asian communism. At the same time Congress adopted measures to counter the growth of communism inside the country. The Mc Carran Internal Security Act of 1950 required the communist front organizations to register with the Attorney General and forbade the foreign communists from entering the country. Senator Joseph Mc Carthy led a crusade against communism, leading to the imposition of rigid restrictions upon all suspects. Mc Carthyism meant suppression of civil liberties. The protracted war apparently without purpose, and the treatment meted out to the popular general, Mac Arthur made the Democratic regime unpopular. This led to the return of the Republicans to power. Finally, the role of China in Korean War so much hardened the American attitude towards her that recognition was postponed and admission to the United Nations was checked for long.

Eisenhower

In the 1952 presidential election Dwight D. Eisenhower elected to the Presidency and his running mate Richard Nixon to the Vice-Presidency. In the succeeding election Eisenhower was re-elected.

President Eisen-hower remained in power from 1953 to 1961. As a Republican he rendered remarkable service to the United States of America during the period.

Internal Administration

The administration of Eisenhower was a period of economic boom. Private enterprise came in for favourable treatment, production continued to expand, workers received higher wages and price controls disappeared. The old age and retirement benefits were not only increased but were given wider application. Large amounts were given wider application. Large amounts were allotted for undertaking house and road building programmes. Alaska and Hawaii were admitted as states into the Union. However, the increased farm production created large surpluses leading to the downward trend in prices. This affected the standard of living of the peasants. The Agricultural Act of 1956 sought to give relief to the cultivators. It introduced the soil bank to pay compensation to the farmers for removing marginal lands from cultivation and raised the price support to farm produce. The Landrum Griffin Act of 1959 required labour unions to report their membership and finances to the government and banned secondary boycotts and picketing. As a true democrat, Eisenhower promoted civil liberties and sought to undo racial segregation.

Dulles and Policy of Containment

During the post war period communism made rapid stride; it gained ascendancy in China, Korea and Indo-China. The Soviets organised communist governments in the countries of Eastern Europe. In 1947 the reds seized control of Hungary and in 1948 Czechoslovakia. The Soviet blockade of Berlin and the Chinese intervention in Korea caused grave apprehension about the designs of international communism. At the suggestion of President Eisenhower a summit conference with Russia was held at Geneva in 1950, but no settlement could be found on the issues of German unification, disarmament and atomic control. Annoyed at this, several leaders demanded the liberation of Eastern European countries from Soviet domination through force of arms and assistance to Chiang Kai Shek to invade mainland China. But the Republicans were reluctant to allot funds and the isolationists were not prepared to allow the country to embark upon another war. As no alternative presented itself, Dulles decided to rely upon a policy of Containment of communism. In accordance with this policy the administration interfered in Guatemala and entered into entangling alliances with amenable powers of Europe and Asia.

Much because of opposition to Yankee expansionism and exploitation, large sections of people in Latin America turned to communism. There came into existence powerful red movements. Guatemala, a Red Indian republic of Central America had been dominated by the Americans for long. In 1954 a pro-communist government came to power and seized the assets of the American United Fruit Company, which had been playing the game of making and unmaking rulers in pursuit of its scheme of exploitation. Washington protested against inadequate compensation given to the giant company but Guatemala ignored. At the same time it was believed that Russia supplied arms to Guatemala. Dulles condemned Russian infiltration into America as a violation of Monroe Doctrine, airlifted arms to Central America to equip an army of mercenaries and engineered an invasion of the state. The pro-red regime collapsed and the state again passed into the orbit of American influence.

In South East Asia Dulles decided to contain spread of communism through a parallel North Atlantic Treaty Organisation, called the South East Asia Treaty organisation. At his initiative, delegates of the United States, Britain, France, Australia, New Zealand, the Philippines, Thailand and Pakistan met in a conference at Manila in 1954 and signed a defence pact. It provided for consultation on mutual defence in the event of any external aggression or internal subversion. However, the SEATO proved no effective an alliance system as the NATO did. It was at the most a consultative agreement with some moral commitment. Eager to gain material benefits, most of the members agreed to join the system but in reality they appeared insincere. Because of its inadequacy to meet the needs of vulnerable areas, the United States signed a mutual defence pact with Taiwan to check the expansion of Chinese communism. The neutral countries like India refused to have anything to do with these defence pacts.

Now it seemed that the Middle East lay exposed to Russian infiltration. Beneath the sands of the Arab world lay the largest deposits of oil. The Western powers were concerned at the possibility of Russian expansion southwards to gain control of the oil fields and to reach the warm waters of the Indian Ocean. In a bid to prevent it there was formed the Middle East Treaty Organisation (METO), other-wise called Baghdad Pact. In 1954 in response to the suggestion of the United States five powers—

Britain, Turkey, Iraq, Iran and Pakistan sent their delegates to Baghdad and signed a defence pact. The United States associated herself with its working. Thus, Russia was confronted with a bloc of powers with their territory extending from the Mediterranean to the Himalayas. However, it represented an alliance of dictators who sought to remain in power with the aid of dollar and arms, supplied by the United States.

In 1956 following the nationalisation of the Suez Canal Company by President Nasser, Great Britain, France and Israel invaded Egypt. The administration feared that Russia would intervene on behalf of Egypt and the U.N.O. would collapse. There upon Eisenhower extended his support to the United Nations to arranges cease-fire and compel the invaders to evacuate Egypt. The success of American diplomacy averted a possible show down with Russia. In 1957 the President announced the Eisenhower Doctrine. It provided for the extension of American economic aid and military support upon request to any country of the Middle East against the threat of communism. Egypt and Syria denounced it, while other countries refused to seek any American aid. The fall of the royal house of Iraq, break away of Bangladesh from Pakistan and conflict between Greece and Turkey dealt a serious blow to the Baghdad Pact.

18

J.F. Kennedy

John F. Kennedy remained in power from 1961 to 1963. As a Democratic President he did a lot to the progress and prosperity of the United States of America.

John F. Kennedy did a wonderful service for world peace in co-operation with Mr. Nehru, the Prime Minister of India.

In the Presidential election of 1960 the Democrats defeated the Republicans. John F. Kennedy, a Senator from Massachusetts and candidate of the Democratic Party, denounced Eisenhower's 'high interest, tight money policy' and charged that the Republicans deprived the country of its military supremacy and allowed Russia to dominate the international scene. As Kennedy was a Catholic of Irish descent, the Protestant clergymen questioned his independence from Vatican, but they failed in making religion a serious issue. Kennedy won the presidency with a narrow margin, defeating his Republican rival, Richard Nixon. The President appointed Dean Rusk as Secretary of State and his own brother, Robert Kennedy, as Attorney-General.

Internal Policy — His Programme

Noted for his dynamism, liberal outlook and enthusiasm for reforms, Kennedy gave executive leadership to Congress in the formulation of a series of social welfare legislations. Progressivism, associated with Theodore Roosevelt, Woodrow Wilson and Franklin D. Roosevelt again found a powerful exponent in the new President. 'New Frontier' as he called his programme, endeavoured to seek a way out of the paradox of poverty and surplus, ignorance and enlightenment. Because of his initiative laws were enacted for the benefit of workers and peasants and steps were taken in defence of the civil rights of the blacks and the remnant Indians. Economic recovery, national defence and foreign aid received special attention.

The President wanted to extend the benefits of social security to more people, unemployment compensation for longer periods, and increased wages to labour. In 1961 Congress gave its approval to several of his suggestions. Thus, an act was enacted to extend employment benefits. The Food for peace Programme provided for the distribution of farm surpluses to the needy peoples throughout the world. An Agricultural Act stipulated a cut in the area of wheat cultivation and granted larger subsidy to the peasants so as to help them maintain a high standard of living. The President employed the army to promote integration in the schools of the South, as Eisenhower did. The administration formulated a scheme aimed at providing funds to the schools for construction of buildings and medical care of the persons above the age of sixty-five. Those were calculated to extend social benefits to more people but Congress refused its support because of the opposition of interested groups and the medical association, which were afraid of losing the privileges that they enjoyed. Nevertheless, the welfare measures caused increased tax burden to the people and greater expenditure for the government.

Foreign Policy

In foreign affairs Kennedy followed a forward policy. He adopted a rigid attitude towards the communist powers, despite his declaration to seek peaceful settlement of disputes. In April 1961 he approved a plan for the invasion of Cuba to overthrow the pro-communist government of President Fidel Castro. In fact the plan had been first formulated during the last months of the administration of Eisenhower by the Civil intelligence Agency, notorious for its international spying and intrigue. The Cuban exiles and refugees were trained and equipped in the American bases located in Florida and Guatemala and sent out for the invasion of the island.

The expedition reached the Bay of Pigs but was beaten off. The people did not rise in rebellion as it was expected and the invasion ended in disaster. Most of the invading parties were killed or captured. The international community condemned die American aggression on Cuba. The Soviet Premier Nikita Khruschev utilised the opportunity to rush missiles and bombers to this highly strategic island. But Kennedy was firm and decided to see the Russians out.

As he instituted a close blockade, threat of a nuclear war loomed large. This so much alarmed the Soviets that they withdrew all offensive weapons from Cuba. In the context of the Cold War this was considered a major victory for the United States. Yet in the process Russia saved a leftist regime.

President Kennedy endeavoured to strengthen the economic structure of the non-communist world. He outlined a ten year plan of economic development and social progress. The American countries, meeting in Uruguay in 1961, adopted a declaration called the alliance for progress aimed at promoting investment of capital for a better life for the people. Despite the fanfare that attended the declaration, the implementation of the programme was tardy. Several of the dictators who accepted the declaration were thrown out of power during the period that followed. Huge amounts were diverted in support of economic progress of the under-developed nations like India but these countries instead of taking advantage of it, turned more dependent and clamoured for more loans to clear the old loans. Kennedy supported the United Nations Organisation in an effort to end the secession of Katanga from Congo. In October 1962 China launched aggression on India across the Himalayan frontiers and pushed the ill-equipped Indian army to the plains of Assam. The President offered American support but China surprised the powers by announcing a quick withdrawal. The Kennedy administration greatly enhanced the prestige of the United States, but his dynamic career was cut short by an assassin on 22 November, 1963.

LYNDON JOHNSON

Vietnam

The Viet-cong dominated the political thinking of the next two Presidents, Johnson and Nixon. The people of Vietnam, harmed the Americans in no way, on the other hand they endeavoured to attain political liberation of their land from colonial domination and national unity against alien machinations. Yet the Americans sent their armies to this little state, bombarded the cities from sea, air and land, dropped hundreds of tons of boms every day and slaughtered the old, the young and the infant indiscriminately. When the Yankees believe that America is for the Americans, the Asiatics are entitled to consider that Asia is for the Asiatics. When they believe in their national unity, other peoples too are entitled to consider that Asia is for the Asiatics. When they believe in their national unity, other peoples too are entitled to do so. But their global politics have imparted the impression that they are not prepared to accept this reciprocity and to leave the other people free.

The Vietnam tragedy had its origin in the American decision to go to the aid of the crumbling colonialism of the French in South East Asia. While the communist powers viewed the possession of this territory as of importance for the promotion of world revolution, the Americans considered it a strategic necessity not only to defend the white racist

Australia against any possible Asiatic advance but also to maintain their communication from the Pacific Ocean to the Indian Ocean. Also U.S.A. was haunted by the domino theory, that if one country would fall to communists, others in the region would follow in a row of dominoes. In consequence the Vietnamese fell victims to power politics. Despite the massive aid furnished by the United States to the enemy, the inhabitants continued their heroic struggle and French imperialism headed towards total collapse. In their attempt to extricate themselves from the anomaly, the French in 1940 persuaded Emperor Bao Dai to organise a government with Saigon as capital. On the otherhand, the communists led by their talented leader Ho-Chi-Minh established government with Hanoi as capital. This divided the country into two opposing camps, the pro-red North Vietnam and the anti-red south Vietnam. The conference of powers held at Geneva in 1954 accepted the 17th parallel as the boundary of the two areas and provided for the holding of elections through out Vietnam for ascertaining the will of the people whether they favoured reunification of the country. However, Dinh Diem, the new ruler of South Vietnam, for fear of reunification of the country under communist leadership and backed by the United States, repudiated the settlement. Driven to disappointment at this attitude the pro-communist Viet-cong organised a parallel administration in this region. President Kennedy, eager to strengthen the anti-communist forces, sent military missions to train the forces of South Vietnam. Yet this had no perceptible impact. Dissatisfied with the leadership of Diem, the pro-American interests with the possible approval of President Kennedy conspired and murdered him in 1963. Subsequently Thieu was elected to the presidency in South Vietnam.

President Lyndon B. Johnson found the situation in Vietnam rapidly moving against American interests. Aid funds went into misuse, desertions from the forces of South Vietnam increased and the Saigon regime moved towards collapse. Determined to prepare the ground for direct military intervention in defence of the tottering regime, Johnson sent the American destroyers to the North Vietnamese territorial waters in the Gulf of Tonkin and provoked a conflict with the communist gun-boats in 1964. The period that followed witnessed a steady escalation of war. Ground forces were sent to Vietnam to fight the communists and the air force and navy were directed to bomb and destroy the North Vietnamese bases and harbours, causing incalculable loss of life. The communist powers of the North did not commit their forces in support of Hanoi. It was left to the Viet-cong to bear the brunt of resistance. The tragedy of vietnam startled the conscience of Asia, yet the United States continued the art of destruction with unabated fury.

In January 1968 the Viet-cong patriots launched the Tet Offensive. They gained a remarkable victory but it proved momentary in March 1968. Johnson announced a halt to the bombardment of North Vietnam beyond the 20th parallel. Subsequently the warring parties agreed to discuss the issues and met in a conference at Paris in May 1968. North Vietnam demanded the evacuation of the alien forces from Vietnam but as aggressors were not prepared to accept it, no progress was made. As the war continued, the Americans were convinced that Vietnam represented a major failure of their foreign policy. Though six lakhs of American troops were committed to the war in support of the south Vietnamese army of seven lakhs, the rising tide of nationalism could not be curbed. As a last resort, Johnson called upon Ho-Chi-Minh, President of North Vietnam, to seek a settlement through negotiation.

Despite the Vietnam debacle, Johnson endeavoured to follow at home the liberal traditions, championed by Kennedy. Architect of the concept of "Great society" he aimed at the liberation of the less fortunate sections of the society from a state of inequality, ignorance and backwardness. In his memories, The Vantage Point he wrote "I knew that as President and as a man, I would use every ounce of strength I possessed to gain justice for the Black American". True to this declaration he enforced a far reaching piece of civil rights legislation in favour of the blacks. Also he launched a programme aimed at providing medical care for the aged, massive aid for education and a crusade against poverty and back wardness. The country maintained its leadership in scientific advancement and the American astronauts landed on the Moon. Like Lincoln and F.D., Roosevelt Lyndon, Johnson is regarded as one of those Presidents who are considered the "best and the worst". For, like the other two, he advocated civil rights and sought peace through war.

Civil Rights Movement

After world War II, Civil Rights Movement took a significant turn in the United States of America. Particularly the Negroes had acquired gains at a rapid speed after World War II.

After the New Deal, the Negroes started supporting any party which promised concrete assistance and so they become an influential factor in times of elections.

Civil Rights Movement aimed at securing equal civil rights with the whites for the blacks and other coloured of the country. It made significant gains during the administration of Eisenhower, Kennedy and Johnson.

For, these Presidents extended their sympathy for the discriminated minorities and sought to rectify their grievances through executive and legislative measures.

The population of the country consisted of whites who traced their descent from Europe, blacks from Africa, Chikanoes from Mexico, Indians from native tribes and Asians mostly from China and Japan. Among the whites the most dominant were the White Anglo-Saxon Protestants (WASP). By 1980 the Afro-Americans with a population of 26.5 million formed 11.7 per cent, the Chikanoes with 14.6 million, 6.4 per cent and the Indians with 1.4 million, 0.6 per cent of the total population. With low income, poor or no education and high morality rate and being discriminated against whites, they lived mostly in the ghetoes. The Indians lived in some 200 reservations, with the highest infant morality and ten times of the national unemployment ratio. The Asiatics, mostly Chinese and Japanese, lived in what were called China towns and little Tokyoes. From India there came an influx of the Sikhs, but it was called as tide of the turbans and beards.

The coloureds were subjected to the worst forms of discrimination. Therefore, after the Civil War, Congress enacted the 14th Amendment to ensure equal protection for all citizens before law and the 15th Amendment to prevent the states from denying votes an account of race, colour or previous condition of servitude.

In 1875 Congress passed legislation guaranteeing to the blacks equal access to hotels, restaurants and public accommodations. But in Plessy *vs.* Ferguson (1896) Supreme Court ruled that separate facilities for blacks did not violate constitutional equality of races. As a result several states enacted what were called Jim Crow Law legalising segregation.

The coloureds were subjected to different forms of discrimination, denied of votes through intimidation or literary tests, required to work for longer hours for poor wages, forced to live in segregated areas and made to sit in separate sections of hotels. Victims of social barriers and ill treatment, the blacks showed no interest in working hard or saving money. While the Negroes surrendered to despair, the white racists displayed an arrogance of the rudest form. However, a number of leaders and associations worked for the eradication of social evils. Among them were blacks as well as whites. Black leaders particularly Franklin Frazier saw a terrible waste of human life in immorality, delinquency and broken homes caused by social prejudices an barriers.

Gunnar Mydral, a Swedish scholar, found the Negro problem as an anachronism in the context of the American ideals of liberty and equality.

In 1909 the National Association for the Advancement of Coloured People (NAACP) was formed. Its programme included voting rights for the blacks, equaltable treatment before law, equal opportunity to work, end to segregated public facilities, abolition of race based pay scales and equal access to trade unions.

Wali Fard founded the Nation of Islam, which condemned all whites as devils and enemies of blacks. Stokely Carmichael and Rap Brown introduced the slogan "block power". In 1943 there was organised Congress of Racial Equality (CORE). It demanded removal of segregating in hotels, transport and other public places and relied on non-violent direct action as a method of struggle.

The movement for civil rights was marked by court battles gheto riots and non-violent direct action. It gained a great victory in 1944, when the Supreme Court in Smith *vs.* Allwright banned segregated dining cars in trains in the South and segregated education at the Universities of Okhlahoma and Texas. In 1954 the Supreme Court in a significant move on Brown *vs.* Board of Education of Topeka declared all racial segregation in public schools as unconstitutional. Encouraged by these decisions, the NAACP sued five school boards and secured an order from the Supreme Court that separate educational facilities were inherently unequal. But the whites through the Ku Klux Klan and White Citizens Council resorted to violence and kept the black students away from white schools. This excited black reaction which led to militancy, sit in demonstrations, freedom rides in bus terminals and boycott. In 1955-56 Martin Luther King Jr. organised a 381 day boycott of the transportation system of Montgomery in Alabama. This forced the city administration to desegregat its buses.

Enlightened presidents appeared sympathetic to the demand for equal rights to all citizens. As the black support was found essential for war effort, F. D. Roosevelt in 1941 signed an order to end discrimination in employment. President Truman issued an order ending segregation in armed forces. President Eisenhower enacted the Civil Rights Act of 1957 and 1960 — the first law created a Civil Rights commission to investigate into instances of denial of votes on ground of colour, race or religion and the second law provided for the punishment of the people who violated the ruling of the Commission. This was followed by rallies and freedom rides for more of equality.

In 1963 Martin Luther King Jr. led a mass rally of more than 150,000 people to Washington. Under Kennedy and Johnson the administration launched a broad abased legislative programme aimed at ending racial segregation and material poverty. Kennedy's sweeping programme for civil rights was bottled up in Congress. However, a wave of sympathy for the assassinated President enabled Johnson to enact the Civil Rights Act of 1964, the Voting Rights Act of 1965 and the Civil Rights Act of 1968. These acts removed discrimination in voting, employment and public accommodation on ground of sex or race. As a result of these measures the coloured found it possible to vote, to seek election, to get jobs and to obtain public accommodation much on an equal basis with the whites.

Having achieved these, by 1967 the Civil Rights Movement declined. Internal conflict among black organisations, the black criticism of American foreign policy and white reaction affected the movement. The whites who opposed extension of civil rights to the coloureds rallied under the Republican Party, leading to the election of Richard Nixon to the presidency. Nixon and Ford opposed federal support to civil rights and curbed black militancy. Many of the liberals appeared content with the progress made so long in the movement, through racial prejudice could not be eradicated completely.

Martin Luther King

In the history of Civil Rights Movement in U.S.A. the name of Martin Luther King is considered highly important by the Negroes. Like our Mahatma Gandhi he followed non-violent methods to achieve his objects. By peaceful means he advocated his teachings and preachings to the people of America. So he earned a very good name and fame in the annals of U.S.A.

Martin Luther King was born in 1929. He was interested in learning when he was very young. As a student he took keen interest in studying the philosophy of Gandhiji, the Father of Indian Nation. He was attracted towards Gandhian philosophy of non-violence and satyagraha.

During his student days the movement for civil rights was marked by court battles, gheto riots and non-violent direct action. It gained a great victory in 1944, when the Supreme Court in Smith *vs.* Allwright banned segregated dining cars in trains in the South and segregated education at the universities of Okhlahoma and Texas. In 1954 the Supreme Court in a significant move on Brown *vs.* Board of Education of Topeka declared all segregation in public schools as unconstitutional. In the meantime the whites through the Ku Klux Klan and white citizens council resorted to violence and kept the black students away from white schools. This excited black reaction which led to militancy, sit in demonstrations, freedom rides in bus terminals and boycott.

In 1955-56 Martin Luther King Jr. organised a 381 day boycott of the transportation system of Montgomery in Alabama. Really it was a great and stunning and striking movement in the history of Civil Rights Movement in America. This forced the city administration to desegregate its buses.

President Eisenhower enacted the Civil Rights Acts of 1957-1960 — the first law created a Civil Rights Commission to investigate into instances of denial of votes on ground of colour, race or religion and the second law provided for the punishment of the people who violated the rulings of the Commission. This was followed by many rallies, and freedom rides for more of equality.

In 1963 Martin Luther King Jr. led a mass rally. It was a great movement for Civil Rights of the Negroes. More than 1,50,000 Negroes participated in the rally. He led the rally to Washington. Under Kennedy already more rights were given to them. On November 20, 1962 he issued an executive order banning racial discrimination in housing constructed with federal funds. Moreover, under Kennedy the administration launched a broad based legislative programme aimed at ending racial segregating and material poverty. However, wave of sympathy for the assassinated President enabled Johnson to enact the Civil Rights Act of 1964. The Negroes under their eloquent and distinguished leader Rev. Dr. Martin Luther King Jr. achieved many more privileges through the non-violent tactics and massive civil disobedience as advocated by our Mahatma Gandhi.

The mass rally led by Rev. Dr. Martin Luther King Jr. created a profound effect and far reaching changes not only in the rank and file of their demonstrators but also in the administration. So the Civil Rights Act of 1964, the Voting Rights of 1965 and the Civil Rights Acts of 1968 were enacted one after another. Thus, Rev. Martin Luther King Jr. rendered remarkable service to the Negroes by these acts. These acts removed discrimination in voting, employment and public accommodation on ground of sex or race. Thereby they got equal rights on par with whites.

The U.S. Negroe Civil Rights Leader for his wonderful and memorable service has earned a very good name and fame in the history of U.S.A. But he was shot dead on 4th April 1968 at Memphis. He was awarded Nobel Peace Prize in 1964. He was awarded posthumously Nehru Peace Prize for his laudable and remarkable service.

19

Nixon Presidency

In the election of 1968 Richard Nixon the Republican candidate became President of U.S.A.

Nixon's foreign policy embodied in Nixon Doctrine, was outlined himself in July 1969. "United States will participate in the defence and development of allies and friends but we will help where it makes of real difference and is considered in our interest".

Policy in Vietnam

Widely considered as a conservative, he believed in strong arm methods. Accordingly he instituted a close blockade of North Vietnam, relied on intensive bombing and extended the war to Cambodia. But finding this policy ineffective, he in May 1969 announced a phased withdrawal of American forces from Vietnam. In a bid to conciliate China and Russia he paid a visit to these countries. This prepared the ground for the replacement of Taiwan by China at the United Nations and conclusion of a Vietnam settlement at Paris in 1973. The terms of the settlement provided for an internationally supervised cease fire in Vietnam and evacuation of American forces from Indo-China. The longest war in U.S. history, the Vietnam War lasted for eleven years and left one lakh Americans and twenty lakh Vietnamese killed. The Americans employed against this state an army of six lakhs men, 600 war planes and a formidable fleet and dropped seven million tons of bombs and shells — more than three times the quantity employed in World War II in pursuit of their diabolic art of slaughter and destruction. Yet Nixon did not learn the lesson of history. In 1971 when the people of Bangladesh launched a liberation struggle, he committed American arms and money to the military junto of Pakistan for the massacre of patriots. Further as reported in the New York Times, he directed the Civil Intelligence Agency to support the opposition factions in their struggle against the leftist regime in Chile.

President Allende of Chile was killed and administration was taken over by the army. Determined to exploit the navel weakness of India, he in 1974 acquired lease of Diego Carcia in Indian Ocean for development of this island into a military base.

Relations with China

Nixcon opened a new chapter by re-establishing relations with China. Dr. Kissinger, the secretary of State visited China in July 1971 and paved the way for Nixon's visit of China in February 1974. Since 1971, the relations between U.S. and China have been comparatively improving. Not only the commercial but also cultural and scientific contact between them are also on the increase.

Relations with Soviet Russia

The first two years Nixon's administration showed a clear trend towards greater understanding between Soviet Union and United States. This trend was interrupted by the tension which arose as a result of the Soviet role in the violation of ceasefire in the Middle East by Egypt. But the strategic Arms Limitations Treaty in May, 1971 agreed by the two countries based on a link between offensive and defensive limitations, is a remarkable achievement.

Soviet Russia and United States had agreed to co-operative in a very extensive field. Henry Alfred Kissinger, the Secretary of State of Nixon had played a vital role in designing the foreign policy of U.S. and became one of the indispensable member of Nixon's administration.

In the field of foreign policy, Kissinger did a lot to increase the image of United States in the eyes of the world. Many diplomatic relations took place due to the sincere and earnest efforts of Kissinger.

At home his policy marked a reaction against Johnson's concept of great society. Though controls were lifted, he gave no consideration to the enlargement of civil rights, extension of educational programme and implementation of foreign aid. Yet his policy was directed towards giving relief from inflation, unemployment and deterioration in balance of payments and towards strengthening the financial system. This greatly contributed to the promotion of economic health of the country.

The fall of Nixon was more sudden than his rise. In the election of 1972 he contested against the Democratic candidate Mc. Govern for the presidency and emerged successful. However, the press and the parties accused Nixon of having gathered information through secret devices about the proceedings of the opposition Democratic Party at its head quarters at Watergate Building in Washington D.C. As the storm gathered momentum and as impeachment appeared certain, the President decided to bow out and resigned. This was the first resignation by a President in the 200 year history of the country. The Nixon episode symbolised a manifestation of the inherent strength of the democratic system.

On the resignation of Richard Nixon, Vice President Gerald Ford was sworn in as the 28th President in August 1974. A man of common sense and expert in finance, he initiated measures for the re-organisation of the monetary system. Though he advocated a better deal for women, they made repeated but futile attempts to take his life out. In Indo-China the communists resumed their offensive, gaining complete control of South Vietnam and Cambodia. President Thieu of South Vietnam and Marshall Lon Nol of Cambodia fled from their states. Taking advantage of this situation, the president closed a tragic chapter in history and asserted that the role of the United States in Vietnam was over. This greatly weakened the American alliance system in South East Asia.

The Watergate Scandal

It was in the early hours of June 17, 1972 that 5 men with surgical gloves, walkie-talkies, a pair of cameras, electronic bugging devices a lock breaking equipment, picked the lock of basement door of a building in Washington's Watergate complex. They left the latch of the door taped open for easy access to and exit from the building. Then they stole up the rear stairwall in the sixth floor headquarters of the Democratic party for the President election in November 1972. Bugging (planting of secret mictophones in the office), photo copying of vital documents and other devices of sabotage, forgery, etc., were resorted to, to give President Nixon an unfair advantage in the election over his democratic rival Mc Govern.

While the political burglars were rifling through the files in the Democratic Party Headquarters, Frank Wills, the night watchman, noticed the tape on the basement door and removed it. Twenty minutes later, when he made another check up round, he found that it was retaped by one of the intruders. Wills called the police, who burst into the Headquarters with guns drawn. Knowing that the game was up, one of the intruders hiding behind a partition shouted, "Don't shoot, you have got us". Then the five came out of hiding and surrendered. The five were, Barnard Barker, Eugenio Martinoz, Frank Fiorini, James Mc Cord and Virgillio R. Gonzales. In the background were G. Gordon, Liddy and E. Edward Hunt. The latter two commanded the espionage task force from another part of the building presumably through walkie-talkies. They fled the building, when the game was up, for the Howard Johnson Motor Lodge across the street, from where, it is believed, conversation in the Democratic Party office was being monitored for several years.

But it did not take the cops long to trace them. While searching the five raiders who broke into the office and their Watergate hotel rooms, where they checked in only a day earlier, a kitful of burglary equipment, cameras, films, tear-gas pens, a radio trans-receiver and two bugging devices were recovered. It was during the hearing of the case that one of the accused Mc Cord blurted out the political connections of the entire scandal. Thereafter the American press, especially the "Washington Post", picked up the threads of the case and insisted on a thorough probe. The Nixon Administration tried to hush up the entire case by giving it a cover up of a burglary. The attempt failed and the scandal exploded with full magnitude.

The Watergate scandal was first probed by Sam Ervin Committee. The Committee started its investigation in May 1973 and one of the most important witnesses was James Mc Cord who along with his other associates had broken into the Watergate complex on June 17, 1972. Mc Cord added a new name to the Watergate break in, John Caulfield, New York City Police detective, who had served as a White House Aide and a CRP official. It was Caulfield, Mc Cord said, who tried to persuade him to plead guilty at the Watergate trial earlier in 1973 and keep silent about the whole affair. According to Mc Cord, a mystery voice summoned him to the telephone and delivered a message from Caulfield, "Plead guilty, you will get executive clemency. Your family will be taken care of and you will be rehabilitated and a job will be found for you". Mc Cord was questioned by the Committee as to why he had gone along with the Watergate raid. According to Mc Cord, Gordon Liddy had assured him that the break-in had been approved by Mitchell, Dean and the Deputy Campaign Director for President's Re-election, Magrunder. Mc Cord conceded that plans smacked of illegality, but has assumed that the Attorney General Mitchell had a valid national security reason for the break-in.

The Watergate scandal was first handed over to Archibald Cox who had insisted on President Nixon surrendering the vital tapes containing relevant material on Watergate to the Jury. President Nixon fired Archibal Cox and appointed Leon Jaworski as special prosecutor. The Grand Jury composed of 23 American citizens submitted its report to the Federal Judge Sirca in March '74. According to the Grand Jury, "they unlawfully, willfully and knowingly did combine, confederate and conspire, agreed together and with each other to commit offences against the United States — they corruptly influenced, obstructed and impeded the due administration of justice — and by deceit, craft, trickery and dishonest means defrauded the United States". They indicted seven include the following :

(1) H.R. Haldeman Nixon's Chief of Staff: He is charged with conspiracy, obstruction of Justice, and 3 counts of perjury in its public testimony before Senator Sam Ervin Seleet Senate Committee.

(2) John D. Ehrlichman, formerly Nixon's Chief Adviser on Domestic Affairs: He is charged with conspiracy, obstruction of justice, and 3 counts of lying to the Grand Jury and to the FBI. He had once acidly termed Congressmen, "a bunch of clowns".

(3) James Colson, formerly Nixon's Special Counsellor: He once declared. "I would do anything that Richard Nixon asked me to do". He has also been indicted for conspiracy and obstruction of justice.

(4) Robert C. Mardian: He was one of the architects of Nixon's southern strategy on School Integration. He was indicted for conspiracy.

(5) C. Strachal — He was Haldeman's Chief Aide in the White House. He later became General Counsellor of the U.S. Information Agency to exert greater control over Federal Bureaucracy. He is charged with conspiracy, obstruction of justice and one count of lying to a Grand Jury.

(6) John Mitchell, the former Attorney General and Head of Nixon's Re-election Committee: He stands indicted on charges of conspiracy; obstruction of justice and 4 counts of making false statements to the FBI and the Senate Watergate Committee for the Grand Jury. He and former Commerce Secretary Maurice Stans are also accused of attempting to intervene with the securities and exchange commissions to help fugitive Robert Vesco to evade massive fraud investigation in return for a secret two lakh dollars contribution to Nixon Re-election Campaign.

Amongst the others who have been charged are John W. Dean, former White House Counsellor. He has pleaded guilty to one count of conspiracy in the Watergate cover up. Herbert W. Kalmbach, one of Nixon's Personal Attorney, has pleaded guilty to violation of the Federal Corrupt Practives Act and to an illegal offer of an Ambassador post in exchange for campaign contribution.

G. Gordon Liddy, former FBI Agent, convicted of conspiracy, burglary and illegal wire trapping at Watergate.

Eugenio Martinez: He has pleaded guilty to burglary, conspiracy, illegal wire trapping and eaves dropping.

James W. Mc Cord — formers CIA Agent — Convicted of conspiracy, illegal wire trapping and eavesdropping.

E. Howard Hunt — one of the White House consultants: He had pleaded guilty to leading the Watergate break-in.

From the long list of the names which included some of the most important names of Nixon administration, it is obvious that practically the entire administration was involved in ensuring re-election of the president.

Impeachment of President Nixon

The most important issue being debated in the United States concerns the extent of involvement of President Nixon in the Watergate cover-up. The report of the Grand Jury may be discussed by the Congress and it may contain enough evidence for impeachment of the American President. The entire issue is to be ultimately decided from President Nixon's talk with Dean in March 73. During these talks Mr. Dean is supposed to have told Mr. Nixon regarding a blackmail demand for one lakh twenty thousand dollars. If involvement of President Nixon is proved, the impeachment would become so much easier. President Nixon has now employed St. Clair as his Personal Attorney. The following assertions have been made by St. Clair in connection with the proposed impeachment of the President.

(1) A President can be impeached only for a crime of a very serious nature in his governmental capacity.
(2) The President can claim executive privilege in withholding requisite evidence from the House Committee.
(3) Because the President is the Chief Law Enforcement Official in the Nation he did not have a legal obligation to report his knowledge of the hush money payments to non else. He must only see to it that the judicial process was initiated.
(4) What is at stake is not President Nixon but the institution of Presidentship.

Another count on which impeachment can proceed in President Nixon's concealment of substantial amounts and evasion of taxes on the same. According to one Congressman, "If Watergate brought pressure on Nixon to resign, our Report will bring about a great deal more pressure. Nixon may well wind up owing more than 5 lakh dollars in taxes and penalties. For the years 1970-71 he paid less than 2,000 dollars on a combined income of 5,26,000 dollars. He also failed to report one 1,42,000 dollars profit on the sale of his apartment in New York in 1969 and did not pay a Capital Gains Tax on the same".

The Watergate scandal has not only shocked the public opinion in the United States, it has also reduced the credibility of president Nixon in the eyes of the Chinese and the Russians. One of the Persistent questions asked from Henry Kissinger during his visit to Moscow in April 1974 was as to whether Nixon will survive or not. He could not transact much business with the Russians mainly on account of political uncertainty within the United States of America.

Cold War

Even before world War II has ended, the victors were competing to achieve the best possible post war position. As long as a powerful common enemy remained in the field, the great coalition held together. The common interest in defeating the Axis States transcended and muted the latent rivalry and conflict between the Soviet Union and the two leading Western powers Britain and the United States.

Rivalry is endemic to the nation-state system. The nature of the system compels every participant to provide its own security; and one nation's security is another nation's insecurity. The logic of the nation-state system breeds in security, distrust, rivalry and hostility. The post-war relationship of the United States and the Soviet Union was conducive to just such and outcome. As the war ended Soviet and American powers confronted each other over congeries of prostrate, exhausted and chaotic societies that provided an invitation to rivalry. Had Germany and Japan not be reduced to impotence by unconditional surrender or had France, Britain and China been able to maintain control of their traditional spheres of influence, the Soviet-American confronting might have been somewhat less threatening. The enormous destruction brought upon the Soviet Union by the war was bound to produce quest for maximum security guarantee. Russia lost 13.6 million soldiers, 1,700 cities and 70,000 towns were devastated and over 6 million buildings were destroyed by the Germans.

The United States was content during the closing months of the war to preserve those advantages with which it was emerging from the war. Roosevelt readily co-operated with Russia and agreed on many points at Yalta and Potsdam. But within six months, after the war's end all pretense of friendship was being dropped. The cold war had begun. On March 5, 1946, Churchill speaking at Fulton in the presence of President Truman denounced the existence of the 'Iron Curtain' and invited America to take up the challenge posed by the Russian occupation of Eastern Europe. At that time no American official endorsed Churchill's assessment.

During 1946 the nature of the cold war shifted from a more or less passive condition to an active one. The Iranian crisis of 1946 was followed by a crisis over the Dardanelles, the shooting down of U.S. transports over Yugoslavia and tense episodes on Triestie and Manchuria. U.S. Secretary of State Byrnes told Germans at Stutgart that United States does not want a desperate an impotent Germany, "The American people want to help the German people to win their way back to an honourable place among the free and peace loving nations of the world". The cold war also spurred the United States to make a vast loan to overcome the economic debilitation of Britain and France.

To save Greece and Turkey from the communists the Truman Doctrine was propounded on March 12, 1947. The United States declared its determination to employ American funds and military advisors to defeat the efforts of communist guerrillas to overthrow those governments. This policy was a radical departure from the methods that the United States had previously employed to contain the Soviet Union.

Marshall Plan

The entire Western Europe was threatened with communism due to destruction of industries, poverty and unemployment. In France and Italy reds were active. Therefore, the American administration decided to extend their plan as explained by Secretary Marshall on June 5, 1947, in his Harward Address. By salvaging Europe and actively recommitting itself to Europe's survival, the United States not only deprived the Soviets of possible victory, but suddenly confronted them with the prospect of Western Europe harnessed to a powerful and dangerous capitalistic power in time to stop the spread of communism, but had also found a powerful ally. Russia first agreed to take part in the European Recovery Plan, but later withdrew. Soviets apprehended that Marshall Plan Aid was likely to be used to promote the economy and hence the political expansion of American influence within Europe, the Marshall Plan meant not only the end to any hopes the Kremlin might have entertained that communism might still triumph through chaos in Western Europe, but it also meant that the West would now begin to challenge Soviet hegemony in Eastern Europe. It would also affect Germany.

The Marshall Plan symbolized the utter dependency of Europe on the United States. Europe now looked exclusively to her for hope and initiative. The Soviets retaliated on June 8, 1948, in a calculated bid to thwart the creation of West German Government and a stable currency for West Germany by a blockade of West Berlin. But the move proved abortive. Another important thing occurred and that was Yugoslavia's revolt against Russia. U.S.A. moved swiftly and by the end of 1948, Yugoslavia was receiving economic and military aid from Washington.

The North Atlantic Treaty

U.S.A. believed that the Soviets recognized only facts and that they would respect only Western positions based upon military and political strength. Hence, U.S.A. pushed ahead with the North Atlantic Treaty. The European dependency on the United States facilitated this strategy. The Treaty was signed on April 4, 1949 obliging the signatories to take up arms immediately against an armed attack threatening the security of any member. This caught the Soviets by surprise.

Victory of Communism in China

On October 1, 1949 People's Republic of China was proclaimed in Peking. Stalin recognized for the first time that a potential Red rival had been born. In U.S.A. the Government was shocked to 'lose' China, but was not averse to recognize it. But the events in Far East made it difficult to do so. In June 1950, North Korea committed aggression against South Korea. In the week following the attack the United States committed its force to the defence of a country hitherto not considered significant. The U.S.A. went to defend South Korea because America feared another Munich. Dictators' appetites grow with eating and it allowed to get away with one aggression, they will be encouraged to perpetrate another. The historical importance of the Korean conflict is two-fold. (1) It signified America's willingness to go to war to defend its allies and (2) It substituted limited war for total war as a test of relative strength and will.

The political advantages of NATO to the United States were immense. It gave the United States a unique potential for supporting its vital interests through a concert of nations. It was the great merit of NATO in its early years that it supported the security and diplomacy of the allies against the Soviet Union and at the same time elicited a high degree of strategic collaboration and political co-operation among the members.

Conflicts Within NATO

As soon as it became apparent that the war in Korea was not a prelude to a general war, the political goals of the members began to take precedence over the collective security and strategic goals of alliance. The economic burdens of large-scale re-armament were heavy in every European society. The Pleven Plan (European Defence Community), that France had proposed as a mean of controlling German re-armament no longer had the same appeal once it became apparent that France was virtually abrogating its national sovereignty. West Germany demanded an end to allied occupation costs and French control of star and a virtual veto power in any East-West talks regarding Germany. In short as a military and security function decreased NATO began to be used to achieve its members' political objectives. The most fundamental contradiction within the alliance is the disparity that exists in size and in objectives for NATO between the United States and Europe. To many Americans also it was not sufficiently dynamic and it gave no promise of yielding immediate victories in the cold war.

The Indo-China and the Geneva Agreements of 1954

Following the defeat of Chiang Kai-Sheck in the Korean war, United States had supplied the French with large sums of money and military equipment to defeat Viet Minh. Eishenhower administration wanted France to continue the hopeless war. French decided to end the war and the Geneva Conference met in April 1954. Dulles came for a week never to return. He abhorred the idea of a Red Victory over West. Dulles also wanted to make it clear to Moscow and Peking that America did not approve of the agreement and did not want the communists to assume at any time that U.S. had washed its hands off Indo-China. In fact the Geneva Agreement terminating the war marked the end of the French phase of the Vietnam story and the beginning of the American phase. It is said Dulles was happy that now U.S.A. would have a free hand in the area. U.S.A. replaced Bao Dai in South Vietnam by Ngo Dinh Diem and gave military and economic help to South Vietnam.

SEATO

The end of French rule in Indo-China brought United States there. American defence strategy was extended to cover S.E. Asia with Pakistan, Thailand and Philippines as Asian Powers. SEATO was created in 1955. It's protection was extended to Laos. Cambodia and South Vietnam. This implicated U.S.A. into Kashmir dispute with which she had no concern.

Death of Stalin

The death of Stalin had its impact on cold war. Kremlin leaders assured Western Europe of their good will towards them. To justify these Korean armistice was concluded, Austrian Peace Treaty signed and accord reached on Indo-China. Normal relations were restored with Yugoslavia. The Western Allies agreed to a Summit Meeting of the four heads — Eisenhower, Eden, Faure and Bulganin.

Geneva Conference (1955)

U.S.A. went to Geneva with contradictions. Whereas Ike went with good faith, Dulles wanted to take full advantage of Russian weakness. Because of his obsessive anti-communism and his fixed notions that the Soviets were coming to conference out of weakness. Dulles felt no compulsion to support Eisenhower's crusade for peace. On July 21, Ike told the meeting, "To give each other a complete blue-print of our military establishments. Next to provide within our countries' facilities for aerial photography to the other country, to verify the facts furnished". This was the 'Open Skies' plan. The Soviet reacted favourably but Dulles sabotaged the whole scheme.

Crisis in the Soviet Camp

The relaxing of Stalinist tensions in Eastern Europe came at a moment when popular force in Poland and Hungary were demanding a greater voice in the regime. The Polish situation at first was regarded as more serious. But Gomulka was shrewd. While he controlled the Poles, he also warned Russia that Poland would resist any armed intervention. In Hungary communist party leader Gero proved unable to master the situation. Leadership passed to revolutionary Imre Nagy who acceded to popular pressure. This led to Russian armed intervention in Hungary. Nagy had wanted the neutrality of Hungary. But Russia ruthlessly suppressed Hungarian revolutionaries. This was a warning to the Eastern satellites that their freedoms were limited in the socialist camp.

Crisis in the Western Bloc

Just when the Soviet camp was shaken by the events in Hungary, the West too was shaken by a most serious post-war crisis. In June 1956 British withdrew from Suez Canal and Nasser nationalized the Suez Canal Company. U.S.A. withdrew its pledge to give a loan of 56 million to Egypt. The nationalization of Suez Canal was a defeat to Britain and France. Eden was anti-Nasser and France wanted to destroy Nasser and thereby cut off the flow of communist bloc arms to the Algerian rebels. U.S.A. did not think in terms of a war. The Anglo-French intervention at a time when presidential elections were due in U.S.A. brought profound antagonism in Washington. Dulles condemned the action. Moscow was able to exploit the situation by supporting Arab cause and winning their sympathies. The Atlantic Alliance was shaken. The British and French were never to foregive Washington for their Suez experience. It reinforced French interest in the European Union and the idea of a European Economic Union.

France had proposed to form a common European defence force in which French and German units would be under a supernational command. But upon closer examination it came to be criticized in France. Dulles delivered threatening notes which antagonized France. The French national Assembly rejected the proposed EDC by a vote of 319 to 264. But on December 28, the National Assembly by a narrow margin approved the plan of Western European Union (WEU). Thus, what was needed in NATO was a new departure, a recognition that Europe's status was changing and that if America was to retain its influence NATO must be developed within a new political framework reflective of these changes.

In France once the common threat for which NATO had been created appeared to recede the nationalist compulsion to remain a great power surged to the fore. Britain continued her special relationship with U.S.A. She had already her Skybolt and Polaris missiles. Thus, France's stature was reduced. The decision of the NATO Council in May 1957 to equip NATO forces with nuclear weapons gave an outward appearance of unity. But many members including France refused to allow the stationing of missiles in their countries.

Cold War Spreads to Under Developed States

The struggle between the revolutionary nationalism of Asia, Africa and the Middle East and the waning empires of Europe has been and almost constant feature of the post-war era. Because most of the new emergent states were in revolt against European imperialism and because they were politically and economically ill-equipped for statehood, they were prime targets of the cold war.

The collapse of European imperialism was viewed as an inevitable stage on the road to world communism. The Soviets came out with the theory of peaceful coexistence. Also to win sympathies they attacked colonialism and propounded the thesis that war was not inevitable and communism could be brought about by parliamentary methods. Since Afro-Asians had a common hatred for west, they fell easily in the Russian trap. American approach was different. U.S.A. thought that since she championed national self-determination, these states would automatically accept her leadership. Also the U.S. thought nationalism would be a potent factor in checking the spread of communism. Whereas Soviets reconciled with the non-alignment policy, Dulles attacked. India and regarded non-alignment immoral. Thus, America launched massive foreign aid programme to win allies in Asia but to no much success. SEATO and MEDO were formed but not many Asian States joined them.

Second Berlin Crisis

Unable to weaken NATO unity, to thwart the emplacement of U.S. rockets in Britain, Turkey and Italy or to attract any NATO government to disengagement, Khrushchev decided to play his most dangerous card! Berlin. On November 27 Tass said six months were being given for an agreement over it. West decided to hold negotiations which opened in Geneva on May 11, 1959 but no results. The same year Khrushchev met Eishenhower at Camp David. Both agreed to resolve the Berlin issue. At the same time U.S.A. told Russia that West was committed to defend Berlin.

Suddenly on May 1, 1960 Russia brought down a U-2 American spy plane. Khrushchev decided to use the incident to torpedo the meeting with Eisenhower. Khrushchev came back from Paris *via* East Germany and told East Germans that Russia would sign a peace treaty with them. American allies were already cracking. France demanded a say in NATO nuclear deterrent. Military coups occurred in Turkey, Thailand and Pakistan. 1951 Treaty with Japan which was to be renewed in 1961 provoked wide spread demonstrations in Japan and Ike had to cancel his visit to Tokyo. The greatest challenge to America came in Cuba, where Castro came to power on January 1, 1959. At first U.S. tried to get along with Cuba but the Cuban exiles assisted by the CIA made the abortive Bay of Pigs invasion, which considerably diminished American prestige.

In 1961 Russia created further troubles in Berlin. Berlin wall came to be erected. De Gaulle did not share Kennedy's view that the risks of war were great over Berlin. Further France thought Russia was only bluffing. The Berlin wall disappointed the West Germans but she has no choice but to stay with the West. But the Berlin crisis also subsided without bringing any hot confrontation between Western States and Russia.

Cuban Crisis

Since the Bay of Pigs invasion Russia had been pouring military equipment and personnal in Cuba. Why Khrushchev did it? The reason was that U.S.S.R. did not have missiles of more than 2,500 miles ranges. U.S.A. was more or less undefeatable whereas West can strike Russia from Europe. It is also generally agreed that there was a connection between the exhaustion and immune of Soviet efforts to dislodge the United States from Berlin and hence the decision to emplace missiles in Cuba. U.S.S.R. thought U.S.A. would not risk a nuclear war over the issue. But American response confounded the Soviet leaders. U.S.A. declared blockade of Cuba in October 1962 and left the next move to the Soviet ships which were already heading for Cuba and there was no time for delay. On October 27, Khrushhev announced to withdraw the missiles entirely from Cuba. Thus, Russia saved the world from a nuclear war.

Meanwhile U.S.A. and U.S.S.R. started negotiations on disarmament. Kennedy said that if unclear weapons' expansion was not checked now, by 1975 at least 15 powers would join the unclear club. The

Treaty was easily negotiated and signed in Moscow on August 5, 1963. It prohibits testing of nuclear devices on earth and space. China and France did not sign this treaty for their own reasons.

France and America

France had long tried to isolate herself from dependency on America. European Common Market, creating of a self-relaint unclear deterrent, demand for withdrawal of NATO bases in France were all attempts in this direction. De Gaulle was not prepared to wait for American green signal, in case of an attack on France. The reasoning behind De Gaulle's decision was his long standing conviction that the cold war developed out of a purely transient situation of bipolariy and then became reinforced by ideological passion. An Atlantic Alliance dominated by the United States could only prolong the ideological confrontation and inhibit a return to a more normal set of relationships. Therefore, it is good both for peace and for Europeans to refuse to remain any longer subordinate to United States' control. In fact De Gaulle has gone out of his way to demonstrate that European nationalism can no longer be disregarded. But he has no answer for German nationalism or the German desire to be united. There will be no real settlement in central Europe so long as Germany remains divided.

Laos and Vietnam

Laos and Vietnam afford prime examples of a type of situation that may become increasingly common in the world. In Vietnam the United States took the French place. North Vietnamese are here equipped with Soviet and Chinese arms aiding the South Veitnamese Vietcong and trying to usurp power. United States has gone to the rescue of South Vietnamese Government along with a few allies. The total American armed forced there are more than 5 lakhs. America is determined to give a challenge to the attempt of the communists to impose military settlement. For the fast few years both the parties have realized the futility of such a venture and are meeting at Paris since 1968 to find out a political settlement.

The End of Sino-Soviet Alliance

Sino-Soviet relations have deteriorated since 1957. The Chinese are not ready to accept Moscow's leadership. Also they reject revisionism of Leninist ideas of class war. Besides, China claims large areas which now constitute a part of Russia. The Sino-Soviet Alliance of 1951 is virtually dissolved. On January 13, 1966 Russia concluded an anti-chinese pact with Mongolia. On March 15, 1969 Russian and Chinese forces clashed over the Urussi River resulting in considerable casualties on both sides.

Soviet Union has even threatened nuclear war, to which Mao has equally responded.

The cold war is now more than 24 years old. Both the American and the Soviets are realizing in futility. Soviet American Dentente is in the offing. Both have agreed along with Britain on July 1, 1968 on a Nuclear Non-Proliferation Treaty. Besides, negotiations are taking pace on the antimissile defence system. The June 1967 Arab Israeli clash once again brought the two super powers as to oppose each other. But the Big Four were busy in finding a settlement for West Asia.

The Sino-Soviet conflict is bound to affect the world situation. There could be two probabilities. Either U.S.A. would come closer to U.S.S.R. or America and China would come closer. Chinese aims are clear. They are: (i) exclusion of all Western influence (including Russian) from Asia, (ii) settlement of Asian affairs by the Asian alone and (iii) hegemony of Communist China over the area.

The cold war has thus crippled the world for the last 24 years and to what gains? Not much. Neither of the two super powers enjoy that much of authority and respect which they did in the years following the war. The Eastern and Western solidarlity is only apparently existing. Neither the Western States have any strong unity nor the Russian satellites have any respect for their master. The Czechoslovakia incident of August 1968 has proved it. The only satisfaction is that the world has so far survived from this cold war.

20

America Under Carter and Reagan

In the presidential election of 1976 Jimmy Carter of the Democratic Party defeated Gerald Ford of the Republican Party. A liberal by conviction, he endeavoured to follow a moralistic policy and dedicated himself to the cause of basic rights of human beings. Accordingly, he withdrew economic and military aid from countries, where human rights were violated and where strategic interests were not involved. While this was done in case of Argentina, Uruguay and Ethiopia, it was not done in case of South Korea. In 1977 two treaties were signed with Panama. By the first treaty Panama was to gain a share of the administration and of income from the Canal. The second treaty provided for the control and operation of the Canal by Panama from 2000 A.D. However, the United States was to share permanently the right to defend the Canal and use it for transit of ships.

In the Middle East the Arab powers fought a major war against Israel. Due to the efforts of Washington and Egypt, Israel settled a peace treaty in 1973. A significant development was the normalisation of relations with China. For the three decades after the communist take over, U.S.A. and China were in a state of confrontation. The two powers fought a major war in Korea. Because of American machinations, China was kept out of the U.N.O. However, as the Communists consolidated their authority, it appeared illogical to deny China her legitimate status. U.S.A. saw the possibility of isolating China from the Soviet camp and promoting trade with that country. Accordingly on March, 1, 1979 the two powers established diplomatic relations. As a result Taiwan ceased to have diplomatic status. In the context of Russo-Chinese clashes, China moved closer to the United States.

Two developments in particular posed threats to the global interests of U.S.A. They were the fall of monarchy in Iran and the Russian intervention in Afghanistan. Washington looked upon the Shah of

Iran as a dependable ally, exploited oil resources and supplied military hardware in the name of defence. However, in the October Revolution of 1972 the Shah fled the country and Ayotollah Khomeini came to power. In protest against the asylum given to the Shah, the Iranians captured the Americans embassy at Teheran and held 49 Americans as hostages. Carter moved the Warships to the Persian Gulf, but his inability to work out the release of hostages tarnished his image. It was only after holding the hostages in captivity for 444 days that Iran released them. This episode coincided with Russian intervention in Afghanistan. As non-aligned country, it served as a barrier to Russian expansion to the Indian Ocean. But in 1979 Russia moved her army to Afghanistan and set up a pro-Soviet government. This introduction brought the Russian presence dangerously closer to the oil rich Persian Gulf.

In the context of the reverses that American arms and diplomacy suffered in Vietnam, Cambodia and Guatemala, the Carter administration decided to check the threatening advances made by Russia. The result was the Carter Doctrine. It declared the Persian Gulf as an area of "vital interests of the United States" and announced the determination of U.S.A. to defend it by all necessary means including force of arms. In support of this doctrine the President strengthened military presence in the Indian Ocean and created the Rapid Deployment Force capable of dealing with any situation in any trouble spot. This represented a hardening of the attitude of the administration against the Soviets. At home there came much unrest against his administration. Huge farm surplus and consequent fall in prices and decline in standard of living made the peasants critical. Keen competition from Japan affected steel industry while Arab oil embargo caused shortage of fuel. As a result, people turned against the Democratic Party.

Reagan

As the presidential election of 1979 drew near, the Democratic Party nominated Jimmy Carter and the Republican Party Ronald Reagan as their respective candidates. In the election campaign Reagan depicted Carter as an advocate of controls and criticised him as soft towards the enemies of the nation. Also, he pointed out that the administration neglected parity in nuclear war heads and missiles with Russia. The hostages issue and the Afghan question too discredited the Democrats. As a result, Reagan won the presidential election with overwhelming majority. People wanted not moralism but realism.

Internal Policy — A Fair Society

A radio announcer and cine actor, Reagan began his political career as a Democrat and then turned a Republican. After serving two terms as

Governor of California, he sought nomination of the Republican Party against Ford but missed it narrowly. He remarked, "It is just one battle in a long war", which Senator K.S. Scheweiker asserted "the country has missed the best leader it had for many many decades". In 1980 he avenged this setback and won the election. More than a conservative, Regan was a realist for he had definite ideas to tackle the situations created by internal and external developments. At home he aimed at the realisation of what he called a 'Fair Society'.

It is essential to correct the dangerous increase in government spending, as it contributed to a sluggish economic growth. This could be done by holding the line on federal spending, checking fraud and waste, saving on defence account and reducing deficit financing.

Secondly, the country should maintain technological leadership. This demanded improvement of the content of education particularly in science and mathematics, family saving as well as federal credits in support of education.

Thirdly, permanent jobs should be generated by extending employment opportunities. This required incentives to employers, assignments for displaced workers, training for unskilled people and expansion of international trade which offered one fifth of the employment potential.

Fourthly, women though were not in minority, were to receive equal justice. There should be no discrimination with men either before law or in wages. Above all, the individual must have his freedom. For, he declared rightly : our strength lies in our values — free election, free press, freedom of the individual and rejection of arbitrary power of the state. The future belongs not to governments and ideologies that oppress their people but to democratic systems of self-government, which encourage individual initiative and guarantee personal freedom.

Keeping in view the examples of South Korea, Taiwan and Singapore, which made progress by leaps and bounds, and the contrast with the outputs in collective farms and state farms in Russia he held out to backward countries-claiming as developing but languishing in the third world that private enterprize was the way to progress.

The administration pointed out that the government "is often an obstacle to development and that donor countries would have to go directly to the people". Guided by these convictions he entertained belief that if the third world countries suffer, it was because of their system. Nevertheless, as the strength of U.S.A. was linked to world economy, he supported free trade and economic health of other countries too.

The policy that he adopted to translate these principles into reality yielded results. Thus, he curbed inflation, effected tax relief to the people, multiplied employment opportunities and promoted educational, industrial and commercial progress. The value of dollar rose to a new high in the monetary system of the world. However, there were victims too. Among the affected were foreign aid programme and contribution to International Development Association. Reagan felt that the UNESCO exhibited hostility towards free market and free press, which were considered as the two basic institutions of free society. On this ground he announced the withdrawal of U.S.A. from this international agency. Reagan's administration made the average American feel proud of himself and confident of a better future.

Foreign Policy

In this external relations Reagan adopted a policy based upon international peace and individual freedom. Yet this was subordinated to strategic considerations. As a result the peace that he wanted to realise was that through strength and the freedom that he recognised was that for allied countries and like-minded democracies. In his words the foreign policy of U.S.A. was based upon realism, strength, full partnership and consultations with our allies and constructive negotiation with potential adversities.

Accordingly, the President reversed the decision of Carter against the production of neutron war heads. This represented a revival of armament race with Russia. More funds were allotted for strengthening the Rapid Development Force and the Indian Ocean Fleet, both initiated by Carter. Also he built up a net work of bases. The allied countries, Whether they supported or suppressed human rights, came in for favoured treatment. Among them were Egypt, Saudi Arabia, Taiwan, South Africa, Argentina, Brazil and Chile. In 1981 the United States entered into a five year arms aid programme with Pakistan. This was calculated to caution Russia as well as India and to counter Soviet presence in Afghanistan.

Reagan gave due importance to friendly relations with the countries of West Europe. He extended military support to Great Britain in the war against Argentina over the Falklands. This made him a suspect in Latin America. In the island of Grenada a military junta killed Prime Minister Maurice Bishop and set up Marxist government. It was feared that Russia and Cuba would establish their influence and convert the island into a base of their operation. Therefore, in October 1983 Reagan sent forces under the cover of protecting "American life and property". The leftist government was overthrown, an interim government was formed and after the objectives were realised, the army was withdrawn. The non-aligned countries led by India criticised the American intervention, but

Reagan dismissed it as that of Soviet client states with no commitment to the principles on non-alignment. In 1984 Reagan defeated the Democratic candidate, Walter Mandale. He won 49 out of 50 States with 525 electoral votes —the highest in history, surpassing F.D. Roosevelt's 523 votes in the election of law. But Democrats retained control of the House and reduced Republican majority in Senate. Yet his victory provided continuity to the policy of realism.

After his re-election Reagan with his usual perseverance has pursued his policy on the progress of third world countries. While he welcomed relaxation of controls and opposed oppressive taxation, he wanted to see them self-reliant with less of aid from his country. He stated in October 1986 that high taxes made the people less free to work, save and invest. His resentment to socialism had its own logic. For, it was the earliest system in history, but being found unsuited to meet the needs of the growing population and craving for individual freedom, it was rejected and replaced by economic democracy. Despite rigorous controls, socialism today is not a success story. It was sound unworkable without a strong admixture of capitalism and yet it caused recurring scarcity instead of continuous boom even in vast and rich countries. While the realism of Reagan was understandable, what had baffled conviction were his opposition to meaningful sanction against apartheid in South Africa, support to racism in Sri Lanka against oppressed Tamils, alliance with dictatorships, whether it was of monarch or military junta or of proletariat, aid to rebel Contras of Nicaragua against the leftist government and refusal to compromise on star wars research. These have caused apprehensions. In October 1986 Congress over-rode a presidential veto and forced the President to accept sanctions against South Africa. Still there remained more of imbalances to be corrected through checks and balances in the American constitutional system.

21

George Bush-End of Cold War

George Bush belonged to the Republican Party. As a Republican candidate he contested in the 1988 presidential election. He won the election with a comfortable majority.

No wonder his administration witnessed many far reaching changes. Let us see one by one in detail.

His administration witnessed great changes, brought by the collapse of communism. The iniquitous system of controls and repression created in support of socialism in U.S.S.R. broke down. U.S.S.R. found it impossible to cope with the strains created by the cold war and armament race with U.S.A. Pulling down of statues of socialist tyrants and breaching of the Berlin Wall gave the signal to the fall of communism. Poland slipped out of Soviet orbit. This was followed by the liberation of the countries of Eastern Europe from communist yoke. East Germany joined with West Germany to form an unified nation. The Soviet intervention in Afghanistan ended in disaster. These developments culminated in the disintegration of U.S.S.R. into fifteen independent republics in 1991.

In consequence U.S.A. found herself as the super power with no rival to challenge its status. Capitalism and free market economy that she upheld triumphed over socialism and state control, marking an end to the cold war. The inherent strength of economy, military powers, advanced technology and treaty relation with the powers of Europe and security system with Japan and Germany gave the country a dominant status in the world.

Two schools of thought, one advocating internal reform while the other seeking external glory, guided public opinion. The isolationists particularly J. Kirkpatrik argued that the country should give up the unusual burdens of the past and return to normal times so that it could take care of the problems at home-education, family welfare, industry and technology. But a more influential school called realism advocated an aggressive policy for protecting the interests and safeguarding the status of America.

After the collapse of Soviet Union no threat to national interests was perceived, yet threat to regional interests was cited as justification for such a line of action. Thus, Dick Cheney, Secretary for Defence in the Bush administration, predicted that by 2000 A.D. more than two dozen developing countries would possess ballistic missiles capable of posing a threat to American interests. Therefore, there should be a system to police these weapons and the powers who brandish these weapons. Such countries are to be denied access to high technology and brought under arms control.

It is the noble task of U.S.A. to lay down the needed rules, enforce these rules by means of her strength and support the new order–the unipolar world. As in the case of the Monroe Doctrine, such a policy was not formulated, yet the Pentagon — the defence headquarters — favoured a line of action envisaging U.S.A. as the leader of the world order and listed potential adversaries including India against which it could strike.

In accordance with this line, U.S.A. proceeded against Iraq in 1990. Saddam Hussain, President of Iraq annexed Kuwait–a territory that formed a province of Iraq in the past but separated into an independent Sheikdom by the British. The Arab countries were prepared to ignore this annexation but not U.S.A. as it posed a threat to her oil based industry and self imposed status as leader of the new world order. President Bush denounced the annexation and at his instance the U.N. Security Council too, supported by the forces of Britain and France and funds from Japan and Saudi Arabia, the United States launched a major offensive. Iraq evacuated Kuwait and surrendered to arms control. As a result the United States consolidated her influence in the oil rich Arab countries. Iraq lost more than two lakh people killed and her status as a major Arab power.

India expected to follow a non-nuclear policy even for self-defence. Nehru and his successors are accused of depending upon bow and arrow warfare and preparing the Indian army as a cannon feed, and reducing the country into a land of verbally powerful Indians. As a result India failed to learn the lesson of history and missed an opportunity for developing advanced technology. Yet she is not spared. The space programme of India is placed under an export ban of items from U.S.A. and New Delhi is brought under increased pressure to sign the Nuclear Non Proliferation Treaty and to improve human rights record.

The high profile foreign policy of the Republican Party under Reagan and Bush has raised the status of U.S. leadership in the new world order and subserved diplomatic and economic interests. Yet at the domestic front the record was not so impressive. Soaring budget deficit, sagging economy, business closures and more than seven per cent unemployment marked some of the weak spots on the Bush administration. Yet the capability of U.S. economy to overcome these difficulties was never in doubt.

22

Social Changes

After World War II significant, even breathtaking social, economic and cultural changes took place in America. Population increased by leaps and bounds. It is considered as dangerous as a nuclear explosion. In 1950 the United States could count 150,697,361 inhabitants, in 1970 over 203,000,000. The mixture had become more uniform, owing to the bubbling of the Melting Pot and the continued slow down of the immigration stream. Among them the largest alien groups were Italian Americans, German Americans, Canadian Americans and Polish Americans.

Population pressure had given strong impetus to "planned parenthood". Oral contraceptives notably "The Pill" came into wide use during the 1960's. Despite official frowns from Pope Paul VI countless Catholics were weakening in their opposition to birth control and legalised abortion. Black population too increased.

During the post war decades fantastic growth took place in the states of Florida, Texas, the Southwest and the Pacific Coast, Incredible California beat out New York as the most populous state in the 1960's with approximately 20,000,000.

Many steps were taken by the Congress to solve the urban problems in the late 1960's. It provided substantial financial support for improved transportation, publicly financed housing and the creation of entirely "new towns" as "model cities". Besides, the only housing surplus was slums. By 1970 there were about 100 million motor vehicles in the United States almost one for every two people, to the envy of the rest of the world.

Traffic deaths were skyrocketing. It was due to drunk driving. It had mounted to some 55,000 lives a year.

By the late 1960's travel by airplane, chiefly on rocket like jets had reached fantastic proportions. All of the major airports were badly congested.

Urban light and suburban sprawl inevitably worsened problems of smog (aerial sewage) water pollution, sound pollution, sight pollution, soil pollution and beach pollution (oil sticks). Rivers and lakes were spoiled considerably.

Youths were degenerated in 1950's and 1960's due to overcrowding in schools and "dropouts". Thousands of them were headed for a life of drug addiction, degeneracy and despondency. Rebellious youth was a world wide phenomenon, fully evident in America even before the 1960's. A "generation gap" had developed. Many of the younger generation were rejecting conventional values. "Trust no one over thirty" was a common warning.

Youthful rebellion in the later 1960's manifested itself in varied ways. Conspicuous were demonstrations in colleges and high schools, designed to achieve a greater "say" in governing social conduct, morals curricula, books and teachers. The "hippie movement" of the late 1960's provided the weired spectacle of long-heired unwashed youths of both sexes rejecting the materialistic, hypocritical values of society and seeking peace and brotherly love through a simple, more relaxed existence. Some lived on marijuana, alcohol, hallucinatory drugs and sex.

Parents themselves were falling short of perfection. Upsurging crimes prevailed during the years 1960 and 1970. By 1970 about one fourth of the states had abolished the death penalty.

During the 1970's economic condition was stable and steady. Nearly one-half of the enormous federal pie was going to the defence establishment. Simultaneously inflation forced war upward the cost of living, with mounting hardship to "senior citizens" and others on fixed incomes.

Farmers continued to raise their crops. In spite of that there was unemployment problem. Besides, thete was labour movement in the country. There were number of strikes by public service employees, policemen, firemen, nurses, teachers and garbage collectors (Sanitary engineers).

Women's Right

Women suffrage, the goal of feminists for many decades, likewise received powerful new support from the progressive early in the 1900's. Political reformers believed that the petticoat vote would elevate the political tone; foes of the saloon felt that they could count on the support of enfranchised females. The "suffragists" crying "votes for women" and "equal suffrage for men and women" protested bitterly against "Taxation without Representation". Many of the States, especially the more liberal ones in the west, gradually extended the vote to women. But by 1910 nation wide female suffrage could still be sheeringly defined as "one who has ceased to be a lady and has not yet become a gentlemen".

Woman suffrage regarded as essential to national unity, was likewise stimulated by the conflict. President Wilson had hitherto opposed to it. ("He kept us out of suffrage"), but at last he supported this concession as "vitally necessary war measure". "Votes for women" achieved a final triumph, when in 1928, the 19th Amendment was written into the constitution. Women tended to vote the same way as men.

American women in some respects the largest minority group of all (though a numerical majority) were continuing their demands for sex equality legislation, including guarantees of equal pay for equal work. Until recent decades wives were reluctant to take jobs lest they reflect shamefully on the bread winning ability of their husbands. This stigma is fast disappearing as millions of women are learning mechanised kitchens to find gainful employment. They seek either to supplement the family income or kept busy after their children are reared. More women have entered politics, including Congress and there is serious talk of some day electing a woman as President. In the late 1960's females broke down the icy-covered walls of masculinity at Yale and Princeton, among a number of colleges, when they were admitted as students.

Ethnic Minorities

The thirteen original colonies were of course inhabited by British immigrants for the most part. The colonial population also had a mingling of races from different countries of the world, who had also contributed their might to the growth of American civilisation. Some illustrious and eminent leaders of this Nation were the descendents of these foreign races. German immigration, Scotch-Irish Presbyterians, French Huguenots Welsh, Dutch, Swedes, Jews, Irish, Swiss and Scots Highlanders and other miscellanious races of America.

By far the largest single non-English group was African predominantly Negro slaves constituting in all about 20 per cent of the total population. In the ladder of colonial society they occupied the lower rings.

The Negroes had acquired gains at a rapid speed after the World War II. Particularly during 1940's and 1950's they had acquired wonderful gains. More Social Rights were given to them during this period. Under Kennedy and Johnson they gained substantially in all fields.

Music, Art and Architecture

Music was gaining popularity from 1900 onwards. America of those days was assembling high quality symphony orchestras, notably in

Boston and Chicago. The famed Metropolitan Opera House of New York was erected in 1863. A marvellous discovery was the reproduction of music by mechanical means. Though the phonograph was an imperfect instrument, had by 1900 reached over 1,50,000 homes. Americans were rapidly being closed with "canned music". By 1968 sixteen of seventeen homes could boast television sets, more than one sixth of them in colour, reaching 96 percent of the population. About 260,000,000 radios existed in 1967 especially the easily portable transistors, or more than one for every inhabitant. Improved techniques of reproduction–such as long playing records, magnetic tapes, high fidelity sets (hi-fi) and stereophonic reproduction were adding to the immense popularity of "canned music".

Rock-'n'-roll derived in part from folk music and the Negro devised blues, was introduced in the 1950's and came to dominate the musical scene in the 1960's.

Another version of the blues that attained wide acceptance in the 1960's was the adaptation known as "soul music". At a different level, the introduction of computer programmed and computer generated music was a significant feature of the mechanised age.

The vitality and virtuosity of local musical organisations in America continued to be most impressive whether operatic, orchestral, or choral. In 1965 the Ford Foundation granted 85 millions to some fifty symphony orchestras. The next year the famed Metropolitan Opera House in New York moved to its palatial new home in the same city. During 1967-68 the Nation could boast 297 opera departments.

Art had been of sickly growth in the rustic years of the Republic, largely because of an absence of leisure and wealth. Several portrait painters of distinction emerged, notably James Whietler (1834-1903). This eccentric and quarrelsome Massachusetts Yankee had earlier been dropped from West Point after failing in chemistry. Another gifted portrait painter, likewise self-exiled in England, was John Singer Sargent (1856-1925). His flattering but some what superficial likenesses of the British nobility were highly prized. George Inness (1825-1894) was America's leading landscapist. Thomas Eakins (1844-1916) attained a high degree of realism in his paintings. Winslow Homer (1836-1910), native of Boston was perhaps the greatest painter of the group.

Probably the most gifted sculptor yet produced by America was Augustus Saint Gandens (1848-1907). Born in Ireland of an Irish mother and a French father, he became an adopted American. Although, he sculptured many noble statues, his most striking work is the "Adams Monument", a shrouded and enigmatic female figure representing grief or a kindred emotion. It was erected in a Washington cemetery by the historian Henry Adams in memory of his beloved wife who had committed suicide.

The most original architects of the era sought to escape the hodge-podge borrowings from Europe by stressing usefulness of design-realism in building. The most noteworthy contribution of this sort was the steel-skeleton skyscraper. Louis H. Sullivan (1856-1924) native of Chicago added muscle to the sky scrapper by his guiding principle, "From follows function".

A revival of classical architectural forms and a set back for realism came with the great Columbian Exposition. Held in Chicago in 1803, it honoured the four hundredth anniversary of Columbus first voyage. This so called "dream of loveliness", which was visited by 27,000,000 people did much to raise American artistic standards and promote city planning, although many of the spectators were attracted primarily by the torsel contortions of a hoochy — kootchy dancer, "Little Egypt".

During the 1960's courses in art appreciation at all levels were attracting thousands of eager learners, and inexpensive painting kite were sending countless amateurs out to the landscapes. Many great galleries were constructed. Manufacturers of cheap reproductions of the classical painters were doing a land — office business.

Many of the younger painters, deemphasising subject matter were moving away from "realism" to pure abstraction, with splashes of colour and angular designs, all presumably expressive of feeling. Some artists were surrealists who painted realistic objects.

American architecture was no pallid prisoner of the past. We can see their modern designs in churches, industrial buildings and other official and public buildings. They consist of glass and plastic materials with pierced decorative scenes.

The "legitimate" theaters still commanded a large following Broadway shows had become big business. Nudity was gaining acceptance. Thigh high mini skirts, peek a bou dresses, bikinis, topless waitresses and underground "stage movies" all found in the 1960's. In New York stage in 1960 both male and female actors began to appear together without clothing. "Adult movies" were stressing nudity and sex, often with foreign imports.

23

America In

(a) Europe; (b) Asia; (c) Middle East; (d) Latin America.

U.S. Foreign Policy

The most prosperous country of the world, United States of America is standing on the continent of North America at a considerable distance from the countries of old world. This situation of America was the only motivating force of U.S. view of foreign relations before World War I. In the First War U.S.A. was dragged by the circumstances and after the war she again shut herself in isolation. In between the two wars she followed the old principle of foreign policy of isolation and this illusion of American isolationism. With it the accompanying dream of remaining aloof from world affairs, died within this war. World War II created two power giants in the world and world found herself divided into two poles of patterns. On the face of the continent of Europe, Soviet Union emerged as the most powerful Nation because the power and prestige of France and United Kingdom had been crushed and made crippled by the Nazi military forces. This emergence of a communist country as a world power was a challenge to American interest which were now vested in all the parts of world. Thus, again the circumstances forced U.S.A. to leave that beaten track of isolationism and now America moulded her foreign relations according to the need of time.

United States of America is a Nation of huge resources — human and material. The far flung and flourished trade and industries of Americans have forced the government to keep a gazing eye on the international events. Today American capital is vested in all the scattered parts of the world and to provide security and safety by means of influence or military might has become the aim of U.S. Government. Thus, far vested interests of America have influenced very much the foreign policy of the country. Americans have influenced very much the foreign policy of the country. American public opinion also influences these relations. The people of America are essentially traders and their minds are filled with the capitalist tendencies. Trade requires peace, for peace is the very first condition for the improvement of the business. Therefore, peace is also the basis of American foreign policy but peace at any price is not the object of the government. Expansion of communism is of dread significance of America because she is a capitalist country. So U.S.A. made the very base of her foreign policy as the "containment of communism". In fact America has no Jealousy for communism but communism is a threatening ghost for U.S. interests. Therefore, the interest of the country is the main objective of her foreign policy especially to attain the National security.

The conduct of foreign relations as provided by the constitutional allocations of authority is also an influential factor on U.S. foreign policy. Separation of Powers has been granted by the American Constitution. Executive and legislative branches of the government are free from each other. But the introduction of principle of Checks and Balances has played an important role even in this field. President, the executive authority, has the powers of head of the State and thus receives and appoints ambassadors of the countries. He also makes the treaties with other nations but they must be ratified by the Senate, the legislative organ of the country. Senate has also the power to declare war and make peace. Thus, the relations of Congress and President determine the principles of U.S. Foreign policy.

Thus, the relations of Congress and President also determine the views of America over events of international importance.

In the practical field of international politics U.S. foreign policy may be divided into three phases. First phase of U.S. policy is upto 1919, when U.S.A. was completely closed in the four boundaries of her Nation and of the continents of North and South Americas. In this period U.S. foreign policy was essentially based on the assumption "America for Americans". During this period United States did not indulge herself in the dirty power politics that was being played on the continent of Europe. In fact, in this phase U.S. international politics was influenced by the far distance which till then was not bridged by the quick and safe means of transportation and communication. During this period America closed herself and was interested only in the matters of the Nations of North and South American continents. In this phase U.S.A. was physically invincible by any of the European power, so she need not to play any of important diplomatic roles in the affairs of European States. American economy was quite infant during this period and she had no claims of business and markets anywhere in the world except in American continents. Monroe Doctrine as propounded by President, Monroe in the year 1823 was the only guiding principle of U.S. policy throughout this period.

In the year 1917 U.S.A. was dragged by circumstances in the World War I and for the very first time interfered in the politics of Europe. In this World War Europe was very badly crushed and this war showed the importance of U.S.A. as the first grade power of the world. In between the wars America helped European Nations for their reconstruction. Millions of U.S. dollars were invested in European countries. American public opinion forced the government to make Kellogg-Briand Pact of 1928 for "outlawing" war itself. U.S. President Woodrow Wilson played an important role in the making of Treaty of Versailles and in the birth of League of Nations. U.S. got herself interested to limit the navy of Japan and wanted to maintain her special position in the Chinese area. So she made her best efforts for Washington Conference of 1921 and could succeed in her efforts. In this way America was desirous to leave the Monroe Doctrine because now it had gone out of time and was not sound for the condition of the world of second quarter of 20th century. Advancement of science and inventions of quicker and safer means of transportation and communication made the entire world a unit and now America was physically visible. Even then U.S. public opinion did not permit the government to indulge herself in the game of power politics of European Nations and American Senate refused to ratify the Treaty of Versailes. Thus, U.S.A. could not become the member of League of Nations and could not play a direct role in international game. During this period U.S.A. tried to have her old isolationism, but that was not completely abandoned. Indirectly America came forward for the safety and security of her vast international interests. In this phase she had an eye over the politics of other Nations for her interests.

The Third phase of U.S. foreign policy begins with World War II. This war resulted in the destruction of power and prestige of chief countries and former big powers of the world. England and France were crushed by German forces and Germany lost all her power in the defeat. Italy already had no real power. Entire continent of Europe was politically disturbed, economically crippled and morally they were frightened. This had also created two major powers in the world. Soviet Union emerged as the most powerful Nation of Eurasia and no country or the group of countries was able to match Muskovite military might. The rise of a communist country as the World power was a challenge of dread significance to America. The Communist imperialism of Soviet Russia give birth to the cold war and now this cold war is the basis of American foreign policy. America does not want the expansion of communism because it is a threatening ghost for the American interests which are now vested around the world. U.S.A. came forward to accept this challenge and now it is following the principle of "containment of communism". Today America has a keen interest in every international importance. To prevent the expansion of communism today U.S.A. is trying at the best. U.S. dollars are going everywhere in the world, U.S. Military bases are in every strategic part of the world and U.S. propaganda is also very harsh to attain her object. Now U.S.A. is playing an active role in international field. In this way this world war again forced Americans to take active part in foreign affairs. The principle "America for Americans" has been replaced by "America for the world". This phase of U.S. foreign policy may be divided into three parts. In first period from 1941 to 1945 U.S. view towards other countries is of co-operation and accommodation in which U.S. and other western powers helped Soviet Union against Nazi attack. Second period deals with patience and firmness with Soviet Union when Yalta and Potsdam Conference were held. Third period deals with the containment of communist bloc in which U.S. makes military parts. This period continues up to present day because today America is following the same principle which she adopted in 1947.

(a) U.S. Foreign Policy in Europe

World War II created Soviet Russia as the most powerful Nation of Europe. Europe was divided into two blocks after this war. Communist countries were the Russia, Czechoslovakia and other Eastern European Nations. France, England, etc. were the capitalistic countries. After the war Soviet Union started her communistic imperialistic attack over the other European countries. No other power of Europe was able to check this military might of Russia, therefore, United States came forward to accept this challenge. United States launched her various plans and schemes for the containment of communism in Europe. On March 4, 1947 U.S. President Truman made his famous Truman Declaration. Greek Civil War was in fact the cause of this declaration. America provided the help of 400 million dollars to Greece and Turkey to make them able to fight communism. On June 5, 1947 Secretary Marshall Plan for the reconstruction of Europe but because of the negative attitude of Soviet Foreign Minister Molotov this plan could not get success and then it helped only 18 Nations of Europe as the name of European Recovery Plan. Thus, in the economic field U.S.A. helped the Nations of Europe, so that they may not become the prey of the cancerous growth of communism. Soviet seizure of power in Czechoslovakia, Blockade of

Berlin and successful Red revolution in China proved that the communist block will not hesitate in the use of even military force for the attainment of her objects. So it was necessary for America to make military pacts to face the possible attack from communist countries. This assumption resulted in North Atlantic Treaty Organization which had very large military force at its disposal. In the year 1949 Soviet explosion of A-Bomb threatened the capitalist block and now America laid a great emphasis on more military might. Marshall Plan was turned into the "defence support funds" and President Truman disposed four divisions of U.S. troops for NATO. To make NATO more effective "European Defence Community" came into existence. Soviet Russia also replied it and made Warsaw Pact in 1955. Thus, U.S. relations in Europe with Soviet Russia were not good up to 1953. The year 1953 is a turning point in the relations of the two leading powers of the world. The commencement of Republican Administration in America, the death of dry-hearted communist Stalin, the truce of Korean war, peace gestures from Moscow and cry to reduce the burden of high taxation in Western democracies caused the change in the Russo-American relations. Both the countries made the efforts to be friends in the Summer Conference of 1955, held at Geneva. Russian premier Krushchev paid visit to U.S.A. in 1959 and the two countries came nearer. But the U-2 incident of 1960 in which the spy plane of United States was shot down 1300 miles within the Soviet territory by the Russians strained their relations. Now again Soviet-American relations became strained and they were at climax point in the year 1963 when on the question of Berlin, NATO forces and Soviet Army were standing at a distance of only 500 yards in Berlin. Now the Berlin problem was solved.

In Europe France is the Military Western country with which the relations of America are not sound. In 1958 when General de Gaulle came to the power, he tried his best to make his relations better with the Eastern European countries and Soviet Union. In his regime France did not remain the member of NATO and opposed the activities of United States in European affairs.

(b) U.S. Foreign Policy in Asia

Rise of Communist China in Far East as a great power caused the attention of U.S.A. divert towards this area. U.S. relations with Communist China are quite strained and U.S. government has still not recognized the new Chinese government. Right from the very beginning of the success of communists in the mainland of China, America is protesting her claims. On the question of Tibet, America opposed the action of China very harshly. In Korean war Chinese clashed with the U.S. military forces.

U.S.A. is the supporter of Nationalist China of Chiang Kai-Sheik. U.S.A. has made military bases in Formosa and VII Fleet of U.S. Navy is sailing the Pacific Ocean on the shore of China. These activities of America are just to see the power of Communist China. Vietnam has become a major and perhaps permanent battle field for the two forces. United States of America has made a Security Pact with Japan in 1965 to get another base in Far East against communist bloc of Soviet Russia and Communist China. United States has always opposed the membership of China in United Nations and China is not the member of U.N. until the relations all improved in 1980. Thus, the relations of United States with a big power of Far East are not friendly. In the regime of President Kennedy, Americans thought to vacate Formosa and of the withdrawal of her military might form Far East. But this withdrawal of U.S.A. from Formosa would vitiate U.S. military might in East Asia, would tend to drive into a position of neutrality or alliance with communist China but at the end she abandoned Nationalist China for communist rule.

U.S. Foreign Policy in South East Asia

South East Asia has become focal point in foreign relations of America. The government of Soviet Russia from a far distance and the Communist China from the heart of Asia, by their activities forced United States to give high priority to the concern, South East Asia. In this zone to prevent the communism, America has been involved since 1950. American forces are fighting in Vietnam against the Communists of North Vietnam. SEATO has been made to improve the military power of U.S. block in South East Asia. ANZUS is also of some importance. U.S. Foreign policy towards the neutrals is to bring them in her block. She is providing tremendous amount of economic help to these Nations, so that they may not join the other group. India is big neutral power of South East Asia and U.S. relations with this sub-continent are not bad. Pakistan is another important country of South Asia and she is the member of SEATO. But in recent years Pakistan is trying and getting the support of China. This is a matter of great anxiety for U.S.A. for Pakistan is important for U.S.A. from military point of view.

(c) U.S. Foreign Policy in Middle East

Middle East has become the storm of international politics since World War II because of her oil resources and strategic situation. The countries of this area are poor and backward, so there is a fertile ground for communists in these Nations. To prevent the communism, U.S.A. has again come here. She has made military pacts and is giving economic help to these Nations for their political stability. The countries of this area are divided into two blocks. First block is of Arab Nationalities which is now tending towards Soviet Union under the leadership of Egypt. The other has the capitalist support and the countries of this group are Israel, Turkey and Iran. U.S. has not left even this area free from the military alliances. In 1955 Baghdad Pact was made with the membership of Turkey, Iran, Iraq, Britain, etc. In 1957 American Congress passed the resolution of Eisenhower principles under which President was empowered to send U.S. troops in Middle East for the prevention of Communism. U.S. relations with Arab community are not good because in the Suez crisis of 1956 and Arab Israel conflict for 1967. U.S.A. has supported the Anti-Arab powers. Anyhow vast American interests are vested in this area and America cannot leave free these areas for Soviet Union. So she has keen interest in the events of Middle East.

(d) U.S. Foreign Policy in Latin America

The countries of the continents of Americans are of great interests for United States. She has been in contact with these Nations right from the very beginning of the new world. Physically these countries are at a less distance and people of United States are in good business with the peoples of Latin America. These Nations are poor and culturally backward. Although, there is no fear of communism in these countries because to extend the communistic imperialism in these far distant Nations is physically difficult for Soviet Union. American relations with these Nations are very good and America has made with them many social, economic and military pacts. Rio Treaty of 1947 has combined the forces of 21 Latin American Nations together with U.S.A. Any kind of Soviet expansion in these Nations is a threat to U.S. Security. So she has very nice terms with these Nations.

True assessment of U.S. foreign relations is that the perennial stream of problems that was generated by the World War II forced United States of America to leave the policy of isolationism. Modern means of communications and transportations have made the entire world a unit and the most prosperous country of the world cannot keep herself away from this unit. Emergence of Soviet Union, the communist power as the most powerful Nation of Europe and her activities of communistic imperialism threatened the U.S. interest especially the security of her freedom. After the World War II, America has followed the policy of encirclement of communist block everywhere in the world to attain her aim of containment of communism. Today America has made her military commitments with the 38 Nations around the world through the regional pacts of Rio Treaty, NATO, ANZUS Treaty, SEATO,

CENTO and by the Bilateral Treaties of Philippines, Japan, South Korea and Taiwan. American interest are vested in every part of the world and America wants to be the most influential Nation of the world. She has got some success in this aim. Peace is the objective of U.S. foreign policy but not at the cost of her interests. She has a great amount of faith in the United Nations. She takes a great part in the activities of this organization. History of U.S. foreign relations is a story of success and failures.

Index